Texas Birds

Where they are and how to find them

Edward A. Kutac

Lone Star Books
A Division of Gulf Publishing Company
Houston, Texas

> *To the women in my life*
> *Albina, my mother, for being everything*
> *a mother should be and more,*
> *Amy, my wife, for 35 wonderful years,*
> *I am hoping for 35 more,*
> *Mary, Anne, and Lucy Kay, my daughters,*
> *who have made fatherhood a great*
> *adventure and totally stimulating*
> *experience.*

Texas Birds

Where they are and how to find them

Library of Congress Cataloging in Publication Data
Kutac, Edward A.
   Texas birds.
   Bibliography: p.
   Includes index.
   1. Bird watching—Texas—Guide-books.
2. Bird refuges—Texas—Guide-books. 3. Wildlife refuges—Texas—Guide-books. 4. National parks and reserves—Texas—Guide-books. 5. Parks—Texas—Guide-books. I. Title.
QL684.T4K88 1982   598'.07'234764   82-9880
ISBN 0-88415-063-1   AACR2

Book design by Doug James
Region maps and cover design by David T. Price

Acknowledgments

A book of this type is impossible without the assistance and contributions of a great number of people. Every person who has contributed to the regional check-lists of Texas birds (particularly the compilers) and all Christmas Count participants have made a direct contribution. The many friends who have traveled around the state with me (they know who they are), local birders who have led or accompanied field trips I have participated in, the Texas Ornithological Society members who have hosted and helped with the 27 meetings in 25 different Texas locations I have attended, and authors mentioned in the Selected References have all enhanced my Texas bird experiences and kept my interest and curiosity level high through the years. The birders are greater than the birds.

The collaborators who have made the most direct contribution by providing information about their particular area, in some cases doing the writing which I edited, or who checked what I had written and provided helpful suggestions are: Peggy Acord, Alma Barrera, Gene Blacklock, Margaret Broday, Kelly Bryan, Russell Clapper, Robert Coggeshall, Charles Crabtree, Maurice and Esther Crawford, Richard Cudworth, Wesley Cureton, Dr. Charles Dean Fisher, Tony Gallucci, Karl Haller, Kelly Himmel, Donald McDonald, James Middleton, Ernest and Kay Mueller, Margaret Parker, Midge Randolph, Steve Runnels, Ken Seyffert, Wayne Shifflett, Jessie May Smith, Clif Stogner, Dan Watson, Clarence Wiedenfeld, Frances Williams, and Kevin J. Zimmer. Information on the Texas Cooperative Wildlife Collections was supplied by Dr. Keith A. Arnold, the Texas Bird Sound Library by Dr. Ralph R. Moldenhaur, and the natural regions of the state by David Riskind. Without their assistance, the scope of this book would be much less comprehensive. It goes without saying, however, that I had the last word, and therefore am solely responsible for any errors, omissions, or shortcomings.

The National Park Service, U. S. Fish and Wildlife Service, Texas Parks and Wildlife Department, Texas Department of Water Resources, U. S. Forest Service, along with all city and county parks departments contacted, were all very cooperative and helpful in supplying promptly all information requested and all have my lasting gratitude. The maps and mileage data are taken from publications of the Texas Department of Highways and Public Transportation.

Special mention is due the following: Deanna Metcalf, who typed and retyped practically the entire manuscript, assisted with proofreading, made many helpful suggestions, and in general kept the project on track and moving; June Osborne, who not only collaborated on the Waco section but also compiled and typed much of the Appendix; Barbara Ribble, who read the entire manuscript and made many corrections and suggestions. Her extensive travels to all sections of the state in search of birds and her vast avian knowledge made her admirably qualified for this task, and I am most appreciative.

I also wish to thank the entire staff at Gulf Publishing Company for their helpful counsel and assistance.

Finally, thanks to my wife, Amy, a bird widow, for helping with typing, proofing, statistical compilations, etc., but mostly for her devotion, encouragement, understanding, and tolerance in putting up with a wandering amateur Texas naturalist for these many years.

Contents

Foreword

The state of Texas is like a country within a country, an area so vast that it can boast the largest avifauna of any of the 50 states, exceeding by a wide margin even California. East meets West, faunally, in midstate, and formerly those bird-watchers who lived near the center line—Fort Worth, Dallas, Waco, Austin, San Antonio, and Brownsville—had to carry into the field both my eastern *Field Guide* and the western *Field Guide*. This changed when the Texas Game and Fish Commission prevailed upon me to put things into one book, just for Texas. Indeed, to this day, Texas is the only state with its own *Peterson Field Guide*.

It was inevitable that still another kind of guide was needed, a directory, or sort of *Baedeker*, which would tell the birder *where* to look for birds and what species to expect. The field observer of today is mobile, and in an area as large as Texas it saves time to know the key places or "hot-spots." Olin Sewall Pettingill's *Bird Finding West of the Mississippi*, first published in 1953, filled the niche for a number of years, but inasmuch as only a limited number of pages could be devoted to any one of the 22 states west of the Mississippi, local guide books soon proliferated. At least four such regional directories were produced for various sections of Texas by Lane, Kutac, and others.

This new book by Ed Kutac is the first to cover the entire state in one volume in a comprehensive way. The author, who has been president of the Texas Ornithological Society and intimately involved with other bird-oriented groups in the state, is familiar with virtually all of the sites described in these pages.

Nearly 800 miles from top to bottom or from east to west and covering some 267,000 square miles, Texas can claim diversity by virtue of size alone, and even more significant than size in determining its rich avifauna is the state's location on the continent. East meets West, biologically, along the 100th meridian, and North meets South, especially along the Rio Grande, where birds from the northern plains meet Mexican types. Altitudes range from sea level along the Gulf to 8000 feet in the Trans-Pecos; rainfall varies from a wet 50-plus inches on the Louisiana border to less than 10 inches in the extreme west.

Truly, Texas is the state above all others that offers the most lively birding, a factor that is now luring binocular-toting tourists from the rest of the United States, especially during spring migration when massive "fall outs" of migrants along the Gulf Coast must be seen to be believed. The varied avifauna of Texas has attracted so many people from out-of-state that several travel agencies have found it profitable to schedule special tours for birders.

Some birders enjoy group companionship or competition with their friends, others prefer to be on their own or with their spouses. It is for both of these groups of bird-watchers that this book has been prepared.

Roger Tory Peterson

Introduction

This book is primarily about bird locations in Texas. The intention is to provide a guide to bird opportunities throughout the state. The reader who is visiting (or plans to visit) a section(s) of the state will find herein a quick reference to a particular area, several favored bird locations in that area, and which birds might be expected, particularly nesting and wintering birds.

It is assumed the reader knows something about bird identification, or "birding" as the hobby or sport of looking for birds has come to be known, and wants to know some places in Texas where certain birds can be found. If learning to identify Texas birds is what is desired, the reader is referred to *A Field Guide to the Birds of Texas* by Roger Tory Peterson, and *Birds of North America: A Guide to Field Identification* by Robbins et al. Both, in my opinion, are indispensable in the field. In addition, all serious Texas bird students should have in their library the two-volume *The Bird Life of Texas* by Oberholser and Kincaid, an encyclopedic treatment of the avifauna of the state. There are also many other fine guides and books which can be obtained, depending on one's interest and financial resources.

Texans are known to boast about how everything in Texas is bigger and better than anywhere else. In the case of birds the boasting is justified. Texas has more bird species recorded within its borders than any other state. The Appendix in this book lists 555 species which have been documented by the Bird Records Committee of the Texas Ornithological Society, along with another 45 hypothetical species. There are several reasons for this large diversity.

Texas is big—after Alaska, the largest state—with 267,000 square miles: 821 miles from Texarkana in the northeast corner to El Paso in the far west, 909 miles from Texline in the extreme northwest to Brownsville at the southern tip. In-between are mountains, desert, pine and hardwood forests, prairies, numerous man-made lakes and farm ponds, extensive farm and ranch lands, the 367-mile coastline of the Gulf of Mexico, barrier islands, estuaries, and the subtropical Lower Rio Grande Valley. Average rainfall varies from 8 inches per year at El Paso to more than 50 inches on the eastern border. The land surface in Texas rises from sea level on the coast northwestward to more than 4000 feet in the northern

Panhandle. In the Trans-Pecos there are at least 20 peaks of more than 7000 feet. Average frost-free days vary from 178 at Dalhart to 341 at Brownsville.

The location of the state in the middle of the North American continent means most migrants of the Mississippi Flyway, the Central Flyway, and the Rocky Mountains pass through some part of the state in spring and fall. In spring many trans-Gulf migrants make landfall along the coast. Add to this number the oceanic birds found in the Gulf, along with strays blown in by Gulf storms (hurricanes), and an impressive total is achieved.

For the purposes of this book, Texas is divided into eight regions: Llano Estacado, Trans-Pecos, Rolling Plains, Edwards Plateau, Central Texas, Pineywoods, Gulf Coast, and South Texas. Some of the regions are divided on the basis of their geology, some on their vegetation, and some are arbitrary and convenient. In some cases the boundary between regions is sharply defined and can be easily recognized, in others the transition is indistinct and may be many miles wide.

Concise descriptions of the regions are included, along with 26 locations administered by agencies of the federal government (national parks, national wildlife refuges, etc.), 37 areas under the jurisdiction of the State of Texas (parks, forests, etc.), 24 Texas cities and towns (22 city parks) and 41 other birding spots in the state—a total of at least 150 sites.

> NOTE: All maps are situated so that the top of each map represents North.

I have personally visited and looked for birds in more than 80% of the locations listed in this book. Of course, Texas is too big for anyone to visit all areas in all seasons; therefore, my experience has been augmented by that of the collaborators named in the Acknowledgments. Regional check-lists have been used extensively to determine abundance, nesting, and other information.

Birds which commonly nest in all eight regions are Turkey Vulture, Killdeer, Mourning Dove, Yellow-billed Cuckoo, Common Nighthawk, Scissor-tailed Flycatcher, Tufted Titmouse, Mockingbird, Eastern Meadowlark, Red-winged Blackbird, Brown-headed Cowbird,

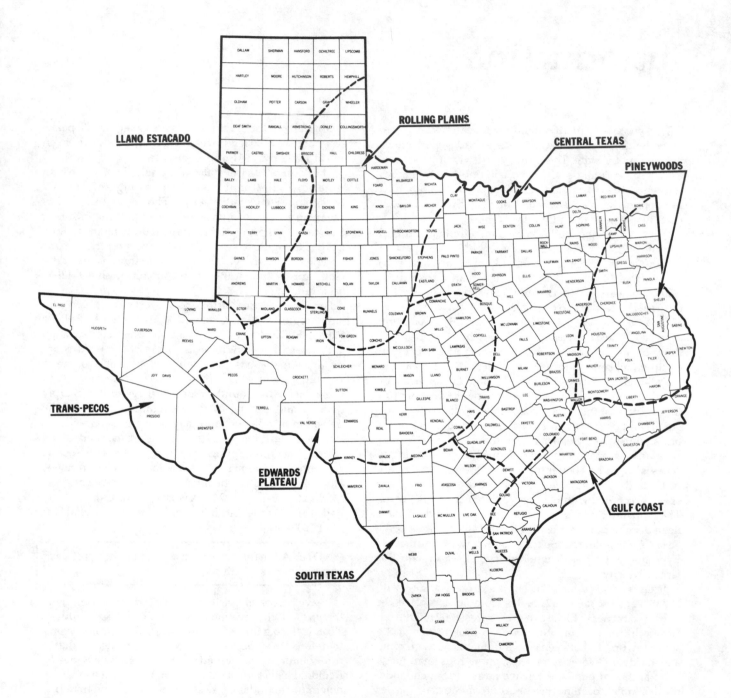

LLANO ESTACADO

ROLLING PLAINS

CENTRAL TEXAS

PINEYWOODS

TRANS-PECOS

EDWARDS PLATEAU

SOUTH TEXAS

GULF COAST

DALLAM   SHERMAN   HANSFORD   OCHILTREE   LIPSCOMB
HARTLEY   MOORE   HUTCHINSON   ROBERTS   HEMPHILL
OLDHAM   POTTER   CARSON   GRAY   WHEELER
DEAF SMITH   RANDALL   ARMSTRONG   DONLEY   COLLINGSWORTH
PARMER   CASTRO   SWISHER   BRISCOE   HALL   CHILDRESS
HARDEMAN
BAILEY   LAMB   HALE   FLOYD   MOTLEY   COTTLE   FOARD   WILBARGER   WICHITA
CLAY
COCHRAN   HOCKLEY   LUBBOCK   CROSBY   DICKENS   KING   KNOX   BAYLOR   ARCHER   MONTAGUE   COOKE   GRAYSON   FANNIN   LAMAR   RED RIVER
DELTA   BOWIE
YOAKUM   TERRY   LYNN   GARZA   KENT   STONEWALL   HASKELL   THROCKMORTON   YOUNG   JACK   WISE   DENTON   COLLIN   HUNT   HOPKINS   FRANKLIN   TITUS   CASS   MORRIS
CAMP
GAINES   DAWSON   BORDEN   SCURRY   FISHER   JONES   SHACKELFORD   STEPHENS   PALO PINTO   PARKER   TARRANT   DALLAS   ROCKWALL   RAINS   WOOD   UPSHUR   MARION
KAUFMAN   VAN ZANDT   SMITH   GREGG   HARRISON
ANDREWS   MARTIN   HOWARD   MITCHELL   NOLAN   TAYLOR   CALLAHAN   EASTLAND   ERATH   HOOD   JOHNSON   ELLIS   HENDERSON   RUSK   PANOLA
SOMERVELL   HILL   NAVARRO   ANDERSON   CHEROKEE   SHELBY
EL PASO   LOVING   WINKLER   ECTOR   MIDLAND   GLASSCOCK   STERLING   COKE   RUNNELS   COLEMAN   BROWN   COMANCHE   BOSQUE   FREESTONE   NACOGDOCHES   SAN AUGUSTINE   SABINE
HAMILTON   MCLENNAN   LIMESTONE   LEON   ANGELINA   NEWTON
HUDSPETH   CULBERSON   REEVES   WARD   CRANE   UPTON   REAGAN   IRION   TOM GREEN   CONCHO   MILLS   CORYELL   FALLS   ROBERTSON   HOUSTON   TRINITY   POLK   TYLER   JASPER
MCCULLOCH   SAN SABA   LAMPASAS   BELL   MILAM   MADISON   WALKER   SAN JACINTO   HARDIN
JEFF DAVIS   PECOS   CROCKETT   SCHLEICHER   MENARD   MASON   LLANO   BURNET   WILLIAMSON   LEE   BURLESON   BRAZOS   GRIMES   MONTGOMERY   LIBERTY   ORANGE
PRESIDIO   SUTTON   KIMBLE   GILLESPIE   BLANCO   TRAVIS   BASTROP   WASHINGTON   WALLER   JEFFERSON
TERRELL   BREWSTER   VAL VERDE   EDWARDS   KERR   KENDALL   HAYS   CALDWELL   FAYETTE   AUSTIN   HARRIS   CHAMBERS
REAL   BANDERA   COMAL   GUADALUPE   COLORADO   FORT BEND   GALVESTON
KINNEY   UVALDE   MEDINA   BEXAR   GONZALES   LAVACA   WHARTON   BRAZORIA
MAVERICK   ZAVALA   FRIO   ATASCOSA   WILSON   KARNES   DEWITT   VICTORIA   JACKSON   MATAGORDA
DIMMIT   LA SALLE   MCMULLEN   LIVE OAK   GOLIAD   CALHOUN
WEBB   DUVAL   JIM WELLS   BEE   REFUGIO   ARANSAS
SAN PATRICIO   NUECES
ZAPATA   JIM HOGG   BROOKS   KLEBERG   KENEDY
STARR   HIDALGO   WILLACY   CAMERON

viii

Cardinal, Painted Bunting, Blue Grosbeak, Lark Sparrow, Rock Dove, Starling, and House Sparrow. It is noteworthy that the last three are introduced birds. Nesting species common in all but one area are Green Heron (uncommon in the Llano Estacado), Bobwhite, Carolina Chickadee, Chimney Swift (not in the Trans-Pecos), Great-tailed Grackle, and Bewick's Wren (not in the Pineywoods). These 24 common species will be minimized in the location accounts, since all are easily found.

The same can be said for wintering birds. A total of 376 species were found on the 73 Christmas Counts conducted throughout the state in 1979. Only two species were found on all 73 counts, while 59 species were found on only one count. The 25 species found on 60 or more counts (the approximate equivalent of being found in all eight regions) are as follows:

No. of Counts	Bird
73	Red-tailed Hawk, Mockingbird
72	American Kestrel, Loggerhead Shrike
71	Ruby-crowned Kinglet
70	House Sparrow, Cardinal
68	Killdeer
67	Marsh Hawk, Mourning Dove, Red-winged Blackbird
66	Great Blue Heron, White-crowned Sparrow
63	Belted Kingfisher, American Robin, Starling, Brown-headed Cowbird
62	Mallard, American Coot
61	Pied-billed Grebe, Yellow-rumped Warbler, Rufous-sided Towhee, Savannah and Field Sparrows
60	Orange-crowned Warbler

What does all this mean? It means if one wants to see most of the birds in Texas, a lot of travel is required. It will be necessary to climb some mountains, tromp through some marshes, take a few boat trips into the Gulf of Mexico, and otherwise cover the wide variety of habitats in the state during different seasons.

National, state, county and city parks, National Wildlife Refuges, and other preserves protect many unique areas of the state, many of which are described in the appropriate sections; however, only 1.4% of the land in the state is afforded this protection. Texas ranks forty-seventh among the 50 states in per capita parkland. If many forms of wildlife are to survive, the cooperation of private landowners is imperative.

Christmas Counts

In the listing of birds which occur in various locations, mention is made of birds found on Christmas Counts. What is a Christmas Count? Christmas Bird Counts are sponsored by the National Audubon Society and have

Mockingbird
(Courtesy Texas Parks and Wildlife Department.)

been conducted annually since 1900. The rules of a count or census are that a "count area must fill or fit entirely within a circle of 15-mile diameter," and be held during a single calendar day within the official Christmas Bird Count period, generally that period of time which includes three weekends before, during, and after Christmas. Recently, the count period was December 20, 1980, through January 4, 1981.

The first count was on Christmas, 1900, with 27 observers on 25 counts in 12 states and two Canadian provinces. Audubon Society official Frank Chapman suggested the first count as a protest against a practice at the time in which "gunners" would compete with one another to see who could shoot the most birds on Christmas Day.

The activity has now grown (in 1979) to 32,292 observers on 1320 counts in 50 states and 12 Canadian provinces. Counts also take place in Central America, South America, the West Indies, and the Atlantic. In Texas in 1979 there were 73 different counts with 1490 observers recording 376 bird species. The results of all counts are published by the National Audubon Society in the journal, *American Birds*, a wealth of information for bird seekers and bird scientists. Because Christmas Count participants are well known for braving cold, wind, rain, and for otherwise disregarding their well-being on their appointed day, *American Birds* once referred to the counts as "North America's premier exercise in mass masochism and cooperative science." The idea of a Christmas Count is to put as many people as possible into the count circle during one 24-hour period and count every species and number of individuals on that particular day. That it is a popular birding activity is attested to by the enormous increase in participation by the birding community.

Nomenclature

The common names of most birds are widely accepted in the scientific and birding communities; however, with continuing and increasing research, it is inevitable that some changes become appropriate.

Species are "lumped" (combined with other species formerly considered separate) and "split" (a species divided into two or more previously considered one). Names are changed to achieve international uniformity and for other reasons. The most widely accepted are those common and scientific names adopted by the Committee on Nomenclature and Classification of the American Ornithologists' Union. The common names used in this book follow those found in the *Check-list of North American Birds, Fifth Edition*, 1957, American Ornithologists' Union, as amended by the 32nd Supplement, 1973, and the 33rd Supplement, 1976.

Which names to use is a dilemma. One problem is that some check-lists and books published before the 32nd and 33rd Supplements use the 1957 names, such as *A Field Guide to the Birds of Texas* and *Birds of North America: A Guide to Field Identification*, the two most widely used field guides in Texas.

In anticipation of expected changes, some new common names for a few species have been adopted by new field guides, such as *A Field Guide to Mexican Birds* and *A Field Guide to Birds, East of the Rockies*.

To complicate matters further, many local check-lists have adopted some changes from the supplements while ignoring others. Sometimes even a new name is coined or a pre-1957 name is used. The American Ornithologists' Union is scheduled to publish a completely new check-list in 1983. This publication should bring about a higher degree of uniformity. To me there is a lot to be said for uniformity, even if a different name is more logical or appealing. It would be helpful if the AOU committee would issue supplements at known five-year intervals and a new check-list every 25 years. If nomenclature change time is known, the publication of guides and check-lists could be timed to help prevent releasing a publication with names that become obsolete soon after printing.

To assist in correlating most of the names that will be encountered, the Appendix lists all birds which have been verified as occurring in Texas plus hypothetical species. The list is given in phylogenetic order, first by the common name as defined previously, then the currently accepted scientific name with the 1957 Check-list name in quotation marks where there has been a change, and finally the probable "new" common name, particularly those listed in *A Field Guide to Mexican Birds* and *A Field Guide to the Birds, East of the Rockies* shown in parenthesis.

No one should assume that the locations included herein are all the places to look for birds in Texas, or that the ones mentioned are even the best places. All habitats are presented, and most of the best public places are included. Some species are most easily found from public roads or on private property, both of which have been minimized here. For example, Barn Swallow are found nesting under highway culverts and bridges in nearly all regions. Also, conditions change and information about roads, trails, and access is that known at the time of publication and should be taken as a general guide. Over time, with habitat modification for urbanization, industrialization, agriculture, and increased preservation through new parks and refuge additions, etc., some changes are inevitable. Some species are aided by these changes and prosper; some suffer and decline. This fluctuation is one of the interesting aspects of bird study. A recent example is the dramatic increase in Cattle Egrets in Texas from none in 1950 to one of our most abundant birds. This increase has taken place with no known assistance from man and with apparently no detriment to any other bird species. Another example is the decrease in Brown Pelicans (apparently the result of man-made pesticides) from tens of thousands to a dozen or so a decade ago, to more than 100 in 1980, with encouraging nesting success.

Also, no attempt has been made to list every bird, whether common or rare, for any particular location, but rather a sampling of what might be expected or has been found in the past.

Edward A. Kutac

Llano Estacado

The Llano Estacado region is the northwest part of the state and covers about 12% of Texas. The region, with minor exceptions, is a flat, featureless, treeless plain, also known as the High Plains or "Staked Plains." Formerly short-grass prairies, it is now extensively devoted to farming with irrigation from deep wells. There are numerous playas—depressions with no outlet which collect rainwater. Some are large and almost permanent.

Playa

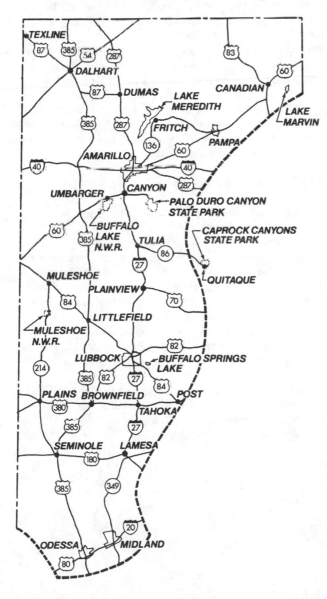

The few drainages and stream crossings have cottonwoods and hackberries as the dominant woody plants. The native grasses of the region are similar to the Rolling Plains to the east. The soils are mostly Tertiary outwash deposits from the mountains of western New Mexico.

The boundary on the east is the Caprock Escarpment, a dramatic elevational change from the Rolling Plains. It extends irregularly south to north from near Big Spring to east of Lubbock and Amarillo, then northeastward to the northeast corner of the Panhandle. The Mescalero Escarpment marks the boundary between the Llano Estacado and the Trans-Pecos. There is no topographic division between the Llano Estacado and the Edwards Plateau, but in this book it is arbitrarily located just south of Odessa and Midland. The elevation increases from 2600 feet to more than 4000 feet, south to north.

The region marks the southern end of the Great Plains which extends north into Canada. The floodplain of the Canadian River is actually geologically and vegetationally a part of the Rolling Plains but is not treated separately here.

Nesting birds include Lesser Prairie Chicken, Long-billed Curlew, Ferruginous Hawk, Scaled Quail, Mississippi Kite, Swainson's Hawk, American Avocet, Burrowing Owl, Horned Lark, and Western Meadowlark.

Lesser Prairie Chicken

Lesser Prairie Chicken are found in the sand hills country near the New Mexico border, and near the Oklahoma border in Lipscomb, Hemphill, and Wheeler counties. All are on private property. Pronghorn are found in the Panhandle north and west of Amarillo, as well as in the sand hills.

Lubbock

Lubbock is located in the heart of the Llano Estacado, and while the plains seem endless and devoid of birds, there are actually many excellent opportunities for birding in the area. In addition to the specific locations detailed in this section, it is beneficial to check the many playas along the highways for waterfowl and shorebirds. Ring-necked Pheasant, which are permanent residents, are often along the roadsides. In winter, Ferruginous and Rough-legged Hawks are seen on power poles, and Mountain Bluebird can be abundant.

West of Lubbock, near the New Mexico state line, Lesser Prairie Chicken are permanent residents in the sand hills country (south Cochran, western Hockley, northern and central Yoakum, and western Terry counties). During March and early April, listen for the "booming" of the males, a part of their courtship behavior. All the land is private property; permission to enter must be obtained. Two good roads for the chickens are FM 1780 between Whiteface and Seagraves, and SH 214 between Lehman and Denver City. When the chickens are not "booming," finding them is a matter of pure luck (but possible).

Mackenzie State Recreation Area

Mackenzie State Recreation Area is owned by the State of Texas but operated by the City of Lubbock. It is located in the northeast section of Lubbock on the North Fork Double Mountain Fork of the Brazos River at the intersection of US 87 (Avenue A) and East Broadway. The park has the most extensive Black-tailed Prairie Dog town on public property in the state, along with a sizable resident population of Burrowing Owl. Mississippi Kite nest here and are present April through September. Playgrounds, a swimming pool, and picnicking facilities are available on the 542-acre site.

Lubbock City Cemetery

From downtown, drive east on 34th Street to the entrance of the Lubbock City Cemetery, which has land birds not always easily found elsewhere in the area. The plains are treeless (except along water courses and those planted by people), so the many ornamental plantings at the cemetery are a magnet for migrating land birds and winter residents. One year a Bohemian Waxwing spent the winter at the cemetery.

Two other areas which are popular intown bird spots are Maxey Park (Quaker Avenue between 24th and 30th Streets), and Clapp Park (University Avenue and 45th Street).

A check-list, *Birds of the Texas South Plains*, 1978, is available from the Llano Estacado Audubon Society, P.O. Box 3603, Lubbock, TX 79450, for 25¢ or five for $1 plus stamped, addressed envelope.

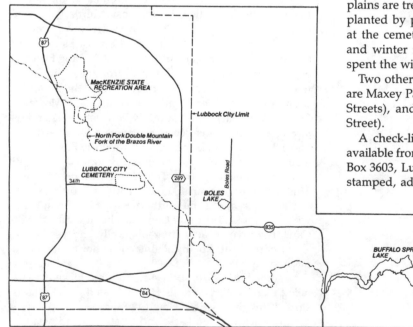

Lubbock

Buffalo Springs Lake

To reach Buffalo Springs Lake, a recreation area, drive 3.5 miles east of Loop 289 on FM 835 to FM 1729, then turn south and go one mile to the entrance of the lake. There is an entrance fee. Western Grebe sometimes winter with the more numerous ducks. Twenty waterfowl species have been recorded on recent Christmas Counts. Below the dam, the shallow ponds, marshes, and thickets should be checked for Sora, Virginia Rail, Long-billed Marsh Wren, and Fox, Harris', and Swamp Sparrows. Brown Towhee, Rock Wren, Verdin, and Rufous-crowned Sparrow are present on the dry slopes. This is one of the favored local areas during spring migration.

On the way to Buffalo Springs Lake, a stop at Boles Lake is sometimes good for the unexpected. To reach Boles Lake from FM 835, turn north on Boles Road about one mile east of Loop 289. The lake, on the west side of Boles Road about one-half mile north of FM 835, is a playa used for treating sewage water for irrigation. Waterfowl, shorebirds, and marsh birds are present in migration and in winter. Many rare waterfowl and shorebirds have been found here, including Whimbrel, Marbled Godwit, White-rumped Sandpiper, Dunlin, Sanderling, and Ross' Goose. Black-necked Stilt and American Avocet have nested here.

Dunlin

Muleshoe National Wildlife Refuge

Muleshoe National Wildlife Refuge has 5809 acres of short-grass prairie, typical of the Llano Estacado before farming and ranching began less than 100 years ago. Established in 1935 to provide resting and wintering areas for Sandhill Crane and waterfowl, the refuge is the oldest national wildlife refuge in Texas.

From the city of Muleshoe, drive south on SH 214 for 19 miles to the refuge entrance on the right (west). From Lubbock, drive northwest on US 84 for 38 miles to Littlefield, west 19 miles on FM 54, four miles west on FM 37, then north on SH 214 about five miles to the refuge entrance on the left.

There are three playa lakes in which the water level varies with the amount of rainfall. In wet years there is approximately 500 surface acres of water. Some years they are practically dry.

The wintering Sandhill Crane are the main attraction. On some Christmas Counts, the number of cranes at the refuge has exceeded 100,000, easily the largest winter concentration of these birds in Texas. From late September through March, the cranes use the refuge for roosting at night and resting during the day. The largest concentrations are present either at dawn or dusk before and as they leave for feeding areas and when they return. The cranes are also frequently seen feeding in nearby fields during the day.

Permanent residents include Bobwhite, Great Horned and Burrowing Owls, Horned Lark, and Cactus Wren. The latter two are often found near the headquarters building.

Other nesting birds, which usually go south in winter, include American Avocet, Snowy Plover, and Cassin's Sparrow.

Rough-legged and Marsh Hawks, Golden Eagle, Prairie Falcon, and Long-eared and Short-eared Owls may be seen during fall, winter, and spring. Canada Geese winter by the hundreds; ducks in the thousands. Some birds found on recent Christmas Counts include Mountain Chickadee, Townsend's Solitaire, and Sage Sparrow. Other birds which may be found in winter are Tree Sparrow, Green-tailed Towhee, Gray-headed Junco, Baird's, LeConte's, and Brewer's Sparrows. McCown's, Chestnut-collared, and Lapland Longspurs winter in the grasslands. Black-tailed Prairie Dog can also be found on the refuge.

A bird check-list of 247 species is available at headquarters. The refuge address is Refuge Manager, Muleshoe National Wildlife Refuge, P.O. Box 549, Muleshoe, TX 79347.

Amarillo

Amarillo, the largest city on the Llano Estacado with a population of 149,000, is centrally located for bird seeking in the Texas Panhandle, as the upper part of the Llano Estacado is known. Ranching predominates north of Amarillo, while farming is more common between Amarillo and Lubbock.

The principal birding locations of the area are Palo Duro Canyon State Park, 20 miles south; Caprock Canyon State Park, 95 miles south; Buffalo Lakes National Wildlife Refuge, 23 miles southwest; Lake Meredith National Recreation Area, 38 miles north; and Rita Blanca National Grasslands, 120 miles northwest of Amarillo.

It is not necessary to leave the city to find nesting Mississippi Kite. They are common in many city parks, particularly Thompson Municipal Park. The park is north of downtown at 24th Street and US 87 and 287. American Robin also nest in the park. The kite can also be easily found in Elwood Park, between West 11th and West 13th Streets and Washington and Jackson.

Lake Marvin is in the Lake Marvin National Grassland, approximately 12 miles east of Canadian on RR 2266 (about 10 miles west of the Oklahoma state line). Many Eastern species reach their western nesting limit here, including Wood Duck, Barred Owl, Warbling Vireo, Northern (Baltimore) Oriole, Field Sparrow, Great Crested Flycatcher, and Least Tern. Lesser Prairie Chicken are also present, but most are found on private land. During March, the "booming" by the males can lead to the places where the chickens carry on their mating rituals. There is an entrance fee.

Palo Duro Canyon State Park

Palo Duro Canyon State Park, the largest state park in Texas (16,046 acres), is located 12 miles east of Canyon on SH 217, or 20 miles south of Amarillo on FM 1541, then east on SH 217. The park preserves a small portion of Palo Duro Canyon, a dramatic western extension of the Caprock Escarpment. The elevation drops approximately 800 feet in a mile or so from the park entrance to Prairie Dog Town Fork of the Red River. Four geological periods representing about 280 million years are exposed in the canyon walls: Permian, Triassic, Tertiary, and Quaternary. To the nongeologist, the walls are a brilliant display of color layers of varying thickness—brick-red, gray, purple, yellow, orange, and tan.

There is picnicking, camping, restrooms with hot showers, a gift shop with snack bar and restaurant, laundry tubs, horseback riding, a miniature train, and an amphitheater. The musical extravaganza, "TEXAS," is presented in the amphitheater nightly (except Sunday) from late June through August. The spectacle depicts the history and culture of the High Plains.

The vegetation of the park is mostly mesquite, Rocky Mountain and One-seeded Junipers, and brush, but large cottonwoods, hackberries, and soapberries are found along the Prairie Dog Town Fork. A hike along this stream can be an excellent way to find the birds of the park.

Nesting birds in the park are Mississippi Kite, Golden-fronted Woodpecker, Ash-throated Flycatcher, Blue and Scrub Jays, Verdin, Bushtit, Cañon and Rock Wrens, Northern (Bullock's) Oriole, and Rufous-crowned Sparrow.

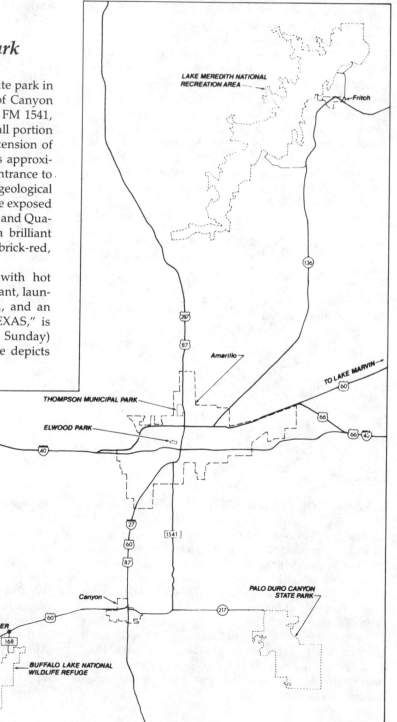

Amarillo

Canada Goose

This is where I found my first Northern Shrike, which occurs in winter with some degree of regularity. Other wintering birds are Common Flicker, Mountain Bluebird, Townsend's Solitaire, Golden-crowned Kinglet, Pine Siskin, Tree Sparrow, and sometimes Golden Eagle.

A bird check-list for the park is available at headquarters. The address is Route 2, Box 285, Canyon, TX 79015 (806) 488–2227.

Lake Meredith

Lake Meredith is on the Canadian River approximately 35 miles north of Amarillo on SH 136. Its purpose is to supply water to several Panhandle municipalities. The lake is created by Sanford Dam, near the town of Sanford, about nine miles east of Borger. At conservation pool level, the lake has 16,505 surface acres and a shoreline of 100 miles.

Though included in this book as part of the Llano Estacado, Lake Meredith is actually in a subregion of the Rolling Plains known as the Canadian Brakes with Rolling Plains vegetation, soil, and bird life. The Canadian River basin here is about 200 feet below the High Plains from which the canyon was carved by the Canadian River.

The National Park Service administers the Lake Meredith National Recreational Area (41,097 acres). The area is divided into eight units with camping, picnicking, boating, fishing, cycling, hunting, and water skiing. The facilities in some units are primitive.

The Alibates Flint Quarries National Monument is near the southeast shore of the lake, the site of prehistoric Indian flint quarries for more than 12,000 years. The flint areas can be visited only on guided tours, presently 10 a.m. and 2 p.m. during the summer months, or by prearrangement during the rest of the year. From archeological evidence, it is known that tools and weapons from alibates flint were widely used by Indians all over the Great Plains and the Southwest.

Common permanent resident birds include Mallard, Pintail, Turkey (Plum Creek), Common Flicker, Horned

Lark, Rock Wren, Western Meadowlark, House Finch, and Rufous-crowned Sparrow. Less common are Golden Eagle and Curve-billed Thrasher.

Common summer residents are Mississippi Kite (Bonita), American Coot, Red-headed Woodpecker, and Cassin's Sparrow. Summer residents which are less common include Green-winged, Blue-winged and Cinnamon Teals, American Kestrel, Virginia Rail, Burrowing Owl, Ash-throated Flycatcher, Hairy Woodpecker (McBride Canyon), Carolina Chickadee (McBride Canyon), and Painted Bunting.

Regular migrant shorebirds are Snowy and Semipalmated Plovers, Long-billed Curlew, Stilt, Baird's, Least, Semipalmated, Western, Upland, and Spotted Sandpipers, Long-billed Dowitcher, Wilson's Phalarope, Greater and Lesser Yellowlegs, and Common Snipe.

Near Alibates at the upper end of the lake, Canada Goose, Gadwall, American Wigeon, Northern Shoveler, Blue-winged, Cinnamon and Green-winged Teals, Redhead, Lesser Scaup, Common Goldeneye, Bufflehead, and Common Merganser winter in large numbers.

In addition to the previous species, winter residents are Golden Eagle, Mountain and Eastern Bluebirds, Townsend's Solitaire, and Tree Sparrow. More difficult to find are Rough-legged Hawk, Prairie Falcon, and Northern Shrike. Bald Eagle are frequently seen over the lake in winter. They roost in the Bonita area where 30–40 birds can be found at one time.

Pronghorn can be found in the grasslands surrounding the lake, and occasionally a coyote comes loping along.

A bird check-list is available from the Lake Meredith Recreation Area, P.O. Box 1438, Fritch, TX 79036.

Buffalo Lake National Wildlife Refuge

Buffalo Lake National Wildlife Refuge (7677 acres) is located on Tierra Blanca Creek approximately 28 miles southwest of Amarillo.

To reach the refuge, drive southwest from Canyon on US 60 for 12 miles to Umbarger. Turn south on FM 168, then go 1.5 miles to the refuge entrance.

The principal feature of the refuge is Buffalo Lake, which has 1100 surface acres when filled with water. Originally built by the Soil Conservation Service, the refuge is now administered by the U.S. Fish and Wildlife Service.

At this time, Buffalo Lake has been drained because the spillway portion of the dam is in need of repairs. The following account assumes that these repairs will occur in the near future, but this is by no means certain. Until the repairs are made, the waterfowl referred to here will not be found.

In summer this has been a very popular recreation area with waterskiing, fishing, picnicking, and camping. In winter Buffalo Lake is home to great numbers of waterfowl. To give an idea of the numbers present, a recent

Christmas Count recorded 108,000 Mallard, 62,000 Pintail, 21,000 American Wigeon, 7500 Canada Goose (with a high-water level—40,000). Common Merganser are usually present also, along with many other waterfowl species in smaller numbers. Other winter residents include Golden and Bald Eagles (sometimes abundant), Long-eared Owl (I found two in the old salt cedar fence row one November day), Tree Sparrow, and occasionally Prairie Falcon.

Nesting birds include Snowy Plover, American Avocet, Black-crowned Night Heron, Bobwhite, Ring-necked Pheasant, and Burrowing Owl.

There is a large and prosperous Black-tailed Prairie Dog town where Burrowing Owl are easily found and Ferruginous Hawk winter.

In winter look for McCown's, Chestnut-collared, and Lapland Longspurs in the fields which surround the refuge. Smith's Longspur occur also but are very rare.

A check-list of the birds of the refuge is available at headquarters. The address of the refuge is Refuge Manager, P.O. Box 228, Umbarger, TX 79091.

Rita Blanca National Grasslands

The Rita Blanca National Grasslands (77,000 acres in Texas and an additional 16,000 in Oklahoma) are located in the extreme northwest corner of the Panhandle. The grasslands are administered by the U.S. Forest Service to demonstrate how marginal land can be restored and managed to produce grass for the benefit of the land, people, and wildlife. Hunting is permitted on certain sections in season.

Ferruginous Hawk

The grasslands are made up of about 38 separate units in Texas, with the largest unit located about eight miles east of Texline at the junction of FM 296 and FM 1879. This unit contains the Thompson Grove Recreation Site, where picnic tables and restrooms are provided. The heavily wooded site is cool in summer and an oasis for a variety of arboreal birds.

Common nesting birds of the grasslands include Long-billed Curlew, Lark Bunting, Ring-necked Pheasant, Ferruginous Hawk, Horned Lark, Cassin's and Lark Sparrows. Some years Mountain Plover can also be found nesting. The Black-tailed Prairie Dog towns are good places for Burrowing Owl and Ferruginous Hawk. Pronghorn and coyote are common residents.

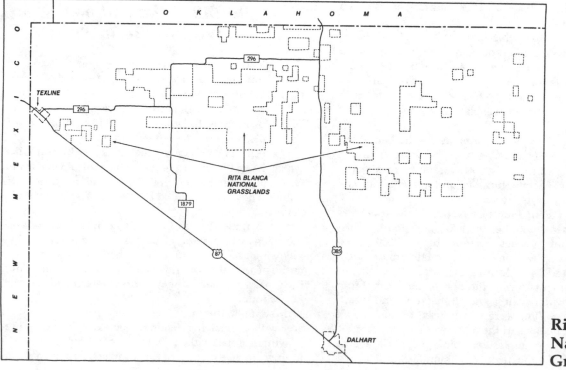

Rita Blanca National Grasslands

The address is Rita Blanca National Grasslands, P.O. Box 38, Texline, TX 79087. The Ranger Station is in Texline, which is 36 miles northwest of Dalhart, or 124 miles northwest of Amarillo on US 87.

Caprock Canyons State Park

Caprock Canyons State Park is located almost equidistant between Amarillo and Lubbock at the eastern edge of the Caprock Escarpment. To reach the park from Amarillo, drive south on IH 27 for 49 miles to Tulia, southeast on SH 86 for 51 miles to Quitaque, then go north on FM 1065 about three miles to the "Lake Theo" sign. Turn left (west) to the park entrance. To get to Quitaque from Lubbock, drive east on US 62 and 82 for 27 miles to Ralls, then north on SH 207 for 52 miles to FM 145. Go east 17 miles to Quitaque.

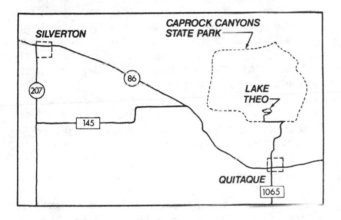

The park is at the southern end of Palo Duro Canyon and has 13,655 acres of rugged canyonlands and creeks. Mesquite is the dominant woody plant in the uplands, while cottonwoods are found along the watercourses. The flora and fauna are similar to that described earlier for Palo Duro Canyon State Park, except for Lake Theo (a 100-acre lake). Lake Theo attracts waterfowl and shorebirds in fall, winter, and spring.

Until 1983, when the park is fully developed, about 300 acres surrounding the lake are open for day use only. Park activities pending the opening are limited to fishing, picnicking, boating, and hiking.

Permanent resident birds include Brown Towhee, Bewick's, Rock, and Cañon Wrens, Scrub Jay, Golden-fronted Woodpecker, Rufous-crowned Sparrow, Bushtit, and Verdin. In summer look for Painted Bunting and Swainson's Hawk. I have seen Mississippi Kite in summer near the entrance to the park.

On Lake Theo, practically all waterfowl found elsewhere in West Texas make an appearance in fall, winter, and spring. Some common species are Canada Goose, Pintail, and Lesser Scaup. Rare waterfowl recorded include Red-throated Loon, Red-necked Grebe, Greater Scaup, and Least Bittern. Osprey, and Forster's and Black Terns are regular migrants.

Mountain Bluebird, Townsend's Solitaire, and many sparrow species winter in the park, including Brewer's Sparrow.

The Aoudad Sheep, first introduced into Palo Duro Canyon State Park from North Africa in 1957, have been successful in adapting to the environment east of the Caprock. Many can be found in Caprock Canyons State Park, with groups of 40-50 sighted regularly in all areas of the park. Other animals include Mule Deer and Porcupine.

The park address is P.O. Box 204, Quitaque, TX 79255 (806) 455-1492.

Midland

(All directions are from the intersection of IH 20 and SH 349, south of Midland.)

Monahans Draw

From SH 349, drive west on IH 20 about 9.5 miles to Exit 126 (FM 1788) just west of the Midland Regional Airport. Drive south on FM 1788 for 4.4 miles to a prairie dog town in a playa on the east side of the road. Continue about 0.2 miles further to a spot where it is safe to turn around. Then come back and park on the east side of the road about halfway to the lowest spot on the road. Burrowing Owl will be on the bare mounds on the slopes of the playa or sticking their heads from the holes in the mounds. The owls are present all year and can be seen almost any time of day, except during very hot summer afternoons. In winter look for Ferruginous Hawk sitting on the ground in the prairie dog colony or sailing overhead. In summer Cassin's Sparrow can be heard on all sides. Look in the direction of the song to see the male skylarking as he sings. Swainson's Hawk, White-necked Raven, and Scissor-tailed Flycatcher are also present in summer. In winter an occasional Prairie Falcon can be seen darting by overhead.

From this spot, continue north on FM 1788 for 1.2 miles to County Road 160. Turn right (east). After one mile, turn right (south) on County Road 1270. One mile from this corner is Monahans Draw. Treated (but odorless) sewage effluent from Odessa flows into the draw. Gadwall, Pintail, Green-winged Teal, American Wigeon, and Northern Shoveler may be seen on the pond on the west side of the road from October through March. Just past the draw, turn left on County Road 170. The first mile of this road is topped with caliche, which is slick when wet (very seldom). The last mile is very sandy, and it is easy to get stuck when dry (usually). But the road crosses Monahans Draw several times past ponds where ducks and shorebirds may be seen. There are also patches of sunflowers, mesquite thickets, and open fields that provide a variety of habitats. Harris' Hawk, Verdin, Ladder-backed Woodpecker, Cactus Wren, and Pyrrhuloxia are present all year. In winter there are Long-billed Marsh Wren, Vesper, Song, Lincoln's, and

Midland

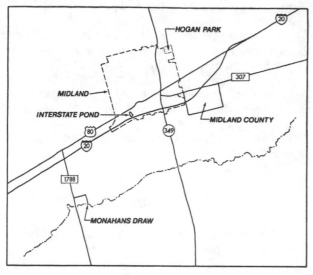

Swamp Sparrows. In some winters Short-eared Owl hunt along the draw at dawn and dusk. In the summer White-necked Raven nest nearby and are frequently seen flying over. When the road becomes too sandy to travel, turn around, go back to County Road 1270, and return to IH 20.

Interstate Pond

From the north end of the Midkiff Road overpass, turn west along the north access road. At 0.6 of a mile, there will be a pond on the right with a dam behind it. Continue another 0.2 of a mile, and turn right on a dirt trail along a fence. Park where most of what the local birders call "Interstate Pond" is visible. DO NOT CROSS THE FENCE. A telescope is necessary to see birds on the pond. Ducks present on the lake from mid-October until late March include Redhead, Ring-necked, Canvasback, and Lesser Scaup, as well as Pied-billed Grebe. Cinnamon and Blue-winged Teals are present in March. During migration, look for American Avocet, Black-necked Stilt, Wilson's Phalarope, Osprey, and Yellow-headed Blackbird.

After viewing the birds on Interstate Pond, take the north IH 20 access road east 2.3 miles to the Petroleum Museum. No birds of interest are here, but there is an excellent museum which explains the history and evolution of the oil industry. There are open-air exhibits of old-time drilling rigs and equipment. Inside is a marine diorama of an ancient ocean reef as well as more of the oil story.

Hogan Park

From Exit 136—Garden City (Two miles east of SH 349)

After exiting, drive north on Fairgrounds Road, although you will not see a sign giving that information until you have traveled a mile. Continue north four miles, go past the golf course, and turn left (west) on Wadley Road. The entrance to Hogan Park is about one-half mile on the right. Turn in, go past the Midland Woman's Club building to a sign, "Outdoor Learning Center." Park, go through the gate, pick up a leaflet from the box in the kiosk, and walk the half-mile trail. Resident birds include Verdin, Cactus Wren, and Pyrrhuloxia. Summer birds are Scissor-tailed Flycatcher, Western Kingbird, Ash-throated Flycatcher, Northern (Bullock's) Oriole, Blue Grosbeak, Lesser Goldfinch, and Cassin's Sparrow. In spring Burrowing Owl is abundant in Hogan Park. They can be seen on telephone poles, mesquite bushes, fence posts, and on the ground. The small grove of trees by the pond is attractive to migrating birds and has provided many exciting rarities for local birders. This is not a good place to go on Saturday or Sunday afternoons—too many people.

Midland County

During winter, another worthwhile birding locality is reached from Exit 136. Cloverdale Road (FM 307) is a mile north of the exit. Turn right (east), go three miles (past Cole Park on the right), and turn right (south) on County Road 1140. On this road, look for Long-billed Curlew, especially when the alfalfa fields are being irrigated. If the alfalfa has been recently mowed, watch also for flocks of Chestnut-collared Longspur flying in and out of the irrigated areas. Sometimes a few McCown's Longspur are present. After traveling two miles on County Road 1140, turn right (west) onto County Road 120. Go three miles on FM 715, turn right (north), and go back to IH 20. Watch overhead for Long-billed Curlew, Sandhill Crane, and Prairie Falcon all through this area.

Trans-Pecos

The Trans-Pecos is approximately 11% of Texas and is generally thought of as that section of Texas west of the Pecos River. However, in this book the Monahans Sandhills east of the river are included in the Trans-Pecos, while Stockton Plateau west of the river is placed with the Edwards Plateau.

The eastern boundary of the Trans-Pecos is roughly a north-to-south line from the New Mexico state line just north of Kermit southeastward between Monahans and Odessa to near McCamey. The boundary line continues to the west and north of Fort Stockton to the eastern edge of the Davis Mountains, and then turns southeast to the Rio Grande.

The area is the northern portion of the Chihuahuan Desert, which extends far south into Mexico between the Sierra Madre Oriental and the Sierra Madre Occidental. The vegetation in the lower elevations of the Chihuahuan Desert is desert scrub, creosote, and tarbush. Extensive structural montane valleys, principally grasslands, are between the desert and the higher elevations.

Several mountain ranges in the desert are biological islands. Well-developed montane woodlands are in the higher elevations, with a mixture of Mexican and Rocky Mountain vegetation, predominantly oaks, junipers, firs, and pines. The geology is complex. The Chisos and Davis Mountains are of igneous origin, whereas the

Guadalupes are composed of sedimentary rocks and block-faulted. Several other mountain ranges are in the Trans-Pecos, but, except for the Franklin Mountains at El Paso, are not included in this book.

The elevation of the desert and grasslands ranges between 1800 and 4000 feet; the mountain peaks range from 5000 to 8751 feet. Rainfall varies from 8 to 12 inches per year, with up to 20-plus inches in the higher elevations.

More bird species will be found near water or where there are trees. If there are both, it is usually an excellent spot for birding.

The Trans-Pecos has more nesting species unique to the region than any other in Texas. Included are White-throated Swift, Crissal Thrasher, Violet-green Swallow, Black-chinned Sparrow, Phainopepla, Black-headed Grosbeak, Western Wood Pewee, Cassin's Kingbird, Hepatic Tanager, Peregrine Falcon, Gambel's Quail, Band-tailed Pigeon, Broad-tailed and Blue-throated Hummingbirds, Western Flycatcher, Western Bluebird, Black-tailed Gnatcatcher, Rufous-sided Towhee, Mexican Duck, Whip-poor-will, Steller's Jay, Mountain Chickadee, Pygmy Nuthatch, Western Tanager, Pine Siskin, and Flammulated Owl. Species with a restricted nesting area are Montezuma Quail, Lucifer Hummingbird, Lucy's, Virginia's, Colima and Grace's Warblers, Mexican Jay, Hermit Thrush, Hutton's Vireo, Gray-headed Junco, and Painted Redstart.

Species which nest throughout the region include Scaled Quail, Roadrunner, Black-chinned Hummingbird, Western Kingbird, Scrub Jay, Cactus and Rock Wrens, Curve-billed Thrasher, Pyrrhuloxia, Black-throated Sparrow, and Black-headed Grosbeak.

Alpine

Alpine, the home of Sul Ross University and Museum of the Big Bend, is the hub for birding in the Trans-Pecos. Big Bend National Park is 78 miles south, the Davis Mountains are 26 miles northwest, and El Paso is 220 miles west. Each highway from Alpine has its bird attractions.

Look for wintering hawks along US 67 northeast to Fort Stockton and US 90 east to Marathon. Red-tailed, Ferruginous, Rough-legged, Harris' Hawks, Golden Eagle, and Prairie Falcon are all regular, and with great luck, a Goshawk.

The Prairie Falcon is fairly common northwest to Fort Davis on SH 118. In winter the roadsides should be checked for Grasshopper, Brewer's, Clay-colored, and Chipping Sparrows, Lark Bunting, and McCown's and Chestnut-collared Longspurs. After summer rains commence, Cassin's Sparrow are very visible. In the first low ridge of mountains the brushy draws can have Baird's Sparrow in winter, while Montezuma Quail are found year-round. Along Musquiz Creek, approximately 20 miles from Alpine at the rest area, summer birds include Bushtit, Cassin's Kingbird, Vermilion Flycatcher, Black

Phoebe, Warbling Vireo, Painted Bunting, and Blue Grosbeak. This location is excellent for observing migrants in spring and fall.

At Paisano Pass, about 13 miles west of Alpine on US 90 toward Marfa, Cliff and Violet-green Swallows and White-throated Swift can be seen overhead. In the oaks look for Cassin's and Western Kingbirds, Black-headed Grosbeak, House Finch, and Western Bluebird. Watch the power lines for White-necked Raven and Swainson's Hawk, both of which nest along this highway.

In the highlands on SH 118 south toward Big Bend National Park, the rest areas should be checked for Phainopepla, Bushtit, Crissal Thrasher, Western Bluebird, and the very light Fuertes race of the Red-tailed Hawk.

Big Bend National Park

Big Bend National Park is one of the "must" birding places in Texas. The park is huge, with more than 700,000 acres—50-plus miles north to south, 60-plus miles east to west. A complete mountain range, the Chisos, is within the park boundaries. The mountains are surrounded by grasslands, which in turn are surrounded by the Chihuahuan Desert.

To reach the park, drive south from Marathon on US 385 (85 miles) to park headquarters. Or, from Alpine, drive south on SH 118 (117 miles) to park headquarters.

Casa Grande, Big Bend National Park

A wide variety of accommodations are available in the park. A modern lodge with dining room (advance reservations recommended, 915–477–2291) and stone cottages with bath are available. Outfitters' horse rides are offered from the Basin to the South Rim and the Window Trail. There are large campgrounds in the Basin, at Rio Grande Village, and at Castolon, as well as service stations and small stores. Float trips on the Rio Grande through Santa Elena, Mariscal, and Boquillas canyons

Big Bend National Park

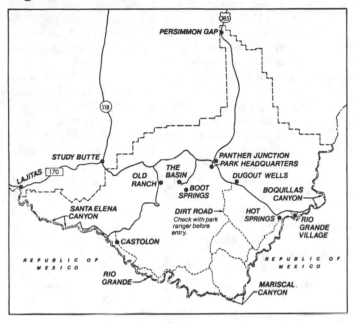

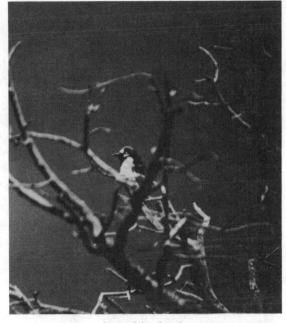

Acorn Woodpecker

may be arranged individually with Ranger approval. Finally, there are 32 hiking trails totaling more than 150 miles. These are listed in the *Hiker's Guide*, published by the Big Bend Natural History Association and available at park headquarters. Also, see *Hiking and Backpacking Trails of Texas* by Mildred J. Little (Lone Star Books) for more information.

Big Bend is a naturalist's paradise of geologic formations, fossils, plants, mammals, birds, reptiles, amphibians, and fish. Many are unique to the area. A stop at headquarters where exhibits, maps, pamphlets, books, and check-lists are available is highly recommended. The desk at headquarters should be checked for recent notable bird sightings.

For the visitor with limited time, the first "must" areas to visit are the Rio Grande Village camping area, the Basin, the Boot Springs area, Santa Elena Canyon, and those few places in the desert where there is water, such as Old Ranch and Dugout Wells. The park is so large it will take several visits in the different seasons before adequate attention can be given to the different habitats.

A hike to Boot Springs (el. 6300 feet) through Laguna Meadow between mid-April and September will take the bird seeker to the nesting area of the Colima Warbler, the park's most famous bird. Big Bend is the only place in the United States where it occurs. It is not always easy to find, but patience will usually be rewarded. Most are found in Boot Canyon, but they can also be seen along the trail near the Pinnacles between the Basin and Boot Springs and between Laguna Meadow and Boot Springs. In recent years Painted Redstart have become regular nesters at Boot Springs—indeed, they are now more easily found than the Colima.

Other nesting birds to watch for on a spring or summer mountain hike are Hutton's Vireo, Acorn Wood-pecker, Mexican Jay, Common Raven, Zone-tailed Hawk, White-breasted Nuthatch, White-throated Swift, Bushtit, Broad-tailed and Blue-throated Hummingbirds. Laguna Meadow is a good spot for Black-chinned Sparrow. Flammulated Owl and Whip-poor-will call in Boot Canyon at night, and at dawn and dusk Band-tailed Pigeon are sometimes present in large numbers. Gray Vireo are reported to nest in the side canyons above Boot Springs. The Pinnacles area on the Boot Springs Trail is a good place to watch for Zone-tailed Hawk, White-throated Swift, and an occasional Golden Eagle.

There are excellent birding possibilities in all seasons for the nonhiker in the Basin (el. 5400 feet)—from the sewage ponds up to the Juniper Flat and Boulder Meadow area. Nesting birds in those areas and along the Window Trail include Lucifer and Black-chinned Hummingbirds, Crissal Thrasher, Violet-green Swallow, White-winged Dove, Elf Owl, Ash-throated Flycatcher, Black-chinned Sparrow, Bell's Vireo, Scott's Oriole, Pyrrhuloxia, Varied Bunting, and Brown Towhee.

In summer the century plant blossoms provide food and moisture for a wide variety of creatures—insects, birds, mammals—and should be watched especially for hummingbirds. Lucifer, Broad-tailed, and Blue-throated Hummingbirds are all possibilities. Scott's Oriole are often seen feeding on century plants. The Lucifer Hummingbird seems to prefer the arroyos of the grasslands and are either increasing or observers are learning better how to find them. In late summer (late August and early September) western hummingbirds migrate through the park. Rufous Hummingbird are common but also Broad-tailed, White-eared, Broad-billed, Costa's, and Calliope have been recorded. Mexican Jay are easily found above the cottages on the trail to Juniper Flat. Cactus Wren call all around the parking lot in the Basin, Phainopepla are sometimes on the power lines, and Black-chinned Sparrow should be looked for in the shrubs near the Boot Springs-Window Trail trailhead.

I have seen Gray Vireo in Campground Canyon, a very steep canyon near the Basin campground. Black-capped Vireo are found in this canyon in summer also. Another location for Gray Vireo is on the slopes at the west end of the Window Trail.

A complete change in bird life occurs at Rio Grande Village campground (el. 1800 feet) on the river at the eastern end of the park. Here Vermilion Flycatcher, Orchard Oriole, Lesser Nighthawk, Elf Owl, Yellow-billed Cuckoo, Verdin, Common Yellowthroat, Summer Tanager, Painted and Varied Buntings, and Bell's Vireo are all common nesters. More Vermilion Flycatcher are here than any other one spot I know of in Texas. Cottontail, Roadrunner, Inca and White-winged Doves walk around the campground like pets. There is an excellent nature trail and several ponds, each of which should be checked for birds. Rio Grande Village is an excellent place to be in late April and early May for spring migration.

The most visible bird in the desert is the Black-throated Sparrow. But a stop at Old Ranch, Dugout Wells, or any of the other springs in the desert will usually add Scott's Oriole, Pyrrhuloxia, Mockingbird, Blue Grosbeak, Ash-throated Flycatcher, and Black-tailed Gnatcatcher. In winter, watch for Green-tailed Towhee. The Varied Bunting is often found at Old Ranch, and occasionally Gray Vireo. Sitting quietly on a bench at Old Ranch and waiting for the birds to come to water is a favorite way for many photographers to get pictures of the birds of Big Bend. In the desert nearby also check for Sage Thrasher in winter and spring.

The park check-list has 35 warbler species as migrants, including such western species as Hermit, Townsend's, Grace's, and MacGillivray's. Nearly every year a rarity or two makes an appearance at Big Bend, such as Aztec Thrush (Boot Canyon), Rufous-capped Warbler (Campground Canyon and Santa Elena Canyon), Coppery-tailed Trogan (Window Trail), Black-vented Oriole (Rio Grande Village), and others.

Roland Wauer, former Chief Naturalist of Big Bend National Park, has written an excellent book which all serious bird seekers should obtain: *Birds of Big Bend National Park and Vicinity*, published by The University of Texas Press, Austin, Texas. It is available at park headquarters, or your local bookstore.

A bird check-list is available at headquarters that lists 360 species plus 37 hypothetical species. The park address is Superintendent, Big Bend National Park, Texas 79834 (915) 477-2251.

Presidio County

Presidio County, west of Big Bend National Park, is a little-known birding area of the state and offers the challenge of discovery to the visiting birder. More than 300 species have been recorded in the county, but many more probably occur and, for those who like remote areas, here is opportunity to add to Texas bird knowledge. This trip follows the Rio Grande from Big Bend National Park to Candelaria and Marfa along what is one of the most scenic drives in Texas. A high-clearance vehicle is recommended for the road from Ruidosa to Candelaria and back.

Take RR 170 (the River Road) from SH 118 just north of the west entrance to Big Bend National Park through Terlingua, Lajitas, and Redford to Presidio. Past Lajitas, a stop at the high overlook in the canyons in summer should turn up Violet-green Swallow and White-throated Swift flying in the updrafts. Cliff Swallow are also present, and Cave Swallow have been found in migration. Cañon Wren can be heard singing their distinctive song. At least one pair of Zone-tailed Hawk nest along this canyon, and a little time spent checking the numerous Turkey Vulture overhead will sometimes result in a good look at the hawk. Common Raven can be recognized by their deep voice and wedge-shaped tail.

Between Lajitas and Redford, the land is characterized by the ocotillo, prickly pear, and lechuguilla—typical plants of the Chihuahuan Desert. In spring Crissal Thrasher, Inca and Ground Doves, and Verdin are common; in winter watch for Sage Thrasher and Sage Sparrow.

At Redford, the Presidio Agricultural Region begins signaling a drastic change in the birdlife. White-winged Dove, a unique race nearly twice the size of all others, makes its appearance here. Cardinal, Yellow-breasted Chat, and Painted and Varied Buntings are common. Check the ditches and drainage pileups for the Mallard/Mexican Duck hybrids. In migration this area can be teeming with waterfowl and shorebirds and sometimes White-faced Ibis. On the western edge of Redford is a packing shed surrounded by tall cottonwoods. Mississippi Kite have nested here.

About nine miles northwest of Redford, at the junction of Alamito Creek and the Rio Grande, is a marshy area which can be overflowing with migrants. Baird's Sandpiper is usually fairly common in spring and fall. Look for them among the Western and Least Sandpipers. Most wintering "peeps" are Least Sandpiper with muddy legs.

Fort Leaton State Historic Site is on RR 170 between Alamito Creek and Presidio and is well worth a visit. Here a fortified trading post dating back to the mid-19th century has been restored for historical study. A bird check-list is available at the site that lists 187 species recorded within five miles of the old fort.

At Presidio turn north to Marfa on US 67 or continue on RR 170 to Ruidosa. On US 67, a worthwhile stop is in the old mining town of Shafter. Drive to the east edge of town to the tall cottonwoods along Cibolo Creek. Ask permission at the house to bird beyond the creek. Nesting birds include Black Hawk, Cassin's and Western Kingbirds. Migration can be very productive.

Drive with care on RR 170 northwest of Presidio. Loose livestock are common, and the road undulates like a roller coaster for much of its 47 miles. The birding is best along this stretch if the departure from Presidio is made about 30 minutes before daylight. The most com-

Presidio County

mon birds along the road are White-winged and Mourning Doves, Crissal Thrasher, Verdin, Roadrunner, Cactus Wren and Turkey Vulture. The only Presidio County flock of Black Vultures (usually about 15) are found in this stretch. A pair of Harris' Hawks is resident about three miles southeast of Ruidosa. The closer to Ruidosa, the more common Gambel's Quail become. There should be no problem finding Gambel's Quail before reaching Candelaria.

The best birding is past Ruidosa to Candelaria, but since the pavement ends at Ruidosa, a high-clearance or four-wheel drive vehicle is recommended. From May until October, washouts and flash floods are not unusual between Ruidosa and Candelaria. Do not drive into the area if the weather appears threatening.

At Ruidosa the pavement gives way to sand and rocky hills, and driving the remaining eight miles to Candelaria is laborious but rewarding. Scan the skies carefully anywhere along this stretch and up into the Chinati Mountains to the north. Zone-tailed and Black Hawks, and Prairie and Peregrine Falcons have all nested in this area. Golden Eagle are a frequent sight, especially in migration.

An oxbow is a prominent feature near Candelaria, and from mid-April to mid-May it is alive with migrants in the runoff and in the bordering salt cedar. This is a good place for waterfowl, including Mallard/Mexican Duck hybrids and shorebirds. In the trees look for local nesters, such as Varied Bunting, Lesser Goldfinch, Common Yellowthroat, Yellow-breasted Chat, Summer Tanager, Bell's Vireo, Hooded and Scott's Orioles, and sometimes Northern (Bullock's) Oriole. Walking one of the sandy draws toward the Rio Grande should reveal these birds in abundance, as well as Ladder-backed Woodpecker and numerous sparrows in winter. During May and June, listen carefully for a high-pitched trill emanating from the salt cedar. Quietly stalk the trill, and perhaps there will be a Lucy's Warbler feeding in the trees. These birds nest in Texas in a small area around Candelaria, and I have been fortunate enough to have recorded them there. I know of no other location in Texas where they can be expected. In migration the most common warblers in this section are Yellow-rumped (Audubon's),

Wilson's, MacGillivray's, Townsend's, Virginia's, Black-throated Gray, Common Yellowthroat, and Yellow-breasted Chat. Lazuli Bunting have been recorded in migration also.

From Candelaria return to Ruidosa, turn left (northeast) on the unpaved road toward the mountains. Follow this road into Pinto Canyon and up through the pass between the Sierra Vieja Rimrock and the Chinati Mountains. Phainopepla can be rather common in this stretch, especially around cottonwoods and junipers. In cottonwood and oak areas watch for Scrub Jay. In winter Steller's Jay and Williamson's Sapsucker have been found.

After going over the pass, the road is paved (RR 2810) and leads to Marfa. The habitat here is high-elevation grassland, and again the birdlife changes. Watch for Golden Eagle, Prairie Falcon, and Pronghorn year-round. In all but the hottest months Lark Bunting should be present, and in winter the roadsides are host to lots of sparrows, including Brewer's, Clay-colored, Vesper, and Chipping, along with McCown's and Chestnut-collared Longspurs. Baird's Sparrow should be looked for in grassy areas near brushy draws. Montezuma Quail occur in a few sheltered spots in the canyon area near Marfa, and sometimes flocks of Piñon Jay can be found in winter. This is a good area to see migrant Yellow-headed Blackbird. Occasionally, Swainson's Hawk nest on power lines south and east of Marfa.

The birds listed on the check-list for the Big Bend National Park should be representative of Presidio County.

Davis Mountains

The Davis Mountains offer a contrast to the Chisos in Big Bend and the more northern Guadalupe Mountains. The difference is explained by the more abundant rainfall, the more thickly forested areas in the higher elevations, the presence of a highly developed riparian system, and the greater number of acres of grasslands surrounding the mountains.

This area offers much for the visitor besides birds: Fort Davis National Historic Site, Davis Mountains State Park, McDonald Observatory atop Mount Locke, and a scenic 74-mile drive which circles Mount Livermore (8382 feet), the highest peak in the Davis Mountains.

The scenic drive is an excellent birding tour with a diversity of montane grasslands, pine forests, and rock outcrops. From Fort Davis, drive north on SH 118, and soon on the left will be the Fort Davis National Historic Site, where the frontier fort established in 1854 and abandoned in 1891 has been restored by the National Park Service.

About four miles further north is Davis Mountains State Park, with camping, picnicking, restrooms with hot showers, and Indian Lodge, a modern motel-type facility with restaurant and pool. The rates are reasonable. Reservations are recommended (915) 426–3254.

The park (1869 acres) is in the foothills between the grasslands and the mountains. The birds to be found are representative of both habitats. There is a four-mile hiking trail connecting the park with the Fort Davis National Historic Site.

Common nesting birds in the park include Scrub Jay, Cassin's Kingbird, Scaled Quail, Curve-billed Thrasher, Cactus and Rock Wrens, Pyrrhuloxia, White-breasted Nuthatch, and Black-headed Grosbeak.

Be on the lookout in the camping area for Montezuma Quail; they often come down for water. This is the only park in Texas where this quail can be expected regularly. Although it is possible to see Montezuma Quail all along the scenic drive, it was my fourth trip to the Davis Mountains before I saw my first one.

In very cold weather high-altitude species, such as Steller's Jay, Mountain Chickadee, Townsend's Solitaire, and Gray-headed Junco, sometimes descend into the lowlands of the park. In the Davis Mountains, Eastern, Western, and Mountain Bluebirds can be found in winter, one of the few places in Texas where all three bluebirds can be expected.

A bird check-list is available at Davis Mountains State Park. The park address is Box 786, Fort Davis, TX 79734 (915) 426–3337.

The next stop, McDonald Observatory, is 13 miles to the west on SH 118. McDonald Observatory is owned

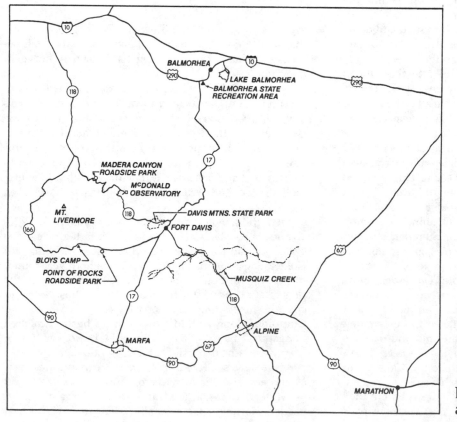

Davis Mountains and Alpine

by The University of Texas. The drive up Mount Locke (el. 6828 feet), where the telescopes are mounted, includes the highest point in the Texas highway system. Scrub Jay are common, and Montezuma Quail can sometimes be seen on the drive up. At this elevation, the Mexican Pinyon Pine and oaks are the dominant trees.

Indian Lodge, Davis Mountains State Park

The Madera Canyon Picnic Area is another seven miles on SH 118, an extensive roadside park maintained by the Texas Department of Highways and Public Transportation. I have always had good luck birding this roadside park. In summer Montezuma Quail, Phainopepla (some years), Hepatic Tanager, Grace's Warbler; in migration western warblers such as Black-throated Gray, MacGillivray's, Townsend's, Hermit, and Virginia's are all possible, as well as some eastern warblers. In winter watch for Mountain Chickadee, Williamson's Sapsucker, and Golden Eagle overhead.

If you cross a fence on this drive, you are on private property. PLEASE DO NOT CROSS FENCES without the owner's permission. Do not give birders a bad reputation by trespassing on private property.

Prairie Falcon are permanent residents and should be watched for anywhere along the drive. Zone-tailed and Black Hawks both nest in the Davis Mountains and should also be watched for as you drive the loop; they move their nests from year to year, so be on the lookout. In general, Black Hawk are in the vicinity of creek bottoms, and Zone-taileds are likely almost anywhere, but neither is very common. In addition, Mountain Plover have been found nesting in the grasslands south of the Davis Mountains.

After turning left on SH 166, you will soon get to the Sawtooth Mountains (to the left). On one February visit, I saw Montezuma Quail and Bald and Golden Eagles within 30 minutes in this area.

Continue on SH 166 back to Fort Davis. Make additional stops at Bloys Camp Meeting Ground (ask permission) and the Point of Rocks Roadside Park. Here Acorn Woodpecker (permanent residents), Gray-headed Junco, Townsend's Solitaire, and sparrows can be found

in winter. Migration can be teeming with birds. In winter there are usually Ferruginous Hawk overhead and McCown's and Chestnut-collared Longspurs in the grasslands.

Pronghorn graze in the grasslands in the vicinity of Fort Davis.

If you are very lucky, you may also encounter a flock of Piñon Jay on the loop in winter. They are usually in a large flock (from dozens to hundreds), but they seem to be constantly on the move. Sometimes they are accompanied by Clark's Nutcracker.

In winter in grassy areas and along creeks the following sparrows are common: Vesper, Cassin's, Dark-eyed (Slate-colored and Oregon) Junco, Gray-headed Junco, Chipping, Clay-colored, Brewer's, Black-chinned, Lincoln's, and Song. Less common are Grasshopper, Sage, Field, and White-throated. With good fortune, there may be Baird's. Near water watch for Black Phoebe and Vermilion Flycatcher.

Balmorhea State Recreation Area

Balmorhea State Recreation Area is near the town of Toyahvale, some 32 miles north of Fort Davis on SH 17, or 50 miles west of Fort Stockton off of IH 10. The main feature of the 48-acre park is San Solomon Springs. The flow of 22-plus million gallons per day from the bottom of the large swimming pool in the park supplies water to Lake Balmorhea, which in turn provides irrigation water to the adjoining area. In addition to swimming, the park has camping, picnicking, and cabins with bath and kitchen. Cave Swallow have been found nesting in the concession stand at the park. When they are on the nest, it is easy to get a clear, well-lighted look at them.

Lake Balmorhea is a mile or so south of the town of Balmorhea, which is about four miles north of Toyahvale. Large permanent bodies of water are scarce in the Trans-Pecos; therefore, the large lake is a mecca for migrating and wintering shorebirds and waterfowl.

The most interesting winter bird here is the Western Grebe, which sometimes occurs in numbers as great as 20 at a time. In midwinter both color phases (perhaps two distinct species) occur here and are easily compared. This is the only place in Texas to see these two color phases reliably.

In addition, Horned Grebe, Common and Red-breasted Mergansers, Mallard/Mexican Duck hybrids, Cinnamon Teal, Common Loon, and Sage and Brewer's Sparrows have been recorded on recent Christmas Counts. Most of the geese and ducks of Texas can be found in winter on the lake at one time or another.

The surrounding fields support a thriving population of Ring-necked Pheasant, and in winter there are large numbers of sparrows, McCown's and Chestnut-collared Longspurs, Lark Bunting, Long-billed and Short-billed Marsh Wrens, and LeConte's Sparrow.

Raptors found on Christmas Counts include Golden Eagle, Red-tailed, Ferruginous, and Rough-legged Hawks, Prairie Falcon, American Kestrel, and Merlin.

Any birding trip to this part of Texas should include a stop at Lake Balmorhea. The address of the Balmorhea State Recreation Area is Box 15, Toyahvale, TX 79786 (915) 375–2370.

Guadalupe Mountains National Park

Guadalupe Mountains National Park (76,293 acres on the Texas-New Mexico line) is one of the unique natural areas of Texas. The park preserves the four highest peaks in the state. The mountains are an exposed portion of the Capitan Reef, an ancient barrier reef laid down at the edge of an inland sea some 200-plus million years ago. At 8749 feet, Guadalupe Peak is the highest point in the state. El Capitan, the southern end of the reef, is a sheer rise of some 2000 feet from the desert below. It is visible for 50 miles and said to be the most photographed natural feature in Texas.

The park is 55 miles southwest of Carlsbad, New Mexico, 110 miles east of El Paso on US 62–180, or 65 miles north of Van Horn on SH 54.

The area is a convergence of natural areas. Here the Rocky Mountains to the north meet the Chihuahuan Desert to the south. The canyons between the low and high country, especially McKittrick Canyon, have a mixture of plants (some endemic) and animals from the mountains in the north and the desert to the south, east, and west.

Some common nesting birds of the higher elevations include Steller's Jay, Mountain Chickadee, Pygmy Nuthatch, Western Bluebird, Broad-tailed Hummingbird, Gray-headed Junco, Band-tailed Pigeon, Hermit Thrush, Violet-green Swallow, and White-throated Swift. Less common are Flammulated Owl, Whip-poor-will, Blue-throated Hummingbird, Brown Creeper, Cooper's Hawk, and occasionally Saw-whet Owl. Red Crossbill are permanent residents.

In the wooded canyons look for Western Flycatcher, Western Wood Pewee, Warbling and Gray Vireos, Grace's Warbler, Western Tanager, Acorn Woodpecker, Spotted Owl, Olive-sided Flycatcher, and occasionally Rivoli's Hummingbird. Virginia's Warbler can be found on dry canyon slopes.

Birds which nest in or near the desert are Black-throated Sparrow, Brown Towhee, Scaled Quail, Rock Wren, Rufous-crowned Sparrow, Roadrunner, Pyrrhuloxia, Black-chinned Sparrow, Scott's Oriole, and Crissal Thrasher. This is the only place in Texas where the Plain Titmouse can be found. I have found it in the draw behind the ranger residence at Frijole Historic Site and in Dog Canyon.

To see Guadalupe Mountains National Park, one must be prepared to hike. There are 63 miles of hiking trails. Two all-day hikes, one to the Bowl and one into McKittrick Canyon, are an excellent introduction to the park and to many birds as well.

No other place in Texas is like the Bowl. With an elevation of about 8000 feet, the Bowl's 2000 acres are sur-

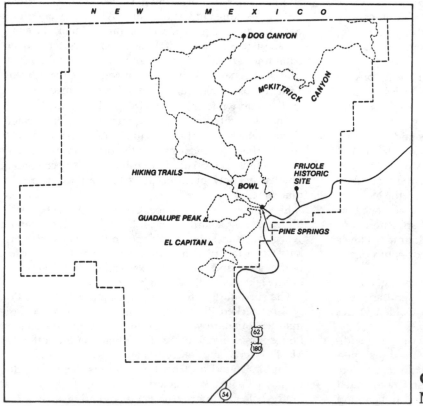

Guadalupe Mountains National Park

El Capitan, Guadalupe Mountains National Park

rounded by the highest peaks of the park. From Pine Springs Campground, it is about a 2.5-mile, steep and strenuous hike up to the Bowl. The increase in elevation is about 2000 feet, but it is well worth the effort. Start early to avoid the heat of the day. When the rim is crossed from the canyon below, a dramatic vegetational change becomes apparent in a matter of a few yards. The very dry, rocky terrain with a scattering of Pinyon Pine, low shrubs, and cacti of the uphill hike suddenly becomes a dense forest of Ponderosa and Limber Pines, 100-foot tall Douglas Firs, a few Quaking Aspens, and grassy meadows. Wildflowers are plentiful in summer. There is a pond or tank (sometimes dry) where many forms of wildlife come to drink at the head of South McKittrick Canyon. Wapiti (elk), Mule Deer, and other animals can be seen at the pond at dawn and dusk. Hike to the Blue Ridge Trail Junction, and look among the tall Douglas Firs in the canyon head for the elusive (for me) Spotted Owl.

McKittrick Canyon has the only perennial stream in the park and is famous for its mixture of desert, plains, Rocky Mountain and southern (Mexican) mountain plant species growing in close proximity. The fall colors of the Big-toothed Maples are spectacular. The McKittrick Canyon hike is the easiest hike for its length as well as the best hike in the park for the greatest variety of birds. Peregrine Falcon have nested on the high cliffs and Spotted Owl in the side canyons. Golden Eagle and Zone-tailed Hawk soar overhead with White-throated Swift and Violet-green Swallow. Pygmy Owl have been recorded in winter.

Manzanita Springs, a short distance behind the Frijole Historic Site, is the only place in Texas where I have seen Goshawk (can be found in the highlands as well). Wapiti come to the springs for water.

A bird check-list is available at park headquarters, as well as maps and other literature explaining the geology, history, and plants of the park.

The mailing address is Superintendent, Guadalupe Mountains National Park, 3225 National Parks Highway, Carlsbad, NM 88220 (915) 828–3385. The park is in the mountain time zone.

El Paso

El Paso, at the western extremity of Texas, is in the valley of the Rio Grande at the base of the Franklin Mountains and surrounded by the Chihuahuan Desert. The combined population of El Paso and Juarez, Mexico, just across the river, is more than 1.5 million. With an average rainfall of about eight inches, finding birds means finding a place where there is water. Nevertheless, there are a variety of habitats within a short drive from the city—mountains of more than 7000 feet elevation, the river, and some man-made ponds and lakes as well as the desert.

Common nesting birds of El Paso County include Gambel's Quail, White-winged Dove, Roadrunner, Burrowing Owl, Poor-will, Lesser Nighthawk, White-throated Swift, Ash-throated Flycatcher, Say's Phoebe, Ladder-backed Woodpecker, White-necked Raven, Verdin, Cañon Wren, Crissal Thrasher, Scott's Oriole, and Black-throated Sparrow. American Kestrel, Phainopepla, Common Yellowthroat, and Hooded Oriole are less common in summer.

The El Paso area is one of the most reliable locations in Texas for the Mexican Duck. However, researchers have determined that almost 100% of the Mexican Ducks in Texas and New Mexico have hybridized with Mallards; therefore, it is virtually certain that the Mexican Duck will be merged with the Mallard on the next A.O.U. check-list revision.

Memorial Park

Memorial Park in downtown El Paso is a favorite of local birders for resident and migrant land birds. From IH 10, drive north on Piedras Street six blocks. Turn right on Grant Street which leads to the park.

Great-tailed Grackle, House Finch, and Inca and White-winged Doves can be found in any season. In spring check the mesquites for warblers (mostly Wilson's, Yellow-rumped, and Orange-crowned; but also MacGillivray's, Townsend's, Virginia's, Yellow, and an occasional Black-throated Gray), Hooded and Northern (Bullock's) Orioles, Black-headed Grosbeak, Western Tanager, Western Wood Pewee, Black-chinned Hummingbird, and various western *empidonax* flycatchers. Fall sees the return of the same migrants but in fewer numbers.

In winter look for Dark-eyed (Oregon) and Gray-headed Juncos, Lesser Goldfinch, Green-tailed Towhee, Red-breasted Nuthatch (rare but regular), Red Crossbill (sporadic), and Yellow-bellied and Williamson's Sapsuckers. One or two Williamson's Sapsucker are present in winter or very early in spring during most years but

El Paso

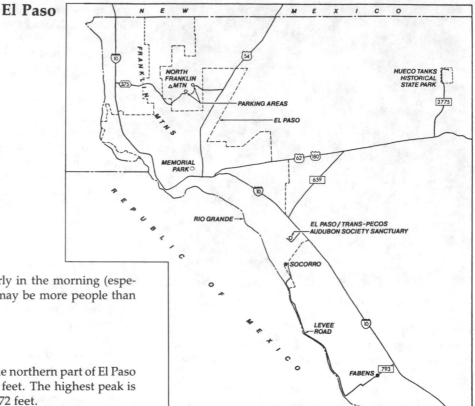

can be hard to find. Arrive early in the morning (especially on weekends), or there may be more people than birds.

Franklin Mountains

The Franklin Mountains in the northern part of El Paso have several peaks above 5000 feet. The highest peak is North Franklin Mountain at 7172 feet.

Good birding can be had in the canyons of the Franklin Mountains off of Trans-Mountain Road, which transects the mountains and connects with IH 10 on the west side of El Paso (Loop 375, Exit #6, Trans-Mountain/Canutillo) and US 54 (Dyer Street) in northeast El Paso. Two favorite canyons can be reached by driving west on Trans-Mountain Road from its intersection with Dyer Street (US 54) east of the mountains. The first canyon is immediately northwest of the large redrock formation as one heads up Trans-Mountain Road (just before the road takes a big bend to the left). This canyon leads to Apache Springs. Park at the pull-off on the right (by the dirt embankment), or further down the hill at the desert museum parking lot. Cross the flats and arroyos, and head northwest into the canyon. Eventually, there will be a conspicuous trail leading up the canyon.

Permanent residents to be found are Cañon Wren, Crissal Thrasher, White-throated Swift, Red-tailed Hawk, House Finch, Verdin, Black-throated and Rufous-crowned Sparrows. Other nesting birds are Blue Grosbeak, Ash-throated Flycatcher, and Scott's Oriole.

In winter, in addition to the permanent residents, watch for Pyrrhuloxia (a few may nest), Lesser Goldfinch (may nest), Black-chinned (a few do nest far up the canyon), White-crowned, Chipping, and Brewer's Sparrows.

The next good birding canyon (there are other canyons in-between) is Whispering Springs Canyon, which is 2.1 miles west of the dirt embankment mentioned previously.

The canyon is on the right, and there is a small pull-off to park a car. A trail leads up the dry wash. Further up where the wash widens, desert willow becomes common. Higher, the canyon narrows into a small but lush oasis surrounding the longest flowing spring in the Franklins. Cottonwood, ash, and black walnut provide shade and nesting sites, as do the profuse tangles of grapevine. The birds are essentially the same as in the Apache Springs Canyon, but Rufous-crowned Sparrow, Bewick's Wren, and hummingbirds are more common. Golden Eagle may be seen soaring overhead anywhere in the Franklins.

El Paso/Trans-Pecos Audubon Society Sanctuary

The El Paso/Trans-Pecos Audubon Society has a bird sanctuary called Feather Lake in the "lower valley" of El Paso County. To reach it, drive south on IH 10 from downtown El Paso and take the Avenue of the Americas exit. Stay to the right (on Avenue of the Americas) toward the end of the exit until you reach the signal light marking the intersection with North Loop Drive (FM 76). Turn right, and drive a short distance to the lake on the left. Pull over here. The lake is surrounded by a chain-link fence, and a caretaker lives in a trailer inside. If the gate is locked, honk the horn, and the caretaker will open the gate. The lake is excellent for migrant and wintering waterfowl, including Cinnamon Teal, several species of migrant shorebirds, and various herons and egrets. White-faced Ibis are commonly seen in migration. Common Merganser are often present in winter, and Whistling Swan will occasionally winter.

Rio Grande

The levee road along the Rio Grande from Fabens to Socorro offers the bird seeker an opportunity to bird irrigated farmland and the river. Drive southeast on IH 10 from its intersection with US 54 (Copia Street) 30 miles to the Fabens exit. Turn right (south) on North Fabens Street to the dead end near the river, and go right (west) onto the levee road. Permanent residents are Gambel's Quail, Mexican/Mallard hybrids, Great-tailed Grackle, and White-winged Dove. Prairie Falcon, Ferruginous, Marsh, Cooper's, and Sharp-shinned Hawks are seen in winter. Summer residents are Burrowing Owl, Blue Grosbeak, and Common Yellowthroat near the ditches. Stay on the levee road headed northwest to Socorro Sewage Ponds (right side of the road). These can be scoped for shorebirds, Cinnamon Teal, and other ducks in migration.

Hueco Tanks State Historical Park

Hueco Tanks State Historical Park is about 32 miles northeast of El Paso. To reach the park, drive east on US 62 and 180, either from Montana Avenue downtown until it becomes US 62, or from IH 10, about 10 miles southeast to RR 659 (Ysleta-Carlsbad Cutoff Road), then northeast about 8.5 miles to US 62 (180). From that point, go east nine miles to RR 2775, which leads north about six miles to the park.

On US 62 (180) in the desert, an area known as the Hueco Basin, Sage Sparrow are found during the winter (some years more easily than others). They prefer patches of creosote bush which are associated with a fair amount of grass and some saltbush (as opposed to the bareground, well-spaced creosote bush areas that are common along the highway). Some of the better areas are in the general vicinity of the El Paso Dragway, which is along the highway a few miles before the turnoff to the park. The dragway itself is closed and should not be entered, but there are some small pipeline roads east of the dragway on the south side of the road that have been open in the past. There are also some conspicuous sand dune-type hills to the right of the highway in this general area. They have good Sage Sparrow habitat at their base, and the dune buggy access roads can be used to park. The sparrows are somewhat shy, and seldom "pish" up into the open like the abundant Black-throated Sparrow. When flushed, watch where they land and RUSH to the spot, slowing down the last several yards. If approached too slowly, the bird will run out of the area. If there are two or more members in a party, they can be surrounded and pinned down. This is the best way to get a good view.

Sage Sparrow can also be found in the first mile of grasslands along RR 2775, the road from US 62 to Hueco Tanks. The area on both sides is very good for wintering sparrows, but this is private ranch land, and visiting birders should exercise appropriate behavior at all times. While driving this road into the park, watch to the left for a small dirt road which angles off to a stock pond and a small clump of mesquite. The mesquite patch should be checked in fall and winter for roosting Long-eared Owl. There is a similar but larger area approximately one mile north of this tank which should also be checked for the owls. The road to this second tank also leads left from the main (paved) road and is easy to see. Eastern Meadowlark are regular around this mesquite-grass-lands association, while Western Meadowlark dominate in other areas.

Nesting birds at Hueco Tanks include White-throated Swift, Black-chinned Hummingbird, Ash-throated Fly-catcher, Say's Phoebe, Verdin, Crissal Thrasher, Scott's Oriole, Poor-will, House Finch, Ladder-backed Wood-pecker, Blue Grosbeak, and Turkey Vulture. Other sum-mer residents are Swainson's Hawk, and Lesser Night-hawk. Burrowing and Barn Owls are sporadic nesters.

Migrants include Western Wood Pewee, Rufous Hum-mingbird, Cassin's Kingbird, Western Flycatcher, Violet-green Swallow, Sage Thrasher, Virginia's, Black-throated Gray, Townsend's, and MacGillivray's Warblers; Black-headed Grosbeak, Broad-tailed Hummingbird, and La-zuli Bunting.

In winter Black Phoebe (rare), Mountain Chickadee, Sage Thrasher, Mountain and Western Bluebirds, Town-send's Solitaire, Phainopepla, Lesser Goldfinch, Pine Siskin, Lark Bunting, Green-tailed Towhee, Gray-headed Junco, and Brewer's Sparrow have been recorded. One winter day I found my first Prairie Falcon at Hueco Tanks perched high on one of the hills on the entrance road.

The park's 860 acres are surrounded by the desert, but a line of rock hills is preserved with many canyons and washes, one of the few water sites for many miles. Used as a water stop by Indians (whose pictographs are also preserved), and later by settlers going west, the water collects in depressions in the rocks which are called "tanks." These "tanks" or ponds attract waterfowl in migration and in winter. In addition, there are several springs located in the rocks.

Picnicking, camping, restrooms with hot showers, hiking, and climbing are all available.

A bird check-list is available at Park Headquarters. The address is Box 16502—Ranchland Station, El Paso, Texas 79926 (915) 859–4100.

Monahans Sandhills State Park

Monahans Sandhills State Park is six miles northeast of Monahans on IH 20, then north on Park Road 41. The park's 3840 acres are an aggregation of large, barren sand dunes, some nearly 100 feet high. Many of the dunes are stabilized by vegetation, including the Havard Oak. Some of the oaks are hundreds of years old, although they are only 3–4 feet tall. Their acorns are the size of

Monahans Sandhills State Park

silver dollars. Facilities are available for picnicking and camping, including restrooms with hot showers, snack bar, a one-quarter mile nature trail, and a natural history interpretative center.

There are two good birding areas within the park. The mesquite thickets near the headquarters building and the nature trail (access through the building) are good places to see birds which are year-round residents of such habitat: Harris' Hawk, Ladder-backed Woodpecker, Verdin, Cactus Wren, Curve-billed Thrasher, Pyrrhuloxia, House Finch, Lesser Goldfinch, and Black-throated Sparrow. Sage Thrasher may be found in winter.

While driving through the park in winter, watch for hawks. Red-tailed, Ferruginous, and Marsh Hawks, and American Kestrel are common. Prairie Falcon winter in the vicinity and are often seen in the park.

It is 1.4 miles from headquarters to the souvenir stand, where a Say's Phoebe may usually be found. Turn left at the souvenir stand, go half a mile past the entrance to the campground to the end of the paved road, and park at the picnic area. There is also an oil well pumping unit here. A road runs west from the picnic area. There is a bar across the road, but its purpose is to keep out vehicles, not hikers. Note there are telephone poles along the road. Walk to the second pole, turn left (south) and walk across the dunes to a row of willow trees. The willows are not visible from the road but are only 50 yards distant. Boots are advisable. At the south end of the row of willows is a small seep, and the combination of trees and water in this sandy desert is a magnet for birds. This area is especially productive during migration. It is also a good place to see summer residents: Western Kingbird, Ash-throated Flycatcher, Northern (Bullock's) Oriole, and Blue Grosbeak. Poor-will and Common Nighthawk may be heard at dusk.

The address of the park is Box 1738, Monahans, TX 79756 (915) 943–2092.

Rolling Plains

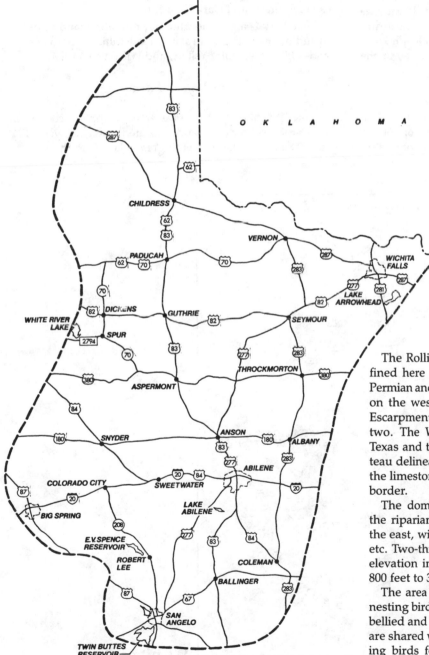

The Rolling Plains region, about 14% of Texas, is defined here as that part of Texas which is underlain by Permian and Pennsylvanian deposits. The area is bounded on the west by the Llano Estacado, with the Caprock Escarpment marking a sharp boundary between the two. The West Cross Timbers and prairies of Central Texas and the Lampasas Cut Plains of the Edwards Plateau delineate the eastern boundary, while on the south the limestones of the Edwards Plateau form a geological border.

The dominant vegetation is mesquite-grasslands. In the riparian areas the vegetation is much like areas to the east, with cottonwood, pecan, cedar elm, hackberry, etc. Two-thirds of the area is devoted to ranchland. The elevation increases southeast to northwest from about 800 feet to 3000 feet.

The area is a transition zone for eastern and western nesting bird species. Ruby-throated Hummingbird, Red-bellied and Downy Woodpeckers, and Common Grackle are shared with the Central Texas region. Common nesting birds found here and in the Llano Estacado and

Trans-Pecos are Mississippi Kite, Scaled Quail, Poorwill, Golden-fronted Woodpecker, Ash-throated Flycatcher, Cactus and Rock Wrens, Lesser Goldfinch, Brown Towhee, and Rufous-crowned Sparrow.

Wichita Falls

Wichita Falls is located approximately 14 miles south of the Red River near the convergence of the Rolling Plains and Central Texas. With a population of 94,000, it is the largest city between Fort Worth and Amarillo.

Mesquite is the dominant woody plant in the uplands of the Wichita Falls area, with hackberry, cottonwood, and cedar elm in the stream bottoms.

Common nesting birds throughout include Great Blue Heron, Carolina Chickadee, Tufted Titmouse, Roadrunner, and Scissor-tailed Flycatcher. Look for Grasshopper and Cassin's Sparrows, Verdin, and Bell's Vireo in the dry uplands in spring and early summer.

Lucy Park

Lucy Park (156 acres) is operated by the City of Wichita Falls Parks and Recreation Department. It is located on the northern edge of Wichita Falls on the Wichita River. Picnicking, swimming, playgrounds, and restrooms are available.

From downtown, drive north on Red River Expressway (US 277, 281, 287) to the Tourist Information exit. Drive south of the Tourist Bureau, park, and enter by the swinging bridge. If driving west on US 82 and 277, turn right (north) on Fillmore Street to the park.

Nesting birds in the park include Red-bellied, Red-headed, Hairy, Downy, and Ladder-backed Woodpeckers, Blue Jay, Mississippi Kite, Great Crested Flycatcher, Northern (Bullock's) Oriole, Indigo Bunting, and Warbling Vireo.

In winter watch for Cedar Waxwing, Orange-crowned and Yellow-rumped Warblers, Common Flicker, American Goldfinch, and Dark-eyed Junco.

Lucy Park is a good location for migrating land birds, including Swainson's Thrush, Philadelphia Vireo, Black-and-white, Nashville, Yellow, and Wilson's Warblers.

Lake Wichita and Jaycee Park

Lake Wichita (2200 surface acres) supplies cooling water for a power plant and is located just southwest of the city on Holliday Creek. To reach Jaycee Park, drive

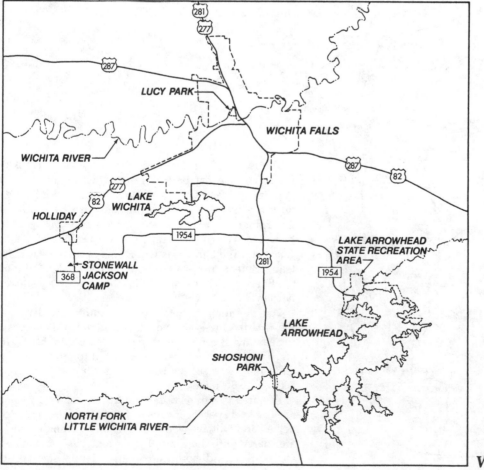

Wichita Falls

south on US 281, take Southwest Parkway (FM 369) west for 4.5 miles to Fairway Road, and turn left (south) 1.2 miles to the lake. The park has 234 acres, is operated by the Wichita Falls Parks and Recreation Department, and offers picnicking, playgrounds, and fishing.

Nesting birds are Great-tailed and Common Grackles, Barn Swallow, and Purple Martin. In winter look for American Kestrel, Common Snipe, Ring-billed Gull, Horned Lark, and Savannah Sparrow. Northern Shrike has been recorded at Jaycee Park, but not in recent years.

Lake Wichita Dam

To reach the lower end of the dam, drive south from the city on US 281, take the Southwest Parkway (FM 369) exit, and drive west 3.3 miles to Kemp Street (FM 2380). Turn south on Kemp, go 0.7 mile to the "Y", and take the right-hand branch of the gravel road to the dam.

Nesting birds include Sora, Long-billed Marsh Wren, Great-tailed and Common Grackles, Common Yellow-throat, Green Heron, and Chimney Swift. Ring-billed Gull, American Goldfinch, Harris' and Song Sparrows are winter residents.

Lake Arrowhead State Recreation Area

Lake Arrowhead is approximately 14 miles southeast of Wichita Falls on the Little Wichita River (16,200 surface acres, 106 miles of shoreline). It is operated by the City of Wichita Falls for municipal water supply. Two popular birding areas on the lake are Lake Arrowhead State Recreation Area and Shoshoni Park.

Lake Arrowhead State Recreation Area (524 acres) is on the northwest shoreline. A boat ramp, boat docks, water skiing, fishing, swimming, picnicking, camping, restrooms with hot showers, and two miles of hiking trails are available. To reach the park, drive south from Wichita Falls on US 281 eight miles to FM 1954, then go east eight miles to the park.

Nesting birds include Red-tailed Hawk, Loggerhead Shrike, Eastern Meadowlark, Western Kingbird, Barn Swallow, and Golden-fronted Woodpecker. In winter look for Tree Sparrow, Ring-billed Gull, Common Flicker, and Double-crested Cormorant.

The park address is Route 2, Box 260, Wichita Falls, TX 76301 (817) 528–2211.

Shoshoni Park

Shoshoni Park (93 acres) is on the southwestern edge of Lake Arrowhead. It is operated by the City of Wichita Falls Parks and Recreation Department. A boat ramp, picnicking, and fishing are available. The park is 12 miles south of Wichita Falls on US 281, or one mile north of Scotland.

Birds found here in summer are Downy Woodpecker, American Robin, Western Kingbird, Swainson's Hawk, and Lark Sparrow.

Wintering species to be expected are Marsh Hawk, Common Flicker, Ruby-crowned Kinglet, Rufous-sided Towhee, Dark-eyed Junco, Harris' and Song Sparrows.

Stonewall Jackson Camp

Stonewall Jackson Camp (25 acres), a Girl Scout Camp and another popular local bird location, is about 14 miles west of Wichita Falls. To reach the camp, drive south on US 281 for eight miles. Turn west on FM 1954, drive 13.4 miles to FM 368, turn south, and go one-half mile to the camp entrance on the east side of the road. Another way to get there is to go south from Holliday on FM 368 for 2.1 miles. There is usually a barricade to keep cars out, but hiking birders are welcome.

Nesting birds include Red-bellied, Downy, and Ladder-backed Woodpeckers, Bewick's Wren, American Robin, Swainson's Hawk, Western Kingbird, Northern (Bullock's) Oriole, and Painted Bunting.

In winter this is a good location for Common Flicker, Brown Creeper, Brown Thrasher, American Goldfinch, Dark-eyed Junco, Tree, Field, Harris', Fox, and Song Sparrows.

A bird check-list covering Wichita and adjacent counties, *The Birds of North Central Texas*, is available from the North Texas Bird and Wildlife Club, 4434 Callfield Road, Wichita Falls, TX 76308, for 20¢ plus a stamped, addressed envelope.

Abilene

Abilene is located in the north-central section of the state on IH 20 between Fort Worth and El Paso. It is near the eastern extreme of the Rolling Plains, with the West Cross Timbers section of Central Texas just to the east. There are elements of the Edwards Plateau represented in the area, particularly the Callahan Divide, the division between the drainages of the Colorado and Brazos Rivers. In the stream bottoms the vegetation and birdlife are representative of Central Texas, while western species are found in the uplands where the mesquite and short-grass prairies occur.

Birding areas south of Abilene include the town of Buffalo Gap, Abilene State Recreation Area, Lake Abilene, and the village of Ovalo. Buffalo Gap is south of Abilene about 10 miles on FM 89. Abilene State Recreation Area is about four miles further southwest on FM 89, Lake Abilene is just west of the park, and the village of Ovalo is 17 miles south of Abilene on US 83.

In and around Buffalo Gap look for Pyrrhuloxia; Bushtit also occur occasionally.

Lake Abilene

At Lake Abilene (653 surface acres operated by the City of Abilene for municipal water), bird seekers are welcome during daylight hours seven days a week.

There are two entrances to the lake, one on the north-west side, and one on the southeast side. In winter Mallard, Gadwall, Pintail, American Wigeon, Northern Shoveler, Canvasback, Ruddy Duck, and American Coot are found. Redhead, Ring-necked Duck, and Bufflehead are less likely. Woodlands consisting of junipers, live oaks, and red oaks surround the lake. Eastern, Western, and Mountain Bluebirds, Pyrrhuloxia, and sometimes Brown Towhee can be found around Lake Abilene in winter.

On the roads in and around the towns, lake, and park, look for Lark Bunting, Curve-billed Thrasher, and Bewick's Wren. Pyrrhuloxia have also been recorded in the village of Ovalo in spring and summer.

Abilene

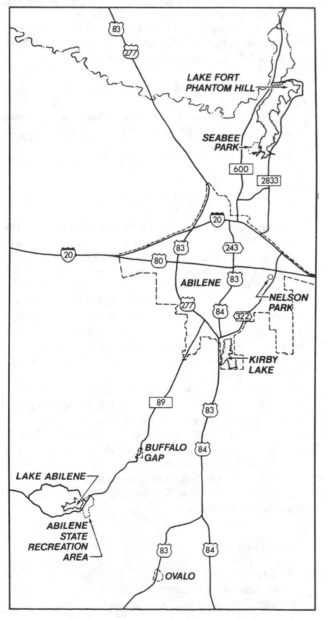

Abilene State Recreation Area

Abilene State Recreation Area is in the low hills near the Callahan Divide. Elm Creek flows through the park. The park's 489 acres, some of which are preserved in a natural state, offer camping, screened shelters, swimming pool with bathhouse, a one-mile hiking trail, and picnicking. Along the wooded sections of the creek, the land birds of the park are most evident.

Nesting birds include Mississippi Kite (present April to September), Yellow-billed Cuckoo, Common Nighthawk, Western Kingbird, Blue-gray Gnatcatcher, Loggerhead Shrike, and House Finch. Less common are Turkey Vulture, Red-tailed Hawk, Roadrunner, Ash-throated Flycatcher, Scrub Jay, White-necked Raven, Cactus Wren, Brown Thrasher, Painted Bunting, Lesser Goldfinch, and Black Vulture. Nine warbler species are listed on the park check-list as migrants, including MacGillivray's Warbler. In addition, 16 sparrow species have been recorded in winter.

There is a bird check-list available at park headquarters listing 136 species occurring in the park or in the immediate vicinity.

The address of the park is Route 1, Tuscola, TX 79562 (915) 572–3204.

Abilene Zoological Gardens

Abilene Zoological Gardens at Nelson Park (13 acres) is on the east side of town on SH 36, just north of the municipal airport and West Texas Fairgrounds. It has a display of amphibians, reptiles, mammals, and 49 species of birds. Ducks winter on the ponds in the park. White-faced Ibis and Yellow-headed Blackbird have been recorded in the park in migration.

Lake Fort Phantom Hill

Lake Fort Phantom Hill has 39,050 surface acres and is operated by the City of Abilene for recreation and

Curved-Bill Thrasher

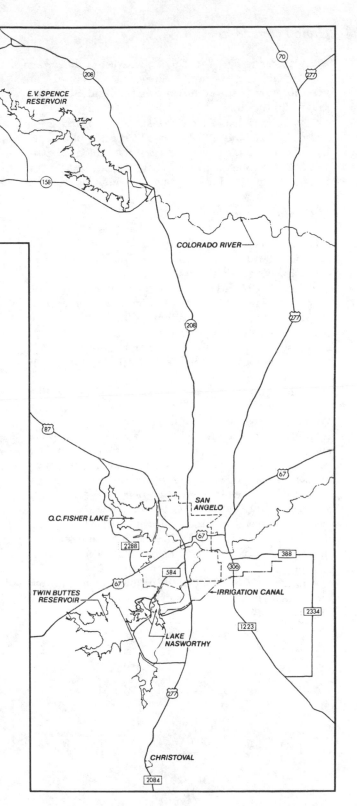

municipal water. The lake is about six miles north of downtown Abilene between FM 600 (west side) and FM 2833 (east side). Seabee Park (184 acres operated by the City of Abilene) is a prime birding spot between FM 600 and the lake. The park has picnicking, camping, and fishing. The wintering ducks on the lake are the same species listed for Lake Abilene. Permanent residents are Great Blue Heron, Roadrunner, Belted Kingfisher, Ladder-backed Woodpecker, Blue and Scrub Jays, Cactus Wren, and House Finch. Water Pipit and many sparrow species are present in winter.

Will Hair Park

Will Hair Park is just north of downtown Abilene, about one-half mile east of Loop 243 on SH 351 (Ambler Avenue). This 25-acre city park has picnicking, restrooms, playgrounds, and a nature trail. Winter residents include Rufous-sided Towhee, White-crowned, White-throated, Field, and Vesper Sparrows, Dark-eyed Junco, and sometimes Fox Sparrow.

Kirby Lake

Kirby Lake (800 surface acres operated by the City of Abilene for municipal water) is at the city's southern edge on US 83 and US 84, just south of the intersection with Loop 322 and about five miles south of downtown. The lake is open to birders during daylight hours seven days a week. Orchard and Northern (Bullock's) Orioles nest in the vicinity, and wintering ducks of the same species as found on Lake Abilene are here too. Phainopepla have been recorded near the lake but are very rare.

San Angelo

San Angelo is located at the the southern extreme of the Rolling Plains, where the North, Middle, and South Concho Rivers join to form the Concho River. The Edwards Plateau is just to the south. San Angelo is the major lamb, wool, and mohair distribution center for the state. Most of the area is devoted to ranching, except for the Lipan Flats area just east of the city where cotton and some grain sorghum are grown.

Short-grass prairies with mesquite and other shrubs are the dominant vegetation near San Angelo, with mid-grasses and live oak and juniper on the Edwards Plateau to the south.

Civic League Park

Civic League Park (on US 67 just west of downtown San Angelo) and Fairmont Cemetery (on Avenue N) are good locations close to downtown for resident and migrating land birds.

A bird check-list, *Field Check-List: Birds of the Concho Valley Region, Texas,* 1979, lists 319 species plus seven hypotheticals and is available from the Biology Department, Angelo State University, San Angelo, Texas 76901. Send a stamped, addressed legal-size envelope.

O.C. Fisher Lake

O.C. Fisher Lake (5440 surface acres), built for municipal water and flood control on the North Concho River, is about 10 miles northwest of the city between US 67 and US 87. FM 2288 connects US 67 and US 87 just west of the lake. It is a good birding road—particularly in the area of Pot Creek—although the creek is usually dry. The roads leading to the lake off of FM 2288 can be driven to gain access to the lake and shoreline, but do not attempt to drive along the shore, as it can be deceptively muddy.

Nesting birds in the vicinity of the lake include Blue Jay, Carolina Wren, Ash-throated Flycatcher, Cactus Wren, Bell's Vireo, Pyrrhuloxia, Brown Towhee, and Black-throated Sparrow. Migrating warblers, Olivaceous and Double-crested Cormorants, and other migrants can be found in spring and fall. In winter check the brushy areas for wintering sparrows (including Fox and Harris' Sparrows), the dead trees for Red-headed Woodpeckers, and the weedy fields for Short-eared Owl. The owls are best seen December through February flying above the fields at dawn and dusk. Rock Wren are common in the rip-rap of the dam in winter; they also occur rarely in summer.

A hike along the road north of the lake should turn up resident Bobwhite, Scaled Quail, and Curve-billed Thrasher.

Orchard Oriole

Brown Towhee

Lake Nasworthy

Lake Nasworthy (1210 surface acres on the South Concho River) and Fish Hatchery No. 2 just below the dam are favorites with local birders. Wintering ducks can be found on the lake as well as the ponds of the fish hatchery. This has been a good spot for Cinnamon Teal in migration. The lake is reached by driving south from town on FM 584 about six miles, or east about three miles on a local road just south of the intersection of US 277 and US 87. In the cattails around the fish hatchery Long-billed Marsh Wren, Common Yellowthroat, and Swamp Sparrow occur in winter. American Bittern are found in migration. Screech and Barn Owls may be found in the area between the dam and the fish hatchery ponds. Long-eared Owl are possible in winter months.

A hike along the top of Lake Nasworthy Dam is usually worthwhile. Night Heron Cove is on the northwest side of the lake. It contains a bullrush and cattail marsh where Green Heron and Least Bittern nest. This is also a good area for migrating Black-crowned Night Heron. Twin Buttes Reservoir is just above Lake Nasworthy. It is a much larger impoundment of 9080 surface acres.

East off FM 584 and just south of Lake Nasworthy, a local road crosses a section of the lakebed known as Ducote's Mud Flat, an excellent location for migrating Yellow-headed Blackbird and shorebirds. Do not cross the fence, since this is private property. The best time to visit Ducote's Mud Flat is in the morning when the light is more favorable than in the afternoon.

East of San Angelo look for Chestnut-collared and McCown's Longspurs (November through February) on the Lipan Flats farmland between FM 388 on the north, FM 1223 on the south, Loop 306 on the west, and FM 2334 on the east. They feed on waste grain sorghum and grass seeds. Drive around in the area until you find grain sorghum stubble, then watch for flocks in flight. Usually, both species are present in the same flock. Sprague's Pipits have been wintering in a small grassy area on the west side of Loop 306 one-quarter mile north of the intersection of Loop 306 and US 87.

Southeast of San Angelo the Bureau of Reclamation has built an irrigation canal where Burrowing Owl can be seen in winter. The owls are not common, but on most days one or two owls can be seen within one to three miles. The best access to the canal is from US 277, where it intersects with Loop 306 south of the city. The canal is more than 25 feet deep here, and huge embankments of excavated soil are on each side of the canal. The owls are usually seen near burrows in the embankments. On windy days they can be hard to find.

Common Raven, which nest on power poles west of the city, and Vermilion Flycatcher, which are common in summer near ranch windmills, are more easily found by driving along roads outside the city. In the sparsely vegetated rangeland listen for Poor-will at night during spring and summer. Lark Bunting are abundant throughout the area in winter.

E.V. Spence Reservoir

E.V. Spence Reservoir (14,950 surface acres), created by a dam on the Colorado River, is north of San Angelo near the town of Robert Lee. To reach the reservoir, drive 30 miles north on SH 208 to Robert Lee, then west on SH 158 to the south shore of the reservoir, or north past Robert Lee on SH 208 to county roads leading to the north shore. Taking FM 1907 west from downtown Robert Lee will lead to the north end of the dam.

Wintering ducks are plentiful. Gadwall, Pintail, Green-winged Teal, American Wigeon, Northern Shoveler, Canvasback, Lesser Scaup, Bufflehead, and Ruddy Duck are the most common. Be on the lookout for Cinnamon Teal, Common and Red-breasted Mergansers, and Common Goldeneye. Sandhill Crane roost in the shallow water at the upstream end of the reservoir in great numbers and are best seen in very early morning before they leave to feed (about sunup), and in late afternoon when they return to roost. Common Loon and Horned Grebe are also present in winter.

Pugh Park

Pugh Park, a county park with more than 1000 acres, is approximately 20 miles south of San Angelo on US 277, just east of the town of Christoval. A permit and fee are required from the Tom Green County Commissioner to enter the east side of the park. A small section west of RR 2084 and adjacent to the South Concho River is open to the public without a fee.

The park is typical Edwards Plateau. Ashe Juniper and live oak are the dominant trees. Scrub Jay, Verdin, and Bushtit are permanent residents.

White River Lake

White River Lake (1800 surface acres) is operated by the White River Municipal Water District to supply water to neighboring cities. It is created by a dam on the White River, a tributary of the Brazos River.

To reach the lake from Lubbock, drive east on FM 40 for 37 miles to the end of the road, then go south on FM 651 for seven miles. Turn east on FM 2794, and go about

Gadwall, Lesser Scaup

eight miles to the lake, or go 13 miles west of Spur on FM 2794. There is an entrance fee. A gravel road leads around both sides of the lake to many overlooks, boat launching sites, three campgrounds with running water and restrooms, and picnic areas.

Located in the mesquite grasslands of the Rolling Plains, the lake is the largest permanent body of water for at least 75 miles in any direction. The wooded, dry water courses, or "draws," leading to the lake provide additional bird habitat to the open water of the lake and its adjacent marshes and the grasslands.

Nesting birds include Curve-billed Thrasher, Northern (Bullock's) Oriole, and Scissor-tailed Flycatcher. Cassin's and Lark Sparrows are abundant in the grasslands surrounding the lake.

In winter sparrows commonly found in the draws and the grasslands are Savannah, Rufous-crowned, Field, Harris', White-crowned, Fox, Song and Dark-eyed Junco. Less common species include Vesper, Tree, White-throated, Lincoln's, and Gray-headed Junco. Other possibilities are Lark, Cassin's, Chipping, Brewer's, Swamp, and Baird's.

Long-eared Owl winter in the dense draws, usually close to the ground. This is one of the few places in Texas where I have seen Baird's Sparrow.

Many wintering hawks can be found in the vicinity of the lake. Sharp-shinned, Cooper's, Red-tailed, Rough-legged, Ferruginous, and Marsh Hawks, Golden Eagle, Prairie Falcon, and American Kestrel are all regular in winter.

The marshy areas support a dense growth of trees, shrubs, and thick herbaceous plants where Long-billed Marsh Wren, Lincoln, Song, and Swamp Sparrows are common in winter.

Water birds recorded on recent Christmas Counts include Common Loon, Horned, Eared, and Pied-billed Grebes, Double-crested Cormorant, Canada Goose, Mallard, Gadwall, Pintail, Green-winged, Blue-winged, and Cinnamon Teals, American Wigeon, Northern Shoveler, Common Goldeneye, Hooded and Common Mergansers. Red-necked Grebe and Red-breasted Merganser are seen occasionally.

Edwards Plateau

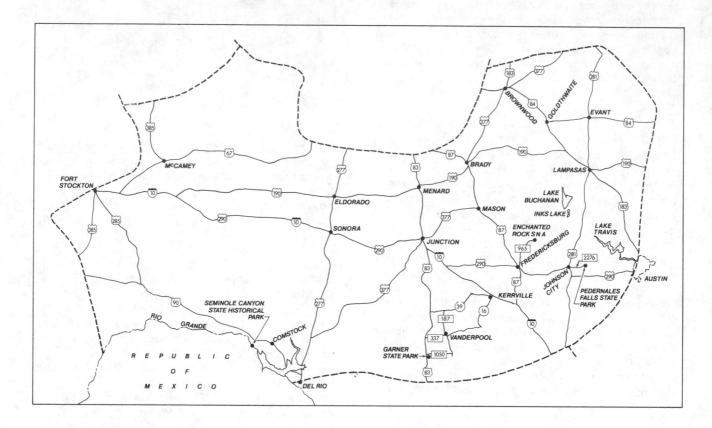

The Edwards Plateau region, approximately 17% of the state, is an elevated area of lower Cretaceous limestone. On the east and south the boundary is the prominent Balcones Escarpment. It runs south from west of Waco through Austin and San Antonio, then west to Del Rio. The northern limit, a very indistinct and discontinuous boundary, is where the limestone meets the Permian and Pennsylvanian deposits of the Rolling Plains. This line runs roughly south of San Angelo, northwestward more or less south of Midland and Odessa, then south to the Rio Grande through Fort Stockton.

The region is underlain by massive limestone strata (in some areas several hundred feet thick), the soil is thin and rocky, and the terrain is very hilly with many deep canyons, except in wide stream bottoms. The Llano area (between the Colorado, San Saba, and Pedernales Rivers), an ancient uplift of Paleozoic sedimentary and Precambrian igneous and metamorphic rocks, is an exception to the general limestone deposits of the rest of the plateau. Examples of these very old formations, among the oldest in the state, can be seen at Inks Lake

State Park and Enchanted Rock State Natural Area. Elevation increases westward from 550 feet at Austin to more than 3000 feet on the Stockton Plateau.

Juniper and oak are the dominant woody plants. Formerly, the uplands were grasslands; now they are heavily invaded by woody plants. Most of the region is devoted to cattle, sheep, and goat ranching. White-tailed deer and turkey are very common. There are numerous springs, which in turn create and feed many streams and rivers. There is less rainfall on the Stockton Plateau west of the Pecos River, where the vegetation is similar to that of the Chihuahuan Desert.

The unique nesting birds of the Edwards Plateau are Golden-cheeked Warbler, Black-capped Vireo, and Green Kingfisher. The latter two are found in two other regions of the state but are perhaps more common and widespread on the plateau than elsewhere. The Golden-cheeked Warbler nests nowhere else in the world. Birdwise, both eastern and western species are found. In the stream bottoms eastern species extend their range west. Examples of western species which are common nesters are Rough-winged Swallow, Poor-will, Black-chinned Hummingbird, Scrub Jay, Bushtit, Bell's Vireo, Golden-fronted Woodpecker, Lesser Goldfinch, and Rufous-crowned Sparrow.

Austin

Austin, the capital of Texas, has a population of more than 320,000 and is located on the Balcones Escarpment where the Colorado River passes from the Edwards Plateau to the Blackland Prairies. The birds of both natural areas are well represented. There are several large man-made lakes in all directions from the city. The Central Mineral Basin, between Burnet and Llano, is only 50 miles northwest, and the "Lost Pines of Texas" at Bastrop is only 30 miles east. These features combine to make Austin an interesting area for birds.

There are more than 8000 acres in parks administered by the Austin Parks and Recreation Department. Most lie along creeks with wooded areas that provide favorable bird habitat. Eastwoods Park has long been one of the favorites for migrating warblers and other land birds. The park is located on Waller Creek at the intersection of 26th Street and Harris Park Boulevard, only a couple of blocks from The University of Texas campus. Another good park for migrants is on the property of the Elisabet Ney Museum, at the corner of 45th Street and Avenue G, also on Waller Creek.

In recent years the best warbler spot has been the Capitol grounds at the intersection of 11th Street and Congress Avenue in downtown Austin. The combination of a wide variety of tall trees (oaks, pecans, elms, etc.), water from fountains, an abundance of insects attracted to the floodlights, and thick shrubs around the Capitol building seems to attract and concentrate the warblers on their journey north in spring or south in fall. Not only are warblers present, but recent migrant records also include Poor-will, Whip-poor-will, Chuck-will's-widow, grosbeaks, thrushes, flycatchers, sparrows, Black-billed Cuckoo, etc. For the largest number of species in a single day, the best time is the first two weeks in May, but some migrants can be found from March through May. About 30 warbler species, including Magnolia and Mourning Warblers, are consistently found on the Capitol grounds during spring migration. Fall migration is a good time also, but the numbers of individuals are much lower than in the spring.

In the Austin area many species are at the periphery of their range. Red-bellied Woodpecker, Ruby-throated Hummingbird, and Blue Jay nest in the city and are common in the east; while Golden-fronted Woodpecker, Black-chinned Hummingbird, Scrub Jay, Green Kingfisher, Black-capped Vireo, and Golden-cheeked Warbler nest in the west section of the city. Other species found west of the city but rarely seen in the east are Northern (Bullock's) Oriole, Lesser Goldfinch, Rufous-crowned

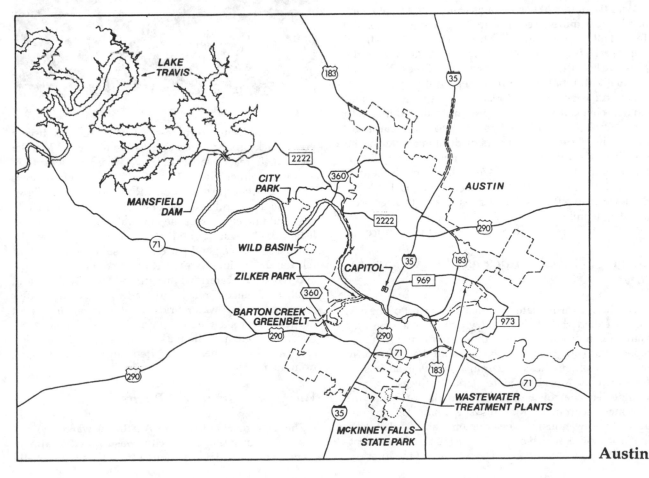

Austin

Sparrow, Poor-will, Ash-throated Flycatcher, Vermilion Flycatcher, Verdin, Bushtit, and House Finch. The Blue Jay seem to be moving west with urban development.

Zilker Park

Zilker Park (350 acres) is located on the south shore of Town Lake and is bisected by Barton Creek. To get there, go west of downtown Austin on Barton Springs Road or south on Loop 1 (MoPac Boulevard). Barton Springs, in the bottom of the swimming pool, flows 37,000,000 gallons of water per day at 68° F, year-round. The pool is a gathering spot for swimmers in great numbers, especially on summer weekends, but it is large enough to accommodate them. The park has ball fields, an excellent garden center with Japanese garden, hike-and-bike trails, picnic areas, miniature railroad, but no camping. Up Barton Creek two-plus miles to Loop 360 is the Barton Creek Greenbelt, an excellent place to hike and look for birds of the area. Here Cañon, Bewick's, and Carolina Wrens and Belted Kingfisher are permanent residents. On Town Lake, Wood Duck and Green Kingfisher can be found in summer; in winter Gadwall, American Coot, and Pied-billed Grebe are very common. Other duck species are less common, except during migration.

Wild Basin

Wild Basin is a 200-acre Travis County Preserve which has been acquired recently to keep a segment of the Texas Hill Country in its natural state for educational purposes. Located in the hills west of Lake Austin, the preserve is in the upper drainage of Bee Creek. The creek is usually dry, but in the rainy season it is very scenic. Yellow-breasted Chat and Black-capped Vireo nest, and Golden-cheeked Warbler are present from mid-March to June. Tours are conducted regularly or by prearrangement. There are no restrooms or drinking water in the preserve. The office address is Commodore Perry Building, Austin, TX 78701 (512) 476–4113. To reach the preserve, drive southwest from Austin on Loop 1 (MoPac Boulevard) to RR 2244 (Bee Caves Road), then go west about four miles to Loop 360. Turn north and drive on Loop 360 for three-quarters of a mile to the entrance.

Golden-Cheeked Warbler and Black-Capped Vireo

On the Edwards Plateau immediately west of the city, locally called the "Hill Country," the Golden-cheeked Warbler can be found where there are mature Ashe Juniper (cedar) and oaks. It is the only bird that nests solely in Texas. Golden-cheeks occur in a narrow band from as far north as Meridian State Park southwest to near Uvalde. This narrow band follows and is just west of the Balcones Escarpment. Mature Ashe Juniper is being ravaged daily by housing developments and "cedar-clearing" conditions which cause the bird to be on the threatened species list of the U.S. Department of the Interior.

In the immediate Austin area, City Park Road has been the favored location for finding Golden-cheeked Warbler and Black-capped Vireo, but unfortunately, the best areas are all on private property, and developments are destroying more of the habitat each year. However, the birds can be found on the road as long as it lasts. On City Park Road, both birds should be looked for after climbing the steep hill upon entering the road from RR 2222. Golden-cheeks can also be found in City Park along Turkey Creek, the only creek that crosses City Park Road. There is a trail up the creek that should be walked until the Golden-cheeks can be heard. The creek is near the entrance to the swimming and camping portion of City Park, about five miles from RR 2222.

Golden-Cheeked Warbler

Mansfield Dam, northwest of Austin, has also been a good Black-capped Vireo and Golden-cheeked Warbler location. To reach Mansfield Dam, drive northwest from Austin on either RR 2222 or US 183. Go about 17 miles to RR 620, then turn west on RR 620 to the dam. Drive over the dam, and take the first road left down the hill, which ultimately crosses the low-water bridge. Look and listen for the warbler and vireo on the way down the hill. This is also a good place for Lesser Goldfinch, Bewick's and Carolina Wrens, Rufous-crowned Sparrow, and whatever waterfowl are around, mostly American Coot, Pied-billed Grebe, and Gadwall in winter. After crossing the low-water bridge, there is a parking lot north of the road where fishermen park. The area between the dam and the parking lot is a good migration spot, and in summer Bell's Vireo can be heard singing from the mesquites.

Wastewater Treatment Plants

The most reliable places in Austin for waterfowl and shorebirds are the three city wastewater treatment plants. Entry regulations change from time to time, and permission to enter must be obtained from the resident manager. Some are accessible on weekends and some are closed.

The Hornsby Bend facility (known locally as Platt's Ponds) is the most popular. To reach these ponds, drive east from IH 35 on FM 969 (MLK Blvd.) about eight miles to FM 973, then go south on FM 973 two miles to Platt Lane. Follow Platt Lane to the entrance. The water level varies, but when mud is exposed, shorebirds are very abundant in July, August, and September, then again in March, April, and May. Some birds are present all year.

American Coot

The Walnut Creek plant is on FM 969 about five miles east of IH 35. The Williamson Creek plant is at the intersection of North Bluff and Nuckols Crossing Road, 1.4 miles east of the intersection of IH 35 and William Cannon Drive (south of the city). The birdlife is usually different at each of the ponds; some species favor one over the others. Many of the notable records for the area have shown up at the Hornsby Bend Ponds, such as Northern Phalarope and Buff-breasted and White-rumped Sandpipers, which occur every year. Some very rare records include Red Phalarope, Sabine's Gull, Hudsonian Godwit, Whooping Crane, Mountain Plover, and Short-billed Dowitcher. During fall, winter and spring, at least 16 duck species and more than 20 shorebirds make regular appearances.

There are several state parks within a one-hour drive of Austin, each offering a completely different habitat for birds. These are McKinney Falls State Park (Edwards Plateau and Blackland Prairies), Pedernales Falls State Park (Edwards Plateau), Palmetto State Park (swamps and woody river bottom in the Post Oak Savannah of Central Texas), Bastrop and Buescher State Parks (Lost Pines of Central Texas), and Inks Lake State Park (Central Mineral Basin of the Edwards Plateau). Each is described more fully elsewhere in this book.

A Check-list of Birds of the Austin, Texas, Region, 1978, is available from Travis Audubon Society, % Mary Martin, 4915 Timberline Drive, Austin, TX 78746, for 25¢, plus stamped, addressed envelope. The check-list has 293 species with an additional 73 accidentals.

A Bird Finding and Naturalist's Guide for the Austin, Texas Area, 1976, E. A. Kutac and S. C. Caran is a detailed guide of birding locations with bird bar charts and habitat descriptions, as well as a list of fishes, amphibians, reptiles, mammals, area campgrounds, etc. It is also available from the Travis Audubon Society.

Inks Lake State Park

Inks Lake State Park is located nine miles west of Burnet on SH 29. There are 1200 acres of picnic sites, camping with restrooms and hot showers, fishing, boating, golfing, and water skiing. The park is on Inks Lake just south of Lake Buchanan and is in the Central Mineral Basin (also called the Llano Uplift).

In winter Lake Buchanan and Inks Lake have Red-breasted Merganser, Common Loon, Horned Grebe, Herring, Ring-billed and Bonaparte's Gulls, Forster's Tern, and a small wintering colony of Bald Eagle. Nesting birds of the area include Brown Towhee, Cactus Wren, Verdin, Black-throated Sparrow, Bell's Vireo, Orchard Oriole, and Golden-cheeked Warbler. Osprey migrate regularly in spring and fall; they sometimes linger along the Colorado River.

The U.S. Fish Hatchery is an excellent location for wintering waterfowl. The hatchery is approximately one mile south of Inks Lake State Park on PR 4 and is open to visitors Monday through Friday during working hours and on Saturday morning.

RR 690 and RR 2341 are on the east side of Lake Buchanan, and SH 261 and RR 2241 are on the west side. These are good roads to check out the birds on and around the lake. Lake Buchanan is 32 miles long and eight miles wide.

The park address is Box 117, Buchanan Dam, TX 78609 (512) 793–2223.

Pedernales Falls State Park

Pedernales Falls State Park is 4860 acres (less than 10% developed) of typical Edwards Plateau habitat with oaks and junipers (cedars) on the dry uplands and bald cypress and sycamores along the river, creeks, and intermittent streams.

The park is 14 miles east of Johnson City on RR 2766. From Austin, drive west 28 miles on US 290, then go six miles north on RR 3232.

Camping, restrooms with hot showers, primitive camping areas, picnicking, canoeing, fishing, swimming, and backpacking are available at the park. There are nine miles of Pedernales River frontage in the park.

Nesting birds include Turkey, Yellow-billed Cuckoo, Green and Belted Kingfishers, Chuck-will's-widow, Ladder-backed Woodpeckers, Carolina Chickadee, Tufted

Pedernales Falls, Pedernales Falls State Park

Titmouse, Bushtit, Bewick's, Carolina, and Cañon Wrens, Mourning Dove, White-eyed Vireo, Golden-cheeked Warbler, Orchard Oriole, Brown-headed Cowbird, House Finch, Chipping and Field Sparrows.

Turkey are abundant and are sometimes seen in the campground in early morning or late afternoon. White-tailed deer are very common.

From the middle of March to the middle of June, look for Golden-cheeked Warbler nesting in the park. A good place to look is at the top of the bluff along the river on the Pedernales Hill Country Nature Trail, on the trail between the parking lot and the overlook at the falls, and in the camping area.

A bird check-list for the park is available at park headquarters. The park address is Route 1, Box 31-A, Johnson City, TX 78636 (512) 868–7304.

Kerrville

Kerrville is in the heart of typical Hill Country habitat 66 miles west of San Antonio on IH 10. It is that part of the Edwards Plateau sometimes called the Balcones Canyonlands, with deeply dissected canyons, clear springs, thin soil, "cedar brakes" with oak, and large ranches with an abundance of white-tailed deer and turkey. The altitude of 1600 feet-plus creates what many local residents say is the best year-round climate in the state. The many springs of the area create creeks which flow into the Guadalupe River, along which there are many resorts and dude ranches that attract numerous vacationers in summer and hunters in fall. The river is a magnet for migrants and water birds.

The area around Kerrville is an excellent place to look for three Texas specialities: Green Kingfisher, Golden-cheeked Warbler, and Black-capped Vireo. The warblers can be heard singing from late March to early June; the vireo from mid-April until mid-July. Close to town, the

Dewberry Hollow section has been good for both birds, and RR 479 between Mountain Home and Harper is a good location for them if traveling north from Kerrville. Green Kingfisher are permanent residents along the river and clear streams.

To reach the Dewberry Hollow section, drive south from Kerrville on SH 16. After the red light at the south end of the Guadalupe River bridge, go 7.3 miles to E. Spicer Road. Turn right on this dirt road, go 1.5 miles to West Spicer Drive, and turn right again. The thick undergrowth (shin oak) starts about here and is the prime habitat of the Black-capped Vireo. The vireo can be heard singing in summer anywhere along West Spicer Drive. If not found, turn right again at 1.2 miles, and look along that road.

For the Golden-cheeked Warbler, do not make the last right turn as just mentioned, but stay on West Spicer Drive for 1.2 miles to Real East. Turn right and go 0.3 mile to a dry wash where there is a culvert and six red-painted metal poles on the left. The warbler will usually come in from the hillside on the left. To return to SH 16, go up the hill, turn right and, just past the yellow house on the left, turn left on E. Spicer Drive.

To reach RR 479 from Kerrville, drive west on SH 27. After 14 miles, turn right (north) on RR 479. From Fredericksburg, the north end of RR 479 can be reached by driving west on US 290 for 28 miles. The Golden-cheeked Warbler can be heard singing during April and May from the road for the first two miles after leaving SH 27. After this interval, there are mostly cleared fields and pasture, but thick undergrowth (shin oak and sumac) starts about 7.5 miles from SH 27. Black-capped Vireo sing from the thick shrubs, especially in the middle of the day. Another favorable location is Reservation Road, a county road east from the "Booster Tower," approximately 5.3 miles north of IH 10, or three miles south of US 290. DO NOT CROSS FENCES IN THIS AREA.

Northern Parula and Yellow-throated Warbler nest throughout the Kerrville area and are most easily found at stream crossings in the tall bald cypress. Locations

Mourning Dove

where they have been found are the county road along Cypress Creek just west of the town of Comfort, and along Prison Camp Road just west of the town of Camp Verde. Comfort is 10 miles southeast of Kerrville on SH 27, and Camp Verde is 14 miles south on SH 173. Another good place is RR 2107, which follows the meanderings of the Medina River (with several crossings) for 8.5 miles to a dead end. RR 2107 is west of SH 16, 3.4 miles north of Medina or 20 miles south of Kerrville.

Kerrville State Recreation Area

To reach the Kerrville State Recreation Area (517 acres), drive south of Kerrville on SH 16 for one-half mile to SH 173, then go east 2.5 miles to the entrance. Camping, restrooms with hot showers, picnicking, fishing, swimming in the adjacent Guadalupe River, and two miles of hiking trails await the visitor. Turkey and white-tailed deer wander along the park roads and in the campground and are easily seen in the early morning and late afternoon. The park has one section along the river and another in the uplands.

The address is 2385 Bandera Highway, Kerrville, TX 78028 (512) 257-5392.

Scenic Drive

There are many scenic drives in the Kerrville area where birding can be excellent in all seasons. One of my personal favorites is an all-day, 150-mile loop trip west from Kerrville. Take SH 27 to Ingram, and go west on SH 39 along the South Fork Guadalupe River to RR 187. Turn south to Lost Maples State Natural Area and Vanderpool. Proceed west on RR 337 over the divide to Leakey, turn south on US 83 to Garner State Park, and then return north on US 83 to RR 1050. Go east to Utopia, and then north on RR 187 back to Vanderpool. From Vanderpool, go east on RR 337 to Medina, then north on SH 16 back to Kerrville. This trip should produce at least 70 bird species any time of the year.

At each river crossing look for Green Kingfisher, which are permanent residents, and in summer Yellow-throated Warbler. Permanent residents to be watched for along the loop include Brown Towhee, Ladder-backed and Acorn Woodpeckers, Common Raven, Turkey, Vermilion Flycatcher, Eastern Bluebird, Scrub Jay, Cactus, Cañon, and Rock Wrens, Black Phoebe, Pyrrhuloxia, Verdin, Field, Chipping, and Black-throated Sparrows. In spring and summer there are Hooded and Scott's Orioles and a rare Zone-tailed Hawk. Wintering birds include Ferruginous Hawk, Dark-eyed Junco, Vesper and Lincoln's Sparrows. Sparrows less commonly found are Harris', White-throated, Fox, Grasshopper, LeConte's, Swamp, and Song. Some winters Red-headed Woodpecker are found. In recent years Blue Jay have become frequent winter residents, sometimes in large numbers.

There are several worthwhile stops along the loop, and brief descriptions of these sites follow.

Lost Maples State Natural Area

Lost Maples State Natural Area is four miles north of Vanderpool on RR 187, one of three natural areas in the Texas Parks and Wildlife Department system. The area (2174 acres) was established to preserve an isolated population of Big-toothed Maple, the most extensive stand of this species east of the Guadalupe Mountains (approximately 400 miles to the west).

The fall colors, always beautiful and sometimes spectacular, are usually best during the first two weeks of

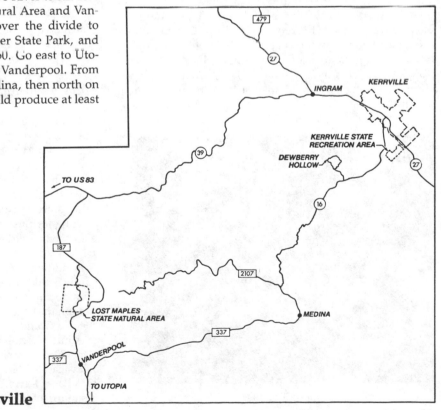

Kerrville

Scrub Jay

November. There is a strenuous six-mile loop hiking trail along Cann Creek and the Sabinal River, the two streams in the park, and the high ground between. The trail provides a good example of the flora and fauna of this section of the Edwards Plateau. In addition, there is camping, restrooms with hot showers, picnicking, and a primitive campground. The developed section is a very small percentage of the park.

Nesting birds include Golden-cheeked Warbler, Black-capped Vireo, and Green Kingfisher. There are not many places in Texas where these three Texas specialities nest in such a small area. April and May should be the best time to find all three. Other common nesters include Ash-throated Flycatcher, Bushtit, Common Raven, Roadrunner, Ladder-backed Woodpecker, Orchard Oriole, Black Phoebe (in the near vicinity if not in the park), Scrub Jay, Pyrrhuloxia, Lesser Goldfinch, and Brown Towhee. Watch for Zone-tailed Hawk from February through July among the many Turkey Vulture soaring overhead.

Tufted Titmouse

This part of Texas, especially west of the park, is the wintering ground for numerous Golden Eagle (November to March), and they are occasionally seen flying over the park.

A preliminary bird check-list is available at park headquarters. The address is Station C Route, Vanderpool, TX 78885 (512) 966–3413.

Garner State Park

Garner State Park is located on US 83, 10 miles south of Leakey and 31 miles north of Uvalde. The park offers camping, restrooms with hot showers, cabins, six miles of hiking trails, picnicking, and swimming on its 630 acres. This is a delightful spot on the clear, spring-fed Frio River, which has immense bald cypress lining its banks in the heart of a scenic section of the Edwards Plateau.

Birds which are present year-round, either in the park or in adjacent areas, include Bushtit, Black Phoebe, Green Kingfisher, Scrub Jay, Black-throated Sparrow, Cactus Wren, Pyrrhuloxia, Common Raven, Brown Towhee, and Verdin.

In summer be on the lookout for Hooded and Scott's Orioles, Yellow-throated Warbler, White-winged Dove, and Vermilion Flycatcher. Zone-tailed Hawk are occasionally seen overhead in summer. If Black Phoebe and Green Kingfisher are not found in the park, check the river crossings north and south of the park where they are sometimes more easily found.

The park is very popular on summer weekends. For birding, any other time is better. The address is Concan, TX 78838 (512) 232–6633.

Cave Swallows

Cave Swallows are increasing their use of highway culverts for nesting north and west of Uvalde. Watch for them from April to July. On RR 187 north of Vanderpool, they can be found nesting in highway culverts and often are seen at the ranch corrals at the Kerr-Bandera County line 4.2 miles south of SH 39. July is an especially good time, since the young birds perch on the utility wires waiting for their parents to bring them food. They have also been recorded in a culvert east of Fredericksburg on US 290.

In addition, Cave Swallows have been reported recently in South Texas under highway culverts in the area bounded on the north by US 90 from San Antonio to Del Rio, on the east by SH 16, and on the south and west by the Rio Grande.

A bird check-list, *Birds of Kerr County and Surrounding Area* (70 miles from Kerrville but excluding San Antonio), is available from Ernest and Kay Mueller, 207 Spanish Oak Lane, Kerrville, TX 78028 (512) 367-2519, for 25¢ and a stamped, addressed return envelope.

Harris Hawk

Seminole Canyon State Historical Park

Seminole Canyon State Historical Park is located two miles east of the Pecos River on US 90. The drive can be made by going 40 miles west of Del Rio, or eight miles west of Comstock. The park was established to protect Indian pictographs which date back 10,000 or more years. The pictographs in the canyon near the head-quarters can be seen only on guided tours which are conducted daily. Time should be allowed to study the excellent exhibit in the headquarters building that depicts the early history of the area.

Camping and picnic areas are provided. The flora and fauna are a mixture of the Edwards Plateau to the north, Chihuahuan Desert to the west, and South Texas to the east. Average annual rainfall is less than 18 inches.

The best birding opportunities are on a 3.5-mile hiking trail from the camping area south along an old road to Amistad Reservoir, which forms the southern boundary of the park.

Since the park has been open only since 1980, the bird list is still being developed, but the following have been observed during summer months: Zone-tailed Hawk, Peregrine Falcon, White-winged Dove, Lesser Night-hawk, White-throated Swift, Varied Bunting, and Brown Towhee.

More common summer birds include Turkey and Black Vultures, Harris' Hawk, Turkey, Poor-will, Common Nighthawk, Green Kingfisher, Black and Say's Phoebes, Ash-throated Flycatcher, Common and White-necked Ravens, Verdin, Cactus and Rock Wrens, Sage Thrasher, Hooded Oriole, Pyrrhuloxia, Cassin's and Black-throated Sparrows. Waterfowl and shorebirds should be looked for along the shore of the lake during spring and fall migration and in winter.

A preliminary bird check-list is available at park head-quarters. As this is a sparsely birded section of Texas, any sightings not on the check-list should be reported to the park office. The address is P.O. Box 806, Comstock, TX 78837 (512) 292–4464.

Central Texas

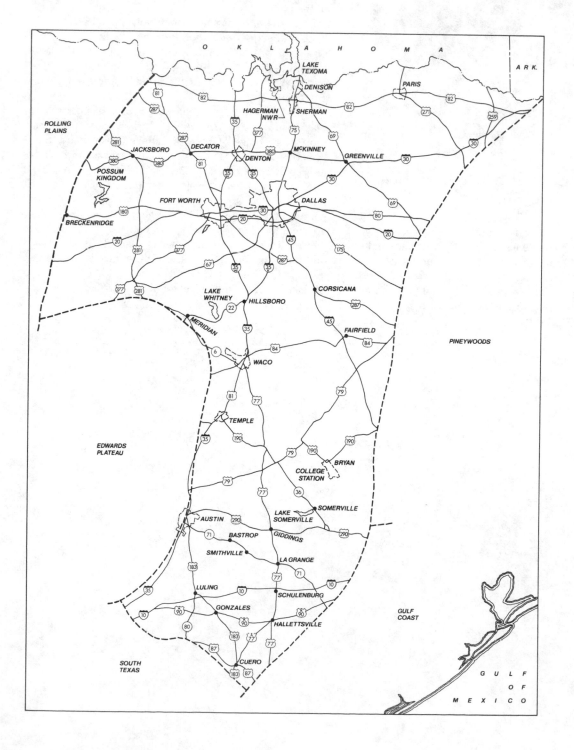

The Central Texas region, about 19% of the state, consists of alternate prairies, woodlands, and savannahs underlain with Tertiary and Upper Cretaceous deposits. The eastern boundary is the beginning of the pine forests of East Texas, roughly from Texarkana through Tyler, Palestine, and west of Huntsville to near Victoria. The southern boundary is very broad and indistinct but generally follows the San Antonio River to San Antonio. The prominent Balcones Escarpment is the western boundary from south of San Antonio north through Austin, Temple, and Waco. The line then proceeds west from the Glen Rose area to north of Brownwood, then north to just east of Wichita Falls.

The major vegetation areas from east to west are the Fayette Prairies, Post-oak Savannah, Blackland Prairies, East Cross Timbers, Grand Prairie, West Cross Timbers, and North Central Prairie. The land becomes more hilly from east to west. The elevation increases from 150 feet in the southeast to about 1500 feet in the northwest.

Originally, tall grass was the dominant vegetation of the savannahs and prairies. Ranching, farming, and urbanization have occurred to the extent that very little, if any, virgin prairie is preserved. The timberlands, mostly post oak and blackjack with a wide variety of other trees and shrubs in the stream bottoms, provide habitat for many of the breeding birds.

Birdwise, the region is a transition zone between the Gulf Coast and Pineywoods (south and east), and the Rolling Plains and Edwards Plateau (west). The numerous man-made lakes attract and provide habitat for many migrating shorebirds and wintering waterfowl.

Eastern species which reach or approach their western limit in the region include Red-shouldered Hawk, Acadian Flycatcher, Blue Jay, Indigo Bunting, Brown Thrasher, Common Grackle, Red-bellied Woodpecker, and Ruby-throated Hummingbird. Western species to be found are Roadrunner, Western Kingbird, Bewick's Wren, and Bell's Vireo.

Dallas

Dallas County (859 square miles) has the highest population density in the state, yet the city has more parkland per person than any other major city in the United States. The county is within the Trinity River drainage basin and is part of the Blackland Prairie vegetational area (with the exception of the extreme northwestern corner of the county which is a part of the East Cross Timbers). With the extensive greenbelt and parkland available, 20,000 acres, many bird species can be found here.

White Rock Lake

White Rock Lake, six miles east of downtown Dallas, offers many different habitats—water, woodlands, and marshy areas—and if there is time for only one place to visit in Dallas, this area would be a good choice. More than 220 species have been recorded on and around the lake.

To reach the lake from downtown, drive east on IH 30 to East Grand exit, then go northeast on East Grand to the lake. The street name changes along the way to Garland Road (SH 78).

The lake is approximately two miles long and one mile wide and is surrounded by parks maintained by the Dallas Parks and Recreation Department.

Dallas

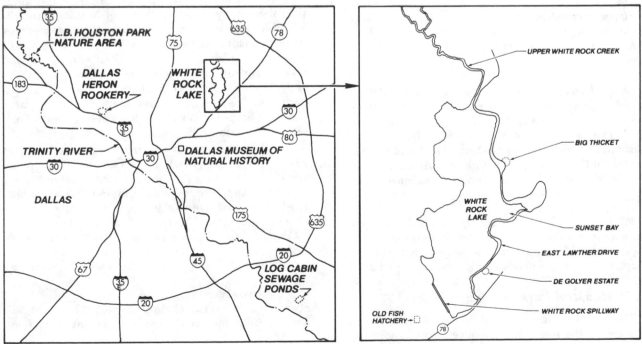

The following areas are a rundown of good birding spots around the lake.

White Rock Spillway. The White Rock Spillway serves as a foraging area for sandpipers and plovers in the spring and fall. Black Tern show up in late summer. Gadwall, Mallard, and other ducks are winter residents, along with hundreds of Ring-billed and occasionally Bonaparte's Gulls. The woods here are a remnant of the original flood plain forest of White Rock Creek, whose abandoned channel may still be seen.

DeGolyer Estate. This 80-acre estate maintained by the parks department is adjacent to the lake off Garland Road. It is especially good for warblers in spring and an occasional Rose-breasted Grosbeak.

East Lawther Drive. This drive is good for spotting some of the lake residents in the winter such as Redhead, Canvasback, Ruddy Duck, Double-crested Cormorant, and occasionally Whistling Swan and Western Grebe. In the fall watch for White Pelican.

Sunset Bay. The shallow water and abundant vegetation here encourage the growth of fish, frogs, and aquatic invertebrates. Wood Duck, grebes, domestic and wild ducks are winter residents. In addition, Brown Creeper and Red-breasted Nuthatch can usually be found. The wide variety of trees and shrubs attract warblers and other land migrants in the spring and fall.

Big Thicket. The Big Thicket area provides an excellent winter habitat for sparrows, wrens, towhees, and thrushes. The trees which make up this grove are Shumard Red Oaks, whose acorns are large and very popular with the Eastern Fox Squirrel.

Upper White Rock Creek. Upper White Rock Creek from Mockingbird Lane north is home to Wood Duck, Green-winged Teal, Great Horned, Barred, and Screech Owls.

Old Fish Hatchery. This heavily wooded area adjacent to the spillway is the home of the Barred Owl and woodpeckers. During the spring, Northern (Baltimore) and Orchard Orioles can be found around the many mulberry trees. This hatchery has been abandoned for many years, but the dried-up ponds are still in evidence. Caution is advised during the spring and summer months because of copperheads.

White Rock Creek Nature Trail. This trail winds through the floodplain forest of White Rock Creek. Woodland birds abound in the large cottonwood, box elder, willow, and elm trees which shade the path.

L. B. Houston Park Nature Area

The L. B. Houston Park Nature Area is located on the Elm Fork of the Trinity River about eight miles northwest

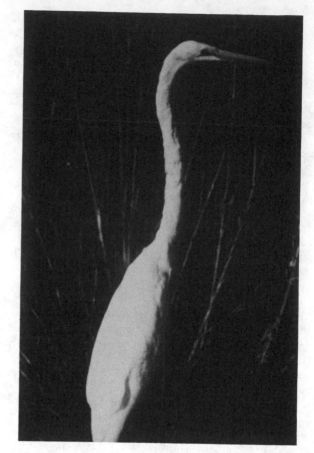

Great Egret

of downtown Dallas. From downtown, drive northwest on IH 35E to Carpenter Freeway (SH 183) then right at SH 114 to Tom Braniff Exit. Continue on the frontage road to Tom Braniff Road, then north about three-quarters of a mile to a parking lot on the right. A trail guide published by the Dallas Museum of Natural History is available at the museum in Fair Park that contains many helpful tips for enjoying the area, including a list of birds and woody plants with descriptions, drawings, and other pertinent information. The area, owned and operated by the City of Dallas Parks and Recreation Department, has a series of five marked trails. It takes about six hours to walk all the trails and cover the habitats of grassland, woodland, swamp, and the river.

This 800-acre primitive nature area is an excellent place to find many local birds year-round. Common nesting birds include Red-headed, Hairy, and occasional Ladder-backed Woodpeckers, Common Crow, White-eyed Vireo, and Tufted Titmouse. In winter look for Common Flicker and Yellow-bellied Sapsucker.

Along the river there are areas where Wood Duck can be found, and in summer Black-crowned Night Heron, Great Egret, Little Blue Heron, and an occasional Snowy Egret.

The area's several grasslands attract many species of sparrows in winter, including Harris', White-throated, Vesper, Chipping, Fox, Lincoln's, Swamp, and Song Sparrows.

Picnic facilities are available at California Crossing Park just north of the nature area on California Crossing Road.

Dallas Heron Rookery

Since 1938, a heron rookery has been located in the Dallas area. It has moved four times during this period and currently is next to the UT Health Science Center between Stemmons Expressway (IH 35E), Inwood Road, and Harry Hines Boulevard, about 3.5 miles northwest of downtown. The rookery has been diminishing in size since 1965 and is now only about one acre.

The first birds arrive by March 20 and leave by the first of October. By far the largest concentrations are the Cattle Egret. They first appeared in Dallas in 1964 and have literally taken over. Other species present include Little Blue Heron, Great and Snowy Egrets, and Black-crowned Night Heron. Please avoid walking into the rookery when the birds are nesting, because they are easily disturbed.

Log Cabin Sewage Ponds

Log Cabin Sewage Ponds, part of the City of Dallas wastewater treatment system, is an excellent place for migrating shorebirds and wintering waterfowl. From downtown, drive south on the Central Expressway (US 75) about three miles to Hawn Freeway (US 175), then turn southeast on Hawn Freeway, and go about 10 miles to Belt Line Road. Turn right (south) on Belt Line Road, and drive about four miles to Log Cabin Road on the right. Drive to the end of the road to the sewage treatment ponds. It is permitted to drive around the ponds, but stay on the road. The ponds are open seven days a week from 8 a.m. to dusk.

During the summer of 1980, 12 Black-bellied Whistling Ducks made this their home. Wintering ducks include Pintail, Green-winged and Blue-winged Teals, American Wigeon, Wood Duck, Ruddy Duck, and Hooded Merganser. Sandpipers include American Golden Plover, Common Snipe, Greater and Lesser Yellowlegs, Upland, Spotted, Pectoral, White-rumped, Baird's, Least, Stilt, Semipalmated, and Western Sandpipers. Also, Wilson's Phalarope and Black Tern can be found in migration.

Dallas Museum of Natural History

One of the finest libraries and exhibits on birds in the state is housed at the Dallas Museum of Natural History in Fair Park. The Museum has more than 30 bird habitat groups ranging from the Bald Eagle to the extinct Ivory-billed Woodpecker. On the second floor of the museum is a synoptic series of birds that represents more than 500 Texas bird species. All birders, whether beginners or experts, are invited to bring their field guides to the museum to compare with the mounted specimens.

In addition to the bird exhibits, the museum has more than 7000 scientific bird specimens, ranking it as one of the largest scientific Texas bird collections. Many of these birds were collected as early as the 1880s. The museum also has a collection of bird nests and bird eggs, and an extensive ornithological library which includes subscriptions to every major ornithological periodical.

Although these collections are of most interest to scientists, they are open to the public as well. Interested persons need only call the Museum Ornithology Department for an appointment.

The museum is open 9 a.m. to 5 p.m., Monday through Saturday, and from 12 noon to 5 p.m. on Sundays and holidays.

Black-capped Vireo nest in southwest Dallas County on private property which is under intensive development. For current information about the possibility of finding the vireo April through July, contact the Ornithology Department at the Dallas Museum of Natural History.

A *Field Check-list of Birds of Dallas County*, compiled by Warren M. Pulich, December, 1977, is available from the Dallas County Audubon Society, % Steve Runnels, Dallas Museum of Natural History, P.O. Box 26193, Dallas, Texas 75226. Include 10¢ plus stamped, addressed envelope.

Fort Worth

Fort Worth (pop. 385,000) is located on the Grand Prairie at the eastern edge of the West Cross Timbers. The city is bisected by the Clear Fork Trinity River and the West Fork Trinity River, which join near downtown to continue east as the West Fork Trinity River. An agricultural, transportation, and manufacturing center, the city also has world-famous art museums, spacious city parks, several large man-made lakes, and the Fort Worth Nature Center and Refuge, the finest example of natural habitat preservation by any city in Texas.

Fort Worth Nature Center and Refuge

The Fort Worth Nature Center and Refuge (3412 acres) is northwest of the city on Lake Worth. To reach the refuge, drive two miles north of the Lake Worth bridge on SH 199 (Jacksboro Highway) to the entrance on the right. It is open 8 a.m. to 5 p.m. daily, except on City of Fort Worth holidays. There are 20 miles of trails from one-half to seven miles long through a wide variety of habitats. These include woodlands with a half-dozen oak species, river bottoms, prairies, extensive marshes, and the lake. Buffalo and black-tailed prairie dog have been reintroduced to an enclosed area and are thriving. White-tailed deer, beaver, and coyote are also resident, but not in enclosed areas. Canoeing is allowed on the river and lake and is the best way to see the birds of these areas. A 900-foot boardwalk over Lotus Marsh has been provided to allow visitors to view the marsh from above.

Nesting birds of the marsh include Prothonotary Warbler, Common Yellowthroat, and Wood Duck. Many duck species spend the fall, winter, and spring here, and shorebirds are common migrants.

The Hardwicke Interpretive Center has natural history exhibits, classes, and wildlife rehabilitation for injured and abandoned wildlife. Check with the office for the times at which regular guided tours are offered. There is no entrance fee to the refuge.

A bird check-list of the refuge is available at headquarters that lists 205 species recorded and an additional 23 accidentals. The mailing address is Route 10, Box 35, Fort Worth, TX 76135 (817) 237–1111.

Fort Worth Fish Hatchery
(6200 Hatchery Road)

From IH 30, drive north on SH 183 about 3.5 miles (or from SH 199, 1.3 miles south) to Roberts Cut-Off. Turn north on Roberts Cut-Off, and drive one block. Turn west on Meandering Drive, and proceed about one mile to Carswell Air Force Base Hospital. Turn right at the hospital, and follow signs to the Fish Hatchery. Drive into the driveway, park, and walk around.

Fort Worth Nature Center

The hatchery has 66 acres with 23 ponds just below the dam that creates Lake Worth. Visitors are welcome from 8 a.m. to 4 p.m., Monday through Friday. For groups of five or more, weekend entry can be arranged in advance by calling (817) 737–6931.

The ponds of the fish hatchery provide a refuge for migrating and wintering waterfowl, and most of the waterfowl that occur in the Forth Worth area (approximately 17 species) can be found here. Usually a pond or two is being drained, which provides favorable habitat for shorebirds on their fall and spring migrations. July and August and March, April, and May are the peak months for shorebirds. Brown Thrasher nest in the area. This is also a favorable location for migrating land birds.

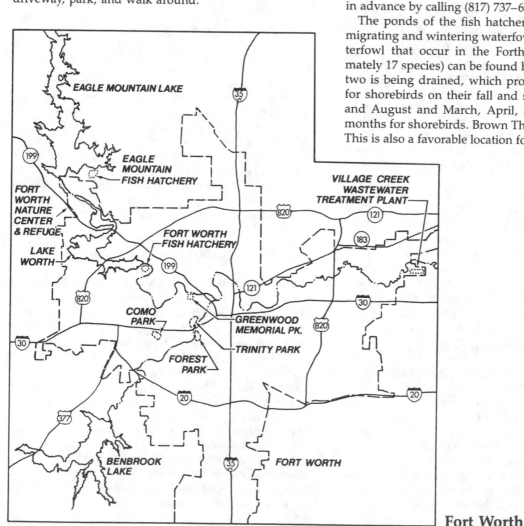

Fort Worth

Eagle Mountain Fish Hatchery

The 78 acres of the Eagle Mountain Fish Hatchery usually attract more waterfowl than the Fort Worth Fish Hatchery. To reach the hatchery, drive northwest from Fort Worth on SH 199 (Jacksboro Highway) to the intersection with Loop 820. Just after the intersection, turn right (north) on FM 1220, drive about two miles, and turn left on 10-Mile Bridge Road (Ten-Mile Azle Road). Drive about 3.5 miles, then turn right (north) on Eagle Mountain Circle. Drive one-half mile to the hatchery entrance on the right. The hatchery is located just below the dam that creates Eagle Mountain Lake on the West Fork Trinity River.

Osprey are regular in spring and fall. Red-tailed Hawk are common in winter, with an occasional Rough-legged Hawk possible.

A walk in the woodlands along the West Fork Trinity River is usually productive. Red-shouldered Hawk have nested in this area.

The hatchery is open to the public from 8 a.m. to 7 p.m. Monday through Friday. However, arrangements to enter on weekends can be made by calling (817) 237–3536 in advance.

Village Creek Wastewater Treatment Plant

The extensive drying area of this sewage disposal system has produced many excellent records and some fine birding. It is located in the Trinity River bottoms east of Fort Worth in Arlington.

To reach the plant, drive east on IH 30 (old Dallas-Fort Worth turnpike), and exit at Fielder. Turn left (north), and go two blocks to a traffic light on Lamar. Turn right (east), and drive 0.4 mile to a traffic light on Davis. Turn left (north), drive 1.0 mile to deadend at Beady. Then go left 0.2 mile to a gate supported by brick towers marked CITY OF FORT WORTH, SOLIDS DRYING AREA, VILLAGE CREEK PLANT. Drive in and continue straight ahead. On the left is an overgrown pond area where herons are sometimes found. Drive to the top of the levee that divides the drying area. Scan the ponds from here. A scope is recommended. The best area is usually to the right (east). Because of the variable water level, stage of treatment, or other factors, birds are sometimes scarce, but during migration (July, August, and September in fall; March and April in spring) when many species of shorebirds, waterfowl, and some passerines are present, it can be excellent. Ring-billed Gull, Spotted and Least Sandpipers, and ducks are winter residents. Common migrants include Franklin's Gull, Upland and Pectoral Sandpipers, and Lesser Yellowlegs. Less common (but expected) are American Golden and Black-bellied Plovers, Common Snipe, Solitary, Baird's, Western, and Stilt Sandpipers, Greater Yellowlegs, Long-billed Dowitcher, American Avocet, and Wilson's Phalarope.

The area is open from 8 a.m. to 5 p.m. weekdays and is normally closed on weekends. Special arrangements can sometimes be made on weekends by calling (817) 277–7591.

Benbrook Lake

Benbrook Lake, a U.S. Army Corps of Engineers flood control and water conservation project, is approximately 12 miles southwest of downtown Fort Worth. From downtown, drive west on IH 30 to US 377, then southwest about five miles to the lake.

The lake has about 40 miles of shoreline (3770 surface acres at conservation pool level,) and six parks with camping, picnicking, fishing, boat ramps, marinas, and restrooms. It is easy to spend a whole day birding around the lake. The creek bottoms are wooded, some short-grass prairie is preserved, extensive mud flats are at the water's edge, and the lake itself offers many birding opportunities, making Benbrook Lake perhaps the best all-round location for birds in the Fort Worth area.

Below and north of the dam and west of the golf course a portion of the short-grass Grand Prairie is preserved, a site where Chestnut-collared and McCown's Longspurs and Horned Larks have been seen in winter. Longspurs have also been found on the drive around the lake.

Driving around the lake one fall day, I found Turkey Vulture, Great Blue Heron, Yellow-bellied Sapsucker, Screech Owl, Blue Jay, Double-crested Cormorant, Pied-billed Grebe, Lincoln's Sparrow, Belted Kingfisher, Bufflehead, Carolina Chickadee, Downy Woodpecker, Red-bellied Woodpecker, Ring-billed Gull, American Coot, Common Snipe, Lesser Yellowlegs, Northern Shoveler, Gadwall, Least Sandpiper, Marsh Hawk, Red-tailed Hawk, Cardinal, Mockingbird, House Sparrow, Loggerhead Shrike, White-crowned Sparrow, Rufous-sided Towhee, Field Sparrow, Bewick's Wren, Dark-eyed Junco,

Red-tailed Hawk

Ruby-crowned Kinglet, Orange-crowned Warbler, American Goldfinch, American Kestrel, and Song and Harris' Sparrows.

The developed parks total 2896 acres, with another 1578 acres undeveloped. All of the parks are good for land birds. Holiday Park has a marked path leading through fields and along woodland edges to a photo blind, where land birds can be found in all seasons. The path is to the right just past the park entrance. Rocky Creek Park (on the east side) and Mustang Park (on the southern end) offer more extensive woodlands and less visitor use, and perhaps better birding. Some portions of Mustang Park are closed in winter. Look for Osprey in migration, shorebirds and ducks on the water, and perching birds in the thickets. Harris' Sparrow are common in winter.

The address of the Benbrook Lake Manager is P.O. Box 26059, Fort Worth, TX 76116 (817) 292-2400.

Greenwood Memorial Park

Greenwood Memorial Park is close to downtown at the intersection of White Settlement Road and University Drive. Enter from White Settlement Road, and drive to the northern end of the cemetery where dense woods and underbrush are preserved between the cemetery and the West Fork Trinity River.

Practically all land birds of the area can be found here. This site is also a favorite place during migration for local birders to see warblers, vireos, tanagers, thrushes, and other land birds.

Winter residents include Dark-eyed Junco, Golden-crowned Kinglet, Brown Creeper, Purple Finch, Pine Siskin, American Goldfinch, and Lincoln's, White-throated, Fox, Field, Song, and Harris' Sparrows.

Trinity and Forest Parks

Trinity and Forest Parks are a mile west of downtown Fort Worth on IH 30 and offer the bird seeker extensive woodlands in the inner city along the Clear Fork Trinity River. From IH 30, Trinity Park is north on University Avenue, and Forest Park is to the south.

Trinity Park (252 acres) is nearly two miles north-to-south and contains the Japanese Garden and the Botanic Garden, both well worth visiting.

Forest Park (233 acres) is just south of Trinity Park. The parks are connected to each other by a road that runs underneath IH 30. Forest Park has large tracts of wooded bottomland and contains the Fort Worth Zoo. In the zoo more than 600 species of birds from all over the world are on display, including a good representation of Texas birds. The rain forest display, where visitors enter the bird area, is well conceived.

Most resident land birds can be found in the parks, and despite some underbush clearance, migrating tanagers, warblers, vireos, and thrushes can be found. Nesting birds of the wooded sections are Cardinal, Tufted

Titmouse, Downy Woodpecker, Great Crested Flycatcher, Carolina and Bewick's Wrens, Brown Thrasher, and Summer Tanager.

Lake Worth and Como Park

If in the general vicinity and time is limited, there are two areas where a few hours can turn up a good list of birds. The first area is east of Lake Worth and south of SH 199. Drive northwest on SH 199 to Loop 820. Continue on SH 199 for three-quarters of a mile to Charbonneau. Drive west on Charbonneau to Malaga Park, which has an inlet to the lake where Wood Duck and shorebirds can be found, and tall trees where warblers and other migrants can be expected.

Pied-billed Grebe

Continue south to Vinca Circle Park, Camp LeRoy Schuman, and Mosque Point Park, birding each as time permits. Follow along the north shore of the lake on Meandering Drive, under Loop 820, and back to SH 199.

Como Park, southeast of the intersection of IH 30 and Camp Bowie Boulevard, is another worthwhile area. There is a small lake, Como Lake, where ducks and sometimes Common Gallinule are found. The thick wooded area below the dam near the picnicking grounds is excellent for resident, migrating, and wintering land birds.

Birds of Tarrant County, second edition, by Warren M. Pulich, 188 pages, 1979, is an excellent annotated checklist of the birds of the county. The book is available from the Fort Worth Nature Center and Refuge, Route 10, Box 53, Fort Worth, TX 76135; The Museum of Science and History; and many area bookstores.

A "Check-list of the Birds of Tarrant County, 1967" is available from the Fort Worth Audubon Society, % Fort Worth Museum of Science and History, 1501 Montgomery, Fort Worth, TX 76107, for 25¢ plus stamped, addressed envelope.

Hagerman National Wildlife Refuge

Hagerman National Wildlife Refuge is on the south shore of Lake Texoma about 12 road miles west-southwest of Denison, 17 road miles northwest of Sherman, or 6.5 miles from Pottsboro. From Sherman, drive west on US 82 three miles to FM 1417. Go north past the FM 691 intersection for 1.5 miles, then west on a county road

Hagerman National Wildlife Refuge

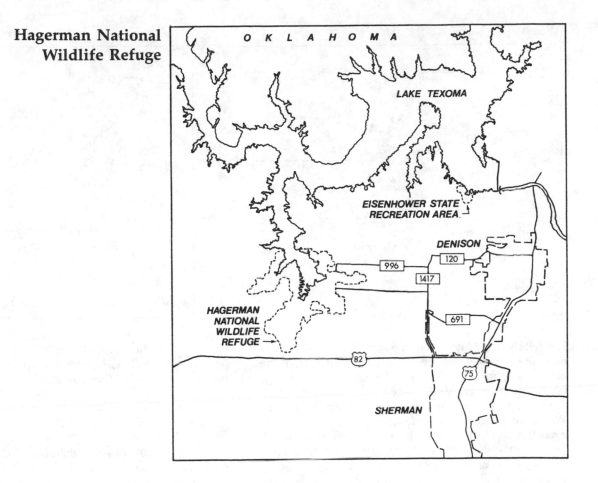

for six miles to the refuge headquarters. FM 1417 can also be reached from Denison by driving west on either FM 120 or FM 691 past Grayson County College.

The refuge is on the Big Mineral Arm of Lake Texoma formed by Denison Dam on the Red River, the boundary between Texas and Oklahoma. The lake has 580 miles of shoreline, 89,000 surface acres at power pool level, and a vast array of recreation areas with camping, boat ramps, drinking water, picnicking, and restrooms. In Texas the Corps of Engineers has 19 such facilities; an additional 25 are in Oklahoma.

The eastern half of the refuge is part of the Blackland Prairie, while the western portion is in the East Cross Timbers. Some of the dominant trees of the Eastern Cross Timbers are elms, eastern red cedar, pecan, hickory, willow, oaks, hackberry, cottonwood, osage orange, box elder, and green ash. The refuge has 11,319 acres—3000 in marsh and water, and 8000 in uplands and farmland.

The primary objective of the refuge is to preserve the natural state of the plant and animal species in the area and to provide wintering and resting areas for migratory waterfowl of the Central Flyway.

Many species of ducks and geese winter on the refuge, with very large numbers of Canada Goose and Mallard. Snow and White-fronted Geese are more common in migration. Some years a few Ross' Goose are winter residents. Brant have been recorded but are very rare.

The only duck expected in summer is the Wood Duck, a regular nester. Pied-billed Grebe nest when there is enough water.

The marshes and mud flats provide habitat for shorebirds during migration, with 30 species recorded on the refuge check-list. Common migrants are Common Snipe, Upland, Spotted, and Solitary Sandpipers, Greater and Lesser Yellowlegs, Pectoral, White-rumped (late spring), Baird's, and Least Sandpipers, Long-billed Dowitcher, Stilt, Semipalmated, and Western Sandpipers, and Wilson's Phalarope.

Sandy Point Access Area at the north end of the road on the refuge is an excellent observation point for finding Bald Eagle fishing over the lake from late October through March. This is also a good place to look for Common Goldeneye, Common Merganser, Horned Grebe, Bonaparte's Gull, Mallard by the thousands, Canada Goose by the hundreds. Other waterfowl winter and migrate in lesser numbers, especially if the lake level is high enough.

Twenty-seven warbler species are on the refuge check-list. Most are seen only during migration; however, Common Yellowthroat nests regularly and Black-and-white, Prothonotary, and Yellow-breasted Chat occasionally.

Pileated Woodpecker are occasionally found in the woods at the Big Mineral Access Area and in the northwest corner of the refuge near Brushy Creek. Look for

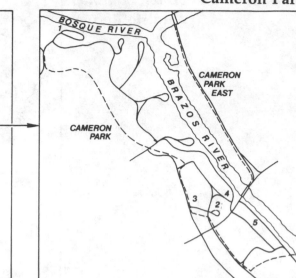

White-breasted Nuthatch in the same locations and also near the Sandy Creek bridge on the west side of the refuge, and from the Meadow Pond west to the refuge boundary at the old steel bridge.

Thirteen species of sparrows winter on the refuge. Watch for them on the road to the refuge also. Dark-eyed Junco, Field (nests also), Harris', White-crowned, Fox, White-throated, and Song are common. Vesper, Lincoln's, Swamp, LeConte's, and Tree (some years in good numbers) are found occasionally. Nesting sparrows usually gone in winter are Grasshopper and Lark. Chipping and Clay-colored are migrants.

The prairies and roadsides of North Texas are wintering areas for Horned Lark and all four species of longspurs. McCown's and Chestnut-collared are the most numerous; Lapland, harder to find; Smith's, difficult at best. Approaches to the refuge, its grassy fields, and indeed, all roads in this part of Texas should be checked.

There is no camping on the refuge, but there are four picnic areas, three with restrooms.

A bird check-list is available at refuge headquarters which lists 282 species. The address is Route 3, Box 123, Sherman, TX 75090 (214) 786–2826.

Lake Texoma

Other public lands on Lake Texoma include Eisenhower State Recreation Area in Texas and Tishomingo National Wildlife Refuge in Oklahoma.

Eisenhower State Recreation Area (475 acres) is about 10 road miles northwest of Denison and has camping, picnicking, a boat ramp, and restrooms with hot showers. There is a bird check-list for the park, but the habitat is much more limited than at Hagerman National Wildlife Refuge.

Tishomingo National Wildlife Refuge has 16,500 acres of open water, marshy lands, and cultivated and natural grasslands on the Washita Arm of the lake. It is 18 miles

northwest of Durant, Oklahoma, or 55 miles north of Sherman. Barnacle Goose have been recorded at Tishomingo National Wildlife Refuge.

Waco

Waco (pop. 101,000) is in the heart of Central Texas at the western edge of the Blackland Prairies near the Balcones Escarpment.

The story of Waco begins with the Brazos River. The Huaco Indians originally established their village on its banks at Indian Spring Park. Visitors to Indian Spring Park will discover a world of history, natural beauty, fun, and good birding.

Birding opportunities in and around Waco are enhanced by the extensive farmlands (hawks and sparrows in winter), several large man-made lakes (waterfowl and shorebirds), and wide and heavily wooded river bottomland (land birds).

Cameron Park

Fort Fisher is just south of the Brazos River on IH 35. It is operated by the Waco Parks and Recreation Department and has excellent facilities for fishing, boating, picnicking, and camping. The Homer Garrison Memorial Texas Ranger Museum and the Texas Ranger Hall of Fame are here, and both are well worth a visit. For camper hook-up information, write to the Waco Parks and Recreation Department, P.O. Box 1370, Waco, TX 76703, or call (817) 754–1433.

To reach Cameron Park from Fort Fisher, drive northwest on University Parks Drive for 2.5 miles. A sign indicates "William Cameron Park," but if the sign is missed, the horse stables on the left will mean the park has been reached. Cameron Park (680 acres), also operated by the Waco Parks and Recreation Department, is spread on both sides of the Brazos River. At the upper end of the park, the Bosque River joins the Brazos, which can be seen from Lover's Leap (#1 on the park map legend). Lover's Leap is one of three cliffs inside the park. From this high vantage point, one can view for miles the farmlands and plains to the east of the city.

The cul-de-sac at Proctor Spring (#10 on the map) is a good place to start birding among the majestic old sycamore, elm, oak, pecan, and cottonwood trees for resident land birds and migrants. During spring migration, the height of warbler passage usually occurs in the first two weeks of May. Starting near the picnic pavilion, follow the stream back toward Lindsey Hollow (#11 on map), and look for birds in the tops of the trees. Migrants found include *empidonax* flycatchers, Eastern Wood Peewee, Veery, Swainson's and Gray-cheeked Thrushes, Northern and Orchard Orioles, Scarlet Tanager, Rose-breasted and Black-headed Grosbeaks, Solitary, Bell's, Philadelphia, and Warbling Vireos, a rare Black-billed Cuckoo, as well as warblers.

The Redwood Shelter (#9 on map) is the only area in the park that is "by reservation only" and requires a small rental fee. However, there are numerous other beautiful picnic spots throughout the park—all free. Across the road from the Redwood Shelter is a large mulberry tree. When there are berries on the tree, there is a good chance of seeing migrants plus a few lingering wintering species, such as Pine Siskin, Lincoln's Sparrow, American Goldfinch, and Cedar Waxwing. Indigo Bunting sometimes nest here as well as directly across the river in Cameron Park East.

Another land bird location is the South Bottom Playground (#14 on the map). From the car bridge, check the creek for Green Heron (a summer resident) and migrating Northern Waterthrush. Overhead watch for Rough-winged Swallow (summer resident), and migrating Mississippi Kite, Franklin's Gull, and Broad-winged and Swainson's Hawks. In recent years Wood Duck have nested in one of the tall cottonwood trees on the bank of the stream near the bridge. The vine-covered tree trunks in this area are good places to find nesting Black-and-white Warbler.

The pecan and oak trees all along the South Bottom Playground are excellent locations for finding warblers. During migration, Nashville, Black-throated Green, Blackburnian, Chestnut-sided, Bay-breasted, Wilson's, American Redstart, Black-and-white, Yellow, Common Yellowthroat, and Yellow-breasted Chat are usually recorded. The last three nest in the park. Less common are Tennessee, Canada, and Northern Parula. Connecticut and Blackpoll are very rare. Look for nesting Pied-billed Grebe and Belted Kingfisher along the water's edge. Shorebirds and waterfowl have been seen in migration along the river.

Nesting species in the park are Carolina Wren, Screech, Barred, and Great Horned Owls, Black-chinned Hummingbird, Eastern and Western Kingbirds, Summer Tanager, and Brown Thrasher.

In the winter the following birds can be found in the park: Hairy, Ladder-backed, and Red-headed Woodpeckers, Common Flicker, Yellow-bellied Sapsucker, Eastern Phoebe, Red-breasted Nuthatch, Brown Creeper, Winter Wren, Blue-gray Gnatcatcher, Hermit Thrush, Purple Finch, Dark-eyed Junco, Whitethroated Sparrow, Yellow-rumped and Orange-crowned Warblers, Cedar Waxwing, and sometimes White-breasted Nuthatch. Chipping Sparrow, Brown Thrasher, and Roadrunner can be found in the higher areas of the park in summer.

The best time for bird seekers to visit Cameron Park on weekends is early morning—before the picnickers arrive with their loud music and frisbees flying in all directions. It is generally very crowded on Saturdays and Sundays, beginning around 11 a.m. and continuing until late evening. However, there is usually no problem on weekdays, except toward the end of May when school picnics prevail.

Steinbeck Bend Area

The Steinbeck Bend area has consistently produced good birding in all seasons. Though in the Waco city limits, the area is rural. Formerly devoted to cropland farming and grazing, this big bend of the Brazos River just north of Cameron Park is now an area of widely spaced private homes with a few cattle.

From Cameron Park, drive east on Herring Avenue (FM 1637), and cross the bridge over Lake Brazos. Turn left onto Lake Brazos Drive at the second traffic light. Eastern and Western Kingbirds, Scissor-tailed Flycatcher, and Painted and Indigo Buntings are easily

Scissor-tailed Flycatcher

Eastern Kingbird

heard and seen in spring and summer between the traffic light and the bridge over the Brazos River. The woods west of the road are in Cameron Park East. From the traffic light, drive north 1.8 miles, and turn right at the flashing light onto Lake Shore Drive. After 0.3 of a mile, turn left at the first gravel road where there is a small abandoned farmhouse, barn, and windmill. Though unmarked at this end of the loop, this is Old Steinbeck Bend Road (not to be confused with Steinbeck Bend Road). From this point, make a right turn at each intersection until back at the starting point, thus completing a loop.

The loop can also be reached from the intersection of IH 35 and Industrial Boulevard (FM 3051) by driving west on Industrial Boulevard and crossing the river. The loop is reached in about one-half mile. Fence rows, open fields, and wood margins along the 2.5-mile loop provide good habitat for a diverse group of bird species.

During spring migration (April and early May), the following birds have been recorded on the loop: Upland Sandpiper (in large numbers in the open fields), Black Tern, Barn and Cliff Swallows, Eastern and Western Kingbirds, *empidonax* flycatchers, Northern and Orchard Orioles, Indigo Bunting, Cattle Egret, Nashville and Yellow Warblers, Common Yellowthroat, White-crowned, Grasshopper, and LeConte's Sparrows. Bobolink are occasionally sighted migrating with the abundant Dickcissel.

Sometimes water stands in these fields for days after heavy rains. On such occasions, shorebirds and wading birds not usually found in abundance in the area can congregate in great numbers. One particularly rainy spring, Wilson's Phalarope, Long-billed Dowitcher, Pectoral Sandpiper, Common Snipe, Little Blue Heron, Greater and Lesser Yellowlegs, Pintail, Northern Shoveler, and Blue-winged Teal were all seen feeding in the shallow water for a period of two weeks or more. In recent years, during the first two weeks of May, Yellow-

headed Blackbird have stopped over to feed with mixed flocks of Brown-headed Cowbird, Red-winged Blackbird, and Great-tailed and Common Grackles.

During winter, look for American Goldfinch feeding in the dried weeds along the fence rows with wintering sparrows: Harris', Lincoln's, White-throated, White-crowned, Savannah, and Vesper.

McLennan Community College

The campus of McLennan Community College (160 acres owned and operated by McLennan County) is located on the crest of a heavily wooded bluff that commands a magnificent view of the valleys of the Brazos and Bosque Rivers. The athletic fields, woods, and frontage along the river offer another opportunity for birding in the city.

From the Steinbeck Bend area, drive southwest on Lake Shore Drive to the Bosque River bridge. Just after crossing the bridge, turn left at the first traffic light (College Drive), then go left again at the first street (Cameron Street). Park in the parking lot next to the athletic fieldhouse beneath the shade trees. Near the river there is an amphitheater.

In spring and summer this is a good area in which to see Great Crested Flycatcher, Red-eyed and White-eyed Vireos, Red-bellied Woodpecker, and an occasional Red-headed Woodpecker. At night, Chuck-will's-widow call in the heavily wooded areas all around the campus.

Near the river in summer look for Little Blue Heron, American Coot, and Pied-billed Grebe. Up river there are Cliff Swallow in great abundance under the bridge. Opposite the marina, the woods on both sides of the road offer excellent habitat for Painted and Indigo Buntings from late April to early August.

Next, walk or drive up the hill, and turn left at the first intersection. Search the wood margins all around the perimeter of the large parking lot at the top of the hill. Here is another favorable location for migrating warblers (same species as mentioned in the Cameron Park section). Inca Dove and Black-chinned and Ruby-throated Hummingbirds are also to be found.

Camp Val Verde

Camp Val Verde, a 400-acre camp located 12 miles west of Waco, is owned and operated by the Huaco Council of Camp Fire, Inc. To reach the camp from the intersection of IH 35 and Valley Mills Drive, go west on Valley Mills Drive for 2.2 miles to Waco Drive (US 84), then drive 9.5 miles to the Val Verde Road exit. Drive north on Val Verde Road 2.5 miles to the camp. There are signs along the road with directions.

The camp is situated on the Middle Bosque River in a predominantly agricultural area. There are two shallow ponds and one small lake on the property as well as intermittent streams flowing through eroded gullies in spring and summer. Permission from the Camp Fire office is required to enter.

Numerous campsites and small cabins with facilities are available for rent. These are scattered throughout the camp. To obtain information or permission for access to the premises for birding, write: Huaco Council of Camp Fire, Inc., Community Services Building, Suite 205, 201 West Waco Drive, Waco, TX 76707; or call (817) 752–5515.

Permanent resident birds of the area include Inca Dove, Roadrunner, Red-headed and Ladder-backed Woodpeckers, Eastern Bluebird, Loggerhead Shrike, Common Grackle, Great Horned, Barred, and Screech Owls, Brown Thrasher, Double-crested Cormorant, Little Blue Heron, Belted Kingfisher, and Black Vulture.

Wintering species include Sharp-shinned and Cooper's Hawks, Common Flicker, Field, Chipping, Clay-colored, White-throated, Fox, Lincoln's, and Harris' Sparrows, Golden-crowned Kinglet, American Goldfinch, Dark-eyed Junco, Eastern Phoebe, Brown Creeper, Yellow-bellied Sapsucker, Common Snipe, Winter and House Wrens, Purple Finch. Occasionals are Vermilion Flycatcher, Green-tailed Towhee, and Say's Phoebe. The wintering species are especially abundant and easy to find around the gravel pit area.

Some summer residents are Great, Snowy, and Cattle Egrets, Chuck-will's-widow, Black-chinned Hummingbird, Eastern and Western Kingbirds, Great Crested Flycatcher, Orchard Oriole, Dickcissel, White-eyed and Red-eyed Vireos, Summer Tanager, Red-headed Woodpecker, and Barn and Rough-winged Swallows.

Migrating birds recorded at the camp include Black-and-white, Yellow, Tennessee, Blackburnian, Bay-breasted, and Canada Warblers, Yellow-breasted Chat, American Redstart, Northern (Bullock's) Oriole, Rose-breasted Grosbeak, Grasshopper and LeConte's Sparrows, Wood and Swainson's Thrushes, Least Flycatcher, Eastern Wood Pewee, Solitary and Warbling Vireos, Blue-gray Gnatcatcher, Gray Catbird, Water Pipit, Western Meadowlark, Spotted, Semipalmated, and Upland Sandpipers, Lesser Yellowlegs, Mississippi Kite, and Sandhill Crane. Black-throated Sparrow, not usually found in the Waco area, have been recorded here.

Lake Waco

Lake Waco is located at the northwest city limits of Waco. It has a shoreline of 60 miles (7270 surface acres at conservation pool) and is operated by the U.S. Army Corps of Engineers. The lake impounds water from the North, Middle, and South Bosque Rivers for the purposes of flood control, water conservation, and municipal water supply. Extra dividends derived from the lake include favorable fish and wildlife habitats, recreational facilities for water sports, hunting, fishing, boating, and birding.

The lake is surrounded by eight Corps of Engineer parks, most of which have camping, restrooms, picnicking, and boat ramps. The north shore can be reached from IH 35 on the north side of Waco. Drive west from the Lake Shore Drive exit on Industrial Boulevard (soon becomes Lake Shore Drive) approximately four miles to

Airport Road. From Waco's south side, take the Valley Mills exit, then go west on Valley Mills Drive approximately 3.5 miles until the road turns north and becomes Lake Shore Drive. To get to the parks on the south and west shoreline, drive northwest about four miles on SH 6 from south of Waco. Signs on the right give directions to the lake.

Airport Park, with its extensive woodlands and protected shoreline, is a good place to start birding the lake. From Lake Shore Drive turn north on Airport Road. Drive north to FM 3051, west to the dead end, then right (north) to where lake headquarters is soon found on the right. Maps and bird information can be obtained at headquarters from the lake rangers. The beach area of Airport Park is on the left about 0.1 mile past headquarters. Airport Road is approximately one mile west of the McLennan Community College campus on Lake Shore Drive.

Soon after crossing the Bosque River bridge while driving north on Airport Road, there is a large pecan grove on both sides of the road where Eastern Bluebird, Great Horned Owl, Red-tailed Hawk, Loggerhead Shrike, and Red-headed, and Ladder-backed Woodpeckers are permanent residents. This is part of Bosque Park.

The beach area is an excellent place for migrating shorebirds and waterfowl. During winter, the gate is sometimes locked; however, visitors can obtain a key at the headquarters office.

Some migrants which have been recorded are American Avocet, Common, Least, Black, and Forster's Terns, Upland, Spotted, Least, Baird's, and Western Sandpipers, Northern and Louisiana Waterthrushes, White Pelican, Sandhill Crane, Willet, Swainson's Hawk, Greater and Lesser Yellowlegs, Sanderling, Semipalmated Plover, Canada Goose, Hudsonian Godwit, and White-faced Ibis. Black Skimmer has been seen occasionally.

Wintering species along the shore, on the water, and in wooded areas include Water Pipit, Pintail, Redhead, Green-winged and Blue-winged Teals, Gadwall, American Wigeon, Canvasback, Northern Shoveler, Double-crested Cormorant, Osprey, Dark-eyed Junco, Lincoln's and Vesper Sparrows, Common Flicker, and Eastern Phoebe. A flock of 20 Canada Geese wintered at Lake Waco during 1980–81.

Summer birds include Little Blue Heron, Snowy, Great, and Cattle Egrets, Great Crested Flycatcher, Grasshopper Sparrow, Barn and Cliff Swallows, Northern (Bullock's) Oriole, Red-eyed Vireo, Dickcissel, Eastern and Western Kingbirds, Chuck-will's-widow, and Broad-winged Hawk.

The wooded areas of Airport Park and Waco Marina are good locations for spring and fall warbler migration. The area designated as 185 Park is especially good for Eastern Bluebird, shorebirds, herons, and White-faced Ibis. In winter hawks are usually present west of the lake.

Speegleville I, II, and III Parks on the west shore, reached by driving northwest from Waco on SH 6, provide the most developed facilities for camping. Woodpeckers are found year-round near the Bosque Bend

Club House in Speegleville I Park. Common Flicker are easily seen in winter. This is also where White Pelican have been found on numerous occasions in both winter and spring. Hawks, Osprey, and land birds are frequently found in the Speegleville Parks.

The address of the Reservoir Manager is Route 10, Box 173-G, Waco, TX 76708 (817) 756–5359.

Meridian State Recreation Area

Meridian State Recreation Area (502 acres) is approximately 42 miles northwest of Waco by way of SH 6, or about four miles southwest of Meridian on SH 22. The park is near where the West Cross Timbers and Grand Prairie of Central Texas meet the Lampasas Cut Plains of the Edwards Plateau. There is an abundance of Ashe Juniper in the uplands, while the vegetation of the floodplain along Bee Creek is similar to that expected in East Texas. The creek has been dammed to form Bosque Lake (70 surface acres), which attracts many shorebirds and waterfowl, particularly in migration.

Camping, restrooms with hot showers, picnicking, swimming, fishing, boat ramps (12-hp limit), and hiking trails are offered.

Rufous-crowned Sparrow

Many eastern and western species occur in the park. Both the Golden-cheeked Warbler and Black-capped Vireo nest; the warbler is probably more abundant than the vireo. This is near the northern limit of the nesting range of the Golden-cheeked Warbler. From mid-March through June, the Golden-cheeked Warbler is usually found in the Ashe Juniper in the northwest section of the park above the lake. The vireo nests in all sections of the park. The vireo is much easier to hear than to see; therefore, it helps greatly to learn its song. Look in the thick oak clumps which are their favored habitat here. Several nests have been found along the Little Forest Junior Trail. I have seen the vireo in the central part of the park in the thick undergrowth.

Permanent residents include Black Vulture, Roadrunner, Barn, Screech, and Great Horned Owls, Ladderbacked Woodpecker, Carolina and Cañon Wrens, Brown

Thrasher, Eastern Bluebird, Lesser Goldfinch, and Rufous-crowned Sparrow. In summer look for Chuckwill's-widow, Poor-will, Western Kingbird, Great Crested Flycatcher, Rough-winged Swallow, Blue-gray Gnatcatcher, White-eyed, Bell's, and Red-eyed Vireos, Blackchinned and Ruby-throated Hummingbirds, Black-and-white Warbler, Yellow-breasted Chat, Orchard Oriole, and Summer Tanager.

In addition to the transient waterfowl and shorebirds attracted to the lake, many land birds migrate through the area. Nineteen warbler species have been recorded, most as migrants, and 14 sparrow species, most of which winter.

A check-list of the birds of the park is available at park headquarters. The park address is Box 188, Meridian, TX 76665 (817) 435–2536.

Lake Somerville

Lake Somerville is located near SH 36 just east of Somerville between Brenham and Caldwell. With 11,460 surface acres at conservation pool, this U.S. Army Corps of Engineers impoundment on Yegua Creek is a mecca for fishing, camping, picnicking, and other water recreational activities. The lake is for flood control, municipal and industrial water supply, and recreation. The Corps of Engineers has seven parks on the lake, two of which are undeveloped. There are facilities for picnicking, camping with restrooms, and boat ramps.

Lake Somerville is in the eastern section of the Post Oak Savannah. Several bird habitats are represented in the parks—grasslands, understory thickets, extensive mud flats, woodlands along the many creeks, and the open water of the lake.

Regular nesting birds include Blue Jay, Lark Sparrow, Screech, Barred, and Great Horned Owls, Red-headed and Downy Woodpeckers, Carolina Chickadee, Tufted Titmouse, Red-shouldered Hawk, Common Grackle, and Painted Bunting.

Wintering birds usually present are Gadwall, Pintail, Green-winged Teal, American Wigeon, Northern Shoveler, Ring-necked Duck, Lesser Scaup, Bald Eagle, Osprey, and many sparrow species.

Shorebirds can be found anywhere along the shoreline, but near Overlook Park and those sections of the lake where boats are excluded are particularly good. Once in early May I saw a migrating Hudsonian Godwit at Rocky Creek Park.

Other birds found are Double-crested and Olivaceous Cormorants, Roseate Spoonbill, and White Pelican. Recent records of unexpected birds include Curve-billed Thrasher, Reddish Egret, Brown Pelican, and Royal Tern.

The address of the Corps of Engineers Resident Manager is P.O. Box 548, Somerville, TX 77879.

Lake Somerville State Recreation Area

Lake Somerville State Recreation Area (5200 acres) is at the western end of the lake. This recreation area is divided into two non-contiguous units: Birch Creek on the north shore, and Nails Creek on the south. Camping, restrooms with hot showers, picnicking, nature trails, and boat ramps are available.

A field check-list of *Birds of Lake Somerville State Recreation Area* is available at the headquarters in each unit. Visitors are requested to report hypothetical species and unusual sightings to the park office.

The address of Birch Creek Unit is Route 1, Box 192-A, Somerville, TX 77879 (713) 535–7763; Nails Creek Unit, Route 1, Box 61-C, Ledbetter, TX 78946 (713) 289–2392.

Bastrop and Buescher State Parks

Bastrop State Park is about 30 miles east of Austin on SH 71 in the "Lost Pines of Texas." The park is one mile east of Bastrop and can be reached from either SH 21 or SH 71 by way of Loop 150, which connects the two highways. There are 2033 acres with two campgrounds, picnic areas, restrooms with hot showers, a swimming pool, golf course, cabins, group barracks with mess hall, and hiking trails. The park preserves an isolated stand of pines in the western section of the Post-Oak Savannah. Here Loblolly Pines occur some 180 miles west of the Pineywoods, with the prairies in-between.

As might be expected, some nesting birds typical of the Pineywoods are found here, such as Pileated Woodpecker, Pine and Black-and-white Warblers, Northern Parula, and Wood Thrush. Hairy Woodpecker are found occasionally. In winter Red-breasted Nuthatch and Golden-crowned Kinglet are usually present, and Red Crossbill have been recorded. Barred Owl, Red-shouldered Hawk, and Common Grackle are more common in the Bastrop area than in Austin.

Park Road 1, which connects Bastrop and Buescher State Parks, is 13 miles long and 200 feet wide: the road is a park in itself. On Alum Creek, the only flowing creek which crosses Park Road 1, Hooded and Kentucky Warblers nest regularly, with Swainson's Warbler found nesting in recent years. Red-headed Woodpecker are permanent residents near Alum Creek.

Buescher State Park (1012 acres) is two miles northwest of Smithville on SH 71 and has a 25-acre lake, screen shelters, campgrounds, restrooms with hot showers, a picnic area, and a recreation building. The wooded creek bottoms leading to the lake offer the best variety of birds. While Black-chinned Hummingbird nest abundantly in Austin, the nesting hummingbird in Bastrop-Buescher parks is the Ruby-throated. Hardwoods are more common in Buescher than at Bastrop, principally Blackjack, Live, and Post Oaks.

The University of Texas Environmental Science Park, a research facility, is located in Buescher State Park.

There is a combined bird check-list for both parks available at both headquarters, listing 26 warbler species nesting, migrating and/or wintering, and 10 sparrow species in winter.

The park addresses are: Bastrop, Box 518, Bastrop, TX 78602 (512) 321–2101; Buescher, P.O. Box 75, Smithville, TX 78957 (512) 237–2241.

Palmetto State Park

Palmetto State Park (263 acres on the San Marcos River) is a small, unique botanical area in the Post Oak-Savannah vegetational area. Camping, restrooms with hot showers, picnicking, and fishing are offered. To drive to the park, take US 183 east from Luling for six miles, or go west from Gonzales 13 miles. From US 183, the park can be reached from either FM 1586 or PR 11.

The park preserves swamps with extensive dwarf palmettos, an artesian well flowing with sulphur-laden water, an oxbow lake nearly one-half mile long, hardwood bottoms along the San Marcos River, thick understory vegetation, and open grassy areas that altogether comprise a remarkable diversity of trees, shrubs, and wildflowers. Formerly, quaking bogs were present that helped make possible the unique flora. More than 500 species of plants have been identified in the park, with western and eastern species growing in close proximity. There are two self-guiding nature trails: one along the San Marcos River, and one in the swampy area near the artesian well. Pick up booklets at headquarters.

Approximately 39 species of birds nest in the park, including Wood Duck, Red-shouldered Hawk, Screech, Great Horned, and Barred Owls, Prothonotary and Kentucky Warblers, Northern Parula, Blue Grosbeak, Indigo and Painted Buntings.

Birds which winter include American Woodcock, Yellow-bellied Sapsucker, Brown Creeper, Brown Thrasher, Hermit Thrush, Golden-crowned Kinglet, Cedar Waxwing, Orange-crowned and Yellow-rumped Warblers, Pine Siskin, and American Goldfinch. In addition, sparrows expected in winter include Savannah, Vesper, Lark, Dark-eyed Junco, Chipping, Field, Harris', White-crowned, White-throated, Fox, Lincoln's, and Song. Other sparrows sometimes found in winter are Grasshopper, Cassin's, Clay-colored, and Swamp. The park is excellent for migrants in spring.

In addition to the trails, the oxbow lake and river, and roads, a walk down PR 11 from the overlook to the village of Ottine will usually turn up most of the land birds present. Caracara and Red-shouldered Hawk can usually be seen flying overhead in the open country surrounding the park.

A bird check-list with 238 species listed is available at park headquarters. The address is P.O. Box 4, Ottine, TX 78658 (512) 672–3266.

McKinney Falls State Park

McKinney Falls State Park (632 acres) is at the southern city limit of Austin. The park offers a campground, restrooms with hot showers, picnic area, four-mile hike-and-bike trail, and visitor's center.

To reach the park from Austin, drive south on US 183 past the intersection with SH 71, then proceed another four miles south on US 183 to FM 812. Turn right (west) on Scenic Loop Road, and go about two miles to the park entrance. The park can also be reached from the south off IH 35 by taking the William Cannon Drive exit. From William Cannon Drive, drive east on North Bluff (same road, different name) to the dead-end. Turn south on Nuckols Crossing Road, then left on Bluff Springs Road. Turn left again onto Scenic Loop Road to the park entrance.

The park has been developed in such a way that the camping and picnic areas, etc., blend with the various habitats to preserve most of them in a natural state, an excellent developmer.t plan. The soil and vegetation are a combination of Edwards Plateau and Blackland Prairie, but the birds are more representative of the eastern sec-tion of the state. Nesting birds include Screech and Barred Owls, Chuck-will's-widow, Cañon and Carolina Wrens, Great Crested Flycatcher, and White-eyed Vireo. A Green Kingfisher or two are usually present along the creek. Also, shorebirds and ducks frequently are found along the creek in fall, winter, and spring. The wide variety of tall trees and underbrush along the creek, open grasslands, and large live oaks in the campground make the park an excellent location for migrating land birds. Wintering birds include Hermit Thrush, Brown Creeper, Golden-crowned and Ruby-crowned Kinglet, Fox, White-throated, Harris', Chipping, Lincoln's, and Vesper Sparrows, and Dark-eyed Junco.

A bird check-list is available at park headquarters. The park address is Route 2, Box 701-B, Austin, TX 78704 (512) 243–1643.

Pineywoods

The Pineywoods region is approximately 9% of Texas. The west boundary of the region is a line from Texarkana through Tyler, Palestine, and west of Huntsville into Waller County. The south boundary is a line extending eastward from just north of Houston to Beaumont and Orange. It is that part of Texas where, because of a combination of climate, soil, and moisture availability, the pine-hardwood forests of the southeastern United States reach their southwestern limit.

The region consists of Tertiary and Quaternary deposits, with the former making up the northern two-thirds. The elevation ranges from 20 to 550 feet, with the terrain gently rolling to hilly. There are many wide rivers, river bottoms, swamps, and bogs.

Loblolly, shortleaf, and longleaf pines are native. Slash pine has been introduced and is grown commercially. There are extensive hardwood forests of oak, beech, maple, magnolia, sweetgum, hickory, and other species with the pines. Large bald cypress swamps are common. The Big Thicket in the southern portion of the region is a meeting ground for many vegetative types, now partially preserved as the Big Thicket National Preserve.

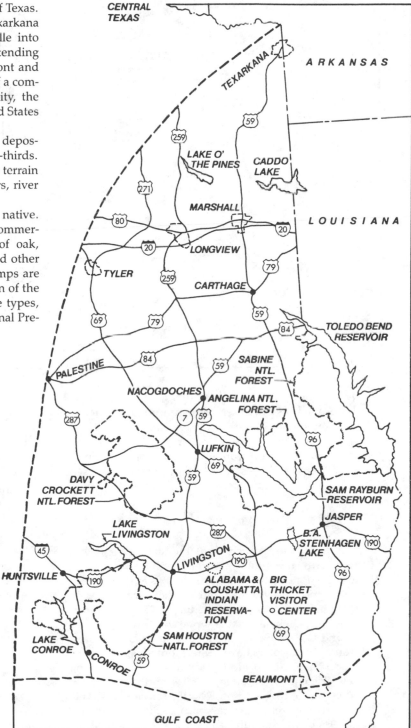

This beautiful wooded area is typical of Pineywoods forests.

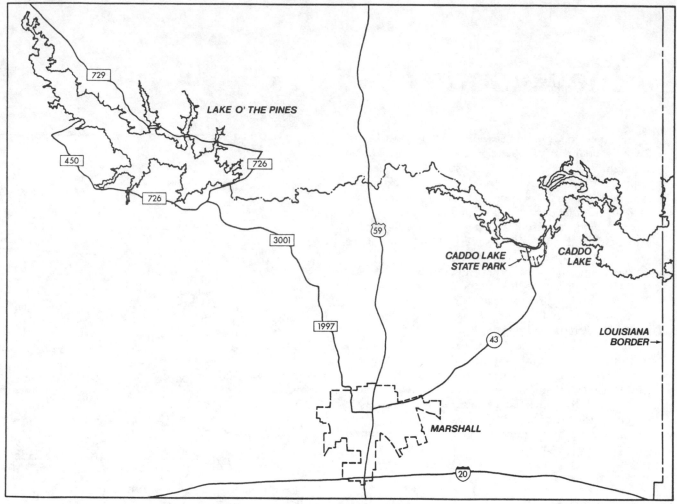

Nesting bird species unique to this region include Red-cockaded Woodpecker, Brown-headed Nuthatch, Prairie Warbler, and Louisiana Waterthrush. Red-shouldered Hawk, Pileated Woodpecker, Pine Warbler, and Wood Thrush are very common nesting species. Fourteen warbler species nest in the Pineywoods.

Marshall

Near the northeast corner of the state, Marshall is between two lakes which are well worth a birding visit. Lake of the Pines (18,700 surface acres) is approximately 30 miles north of Marshall and excellent for wintering waterfowl, particularly diving ducks. Common Loon and Horned Grebe are usually present in winter; Black Duck and Greater Scaup are regular in small numbers; Oldsquaw and scoters have been recorded.

Caddo Lake (20,700 surface acres) is on the Louisiana border. By road, it is about 14 miles northeast of Marshall on SH 43, then east on FM 2198 for one mile. This is a fascinating area with large, picturesque bald cypress trees. Originally a natural lake, it is now dammed for

flood control. Fish Crow occur here throughout the year. Elsewhere in the state this species is found regularly only on the lower Sulphur River and the lower Neches River near Beaumont. Yellow-throated Warbler are abundant in spring and summer.

Caddo Lake State Park

Caddo Lake State Park (480 acres) is on the south shore of Caddo Lake. Camping, cabins, restrooms with hot showers, picnicking, fishing, boat ramps, and a hiking trail are available. The lake is probably easier to see and bird from a boat or canoe, and the park is a good starting spot.

The park address is Route 2, Box 15, Karnack, Texas 75661 (214) 679–3351.

Nacogdoches

Located approximately in the center of the Pineywoods, in what some Texans refer to as "Deep East Texas," Nacogdoches is an excellent base from which to

Nacogdoches

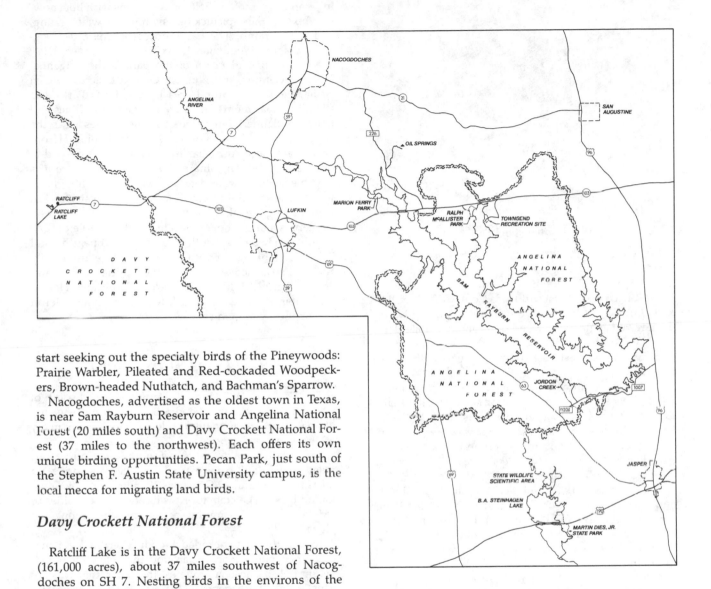

start seeking out the specialty birds of the Pineywoods: Prairie Warbler, Pileated and Red-cockaded Woodpeckers, Brown-headed Nuthatch, and Bachman's Sparrow.

Nacogdoches, advertised as the oldest town in Texas, is near Sam Rayburn Reservoir and Angelina National Forest (20 miles south) and Davy Crockett National Forest (37 miles to the northwest). Each offers its own unique birding opportunities. Pecan Park, just south of the Stephen F. Austin State University campus, is the local mecca for migrating land birds.

Davy Crockett National Forest

Ratcliff Lake is in the Davy Crockett National Forest, (161,000 acres), about 37 miles southwest of Nacogdoches on SH 7. Nesting birds in the environs of the lake are Wood Duck, Common Yellowthroat, and an occasional Pied-billed Grebe.

In the mixed pine-hardwood forest adjacent to the lake, nesting birds include Barred Owl, Chuck-will's-widow, Red-shouldered and Broad-winged Hawks, Pileated Woodpecker, Acadian Flycatcher, Summer Tanager, Wood Thrush, Red-eyed and Yellow-throated Vireos, Northern Parula, Black-and-white, Yellow-throated, Pine, Kentucky, and Hooded Warblers, and with luck and persistence, Worm-eating and Swainson's Warblers, and Louisiana Waterthrush.

Northeast of the lake is an area of shortleaf and loblolly pines with resident Red-cockaded Woodpecker and Brown-headed Nuthatch. Areas cleared by lumbering or fire several years ago with small, second-growth pines should be birded for Prairie Warbler, Yellow-breasted Chat, Indigo Bunting, and Blue Grosbeak.

Oil Springs

Oil Springs is 21 miles southeast of Nacogdoches, and the site of the first oil well in Texas (1866). To reach the historical site, drive east on SH 21 to Oak Ridge, then turn south on FM 226 to Woden. Go south of Woden seven miles to the turnoff to Oak Springs. Drive east on the dirt road 3.5 miles to Oil Springs. This dirt road can be impassable after a hard rain. Swainson's, Worm-eating and Prairie Warblers, and Louisiana Waterthrush are usually nesting but not always easy to find. Again, the Prairie Warbler is usually found in small regenerating pines.

Northern Shoveler

Sam Rayburn Reservoir

Sam Rayburn Reservoir (560 miles of shoreline) is at the southern end of Nacogdoches County. The northern end of the lake is located about 20 miles south of Nacogdoches, but actually the reservoir is about 50 miles long, north to south (114,500 surface acres at power pool), making it the largest lake completely within the state's boundaries.

Bald Eagle, Common Loon, Eared, Horned, and Pied-billed Grebes, ducks, and cormorants winter on the lake. Red-cockaded Woodpecker, Brown-headed Nuthatch, Prairie Warbler, and Bachman's Sparrow nest near the southern end of the lake in the Jordan Creek area of the Angelina National Forest (153,000 acres). This area contains many pitcher plants and longleaf pines.

Marion Ferry Park (12 miles east of Lufkin on SH 103, and two miles north on FM 1669) is one of the better places on the lake for shorebirds July through November. It is also good for large wading birds and wintering waterfowl. Wood Stork and Roseate Spoonbill have been found in late summer.

Ralph McAllister Park and Townsend Recreation Site (just south of SH 103, and 2.3 miles west of FM 1277) are on a northeast arm of the lake and are both good locations for Red-headed Woodpecker, Yellow-throated Warbler, and sometimes, Prothonotary Warbler. These locations offer an excellent view of the lake for wintering ducks and spring and fall migrants.

A bird check-list for Nacogdoches County is available from the University Bookstore, Stephen F. Austin State University, Box 3057, Nacogdoches, Texas 75962, for 10¢ plus stamped, addressed envelope.

Martin Dies, Jr. State Park

Martin Dies, Jr. State Park (705 acres) preserves pine and river-bottom hardwoods along US 190 between Woodville and Jasper on the shores of B.A. Steinhagen Lake (a U.S. Army Corps of Engineers project with 13,700 surface acres). It is located about three miles north of the Upper Neches River Corridor of the Big Thicket National Preserve. The park is in three units, with fishing, camping, screen shelters, restrooms with hot showers, hiking trails, picnicking, swimming, water skiing, and a boat ramp. The park address is Box 1108, Dogwood Station, Woodville, Texas 75979 (713) 384–5231.

Adjacent to and north of the park is the Angelina-Neches Scientific Area Number One (4042 acres), which is managed as a natural area by the Texas Parks and Wildlife Department. There are no trails or facilities and none are planned. Numerous heron rookeries are in the large stands of bald cypress, with Great Blue Heron, Great Egret, and Anhinga. To enter, a boat is needed to cross either the Angelina or Neches River, where it is possible to hike around and explore. Look for Pineywoods birds in the forested sections and waterfowl in winter along the lake.

There is a large rookery located in the middle of B.A. Steinhagen Lake just south of US 190. A scope is helpful if you are looking from the highway. There are usually 10,000–20,000 active nests in the spring. Cattle and Snowy Egrets, Little Blue Heron, Louisiana Heron, White Ibis, Anhinga, and Yellow-crowned Night Heron are the most common species.

W.G. Jones State Forest

The 1700-acre W.G. Jones State Forest is just south of Conroe. Red-cockaded Woodpecker and Brown-headed Nuthatch are permanent residents, along with many other Pineywoods species.

To reach the state forest, drive south from Conroe four miles on IH 45. Turn west on FM 1488, and drive 1.5 miles to the entrance. Conroe is 39 miles north of Houston on IH 45. The state forest is located on both sides of FM 1488 and has camping and picnicking among the pines.

To find the Red-cockaded Woodpecker, look for mature pines with sap oozing around and below the woodpecker holes. These are the nest trees, and the birds are usually nearby. In general, the woodpeckers are easier to find in early morning. If you are unable to find them, the forest personnel often know where they can be located. Bachman's Sparrow has been recorded here in winter, and the nuthatch is common throughout.

Huntsville

Huntsville is located on the western edge of the Pineywoods. It is within easy driving distance of Huntsville State Park, Sam Houston National Forest, Lake Livingston, and Lake Conroe.

Sam Houston Park, just west across Sam Houston Avenue from Sam Houston State University in downtown Huntsville, is an excellent location for land migrants—warblers, vireos, tanagers, flycatchers, thrushes,

Martin Dies, Jr. State Park

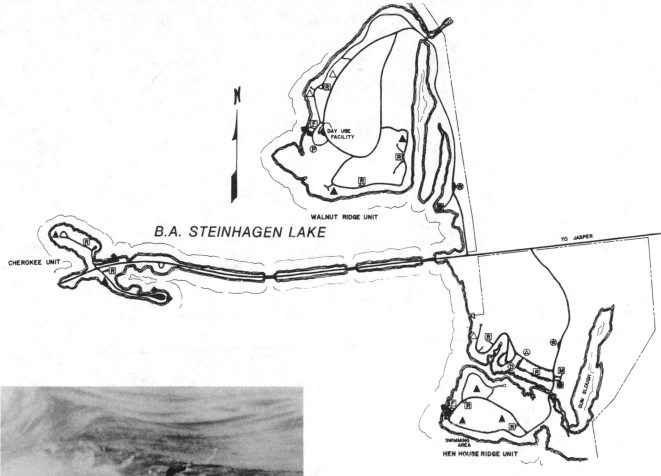

B.A. STEINHAGEN LAKE

WALNUT RIDGE UNIT

DAY USE FACILITY

CHEROKEE UNIT

TO JASPER

GUM SLOUGH

SWIMMING AREA

HEN HOUSE RIDGE UNIT

Louisiana Heron

orioles, grosbeaks, and buntings. The peak of spring migration is from mid-April to mid-May.

There is a check-list of birds for Walker County available from the University Bookstore, Sam Houston State University, Huntsville, Texas 77341, for 15¢ plus addressed, stamped envelope.

Huntsville State Park

Huntsville State Park (2083 acres of pines and hardwoods) is located eight miles southeast of Huntsville on IH 45. It has picnicking, camping, restrooms with hot showers, fishing in Lake Raven, nine miles of hiking and nature trails, and a good representation of typical East Texas birds.

Summer is the most interesting bird season, with the many breeding birds in full song throughout the forest. Common nesting birds include Wood Duck, Red-shouldered Hawk, Barred Owl, Pileated, Red-bellied, and Downy Woodpeckers, Great Crested and Acadian Flycatchers, Eastern Wood Pewee, White-breasted and Brown-headed Nuthatches, Wood Thrush, Blue-gray Gnatcatcher, White-eyed, Yellow-throated, and Red-eyed Vireos, Indigo and Painted Buntings, and Chipping Sparrow. In addition, 12 warbler species have been recorded nesting in the park: Black-and-white, Prothonotary, Swainson's, Northern Parula, Yellow-throated, Pine, Louisiana Waterthrush, Kentucky, Common Yellowthroat, Yellow-breasted Chat, Hooded, and American Redstart. Worm-eating and Prairie Warblers have also spent the summer here at least once.

Huntsville

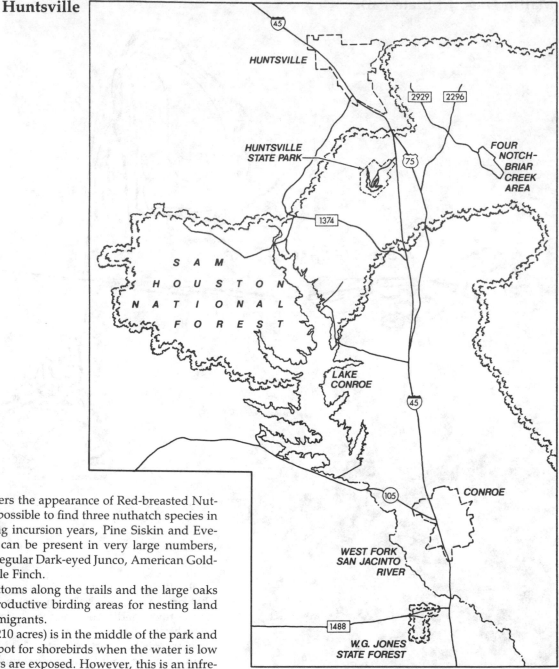

In some winters the appearance of Red-breasted Nuthatch makes it possible to find three nuthatch species in the park. During incursion years, Pine Siskin and Evening Grosbeak can be present in very large numbers, along with the regular Dark-eyed Junco, American Goldfinch, and Purple Finch.

The creek bottoms along the trails and the large oaks are the most productive birding areas for nesting land birds and land migrants.

Lake Raven (210 acres) is in the middle of the park and can be a good spot for shorebirds when the water is low and the mudflats are exposed. However, this is an infrequent occurrence.

A bird check-list is available at park headquarters. The park address is P.O. Box 508, Huntsville, Texas 77340 (713) 295–5644.

Lake Conroe

The dam area of Lake Conroe (20,985 surface acres) offers good birding, especially in fall, winter, and spring. Permission to enter should be obtained from the San Jacinto River Authority personnel at the dam just north of SH 105 (approximately seven miles west of Conroe). Permission is readily granted Monday through Friday, 8 a.m. to 5 p.m.

By driving across the dam during fall, winter, or spring, large rafts of waterfowl can often be found just off the riprap. The grassland below the dam is a good place for Savannah, LeConte's, and Grasshopper Sparrows. In migration check the rows of willows which seem to be good migrant traps.

The upper portion of Lake Conroe in the Sam Houston National Forest has nesting warblers, including Swainson's and American Redstart. The area around Stubblefield Lake Recreation Area can be very rewarding. Look for Broad-winged Hawk and Anhinga in summer, and Bald Eagle in winter. There are numerous Red-cockaded

Woodpecker colonies in the national forest surrounding upper Lake Conroe.

Sam Houston National Forest

The Sam Houston National Forest (158,411 acres) is south and east of Huntsville. Birds are comparable to those found in Huntsville State Park. The national forest contains the 100-mile Lone Star Hiking Trail that extends from about the western edge of the forest northwest of Lake Conroe to the southeastern border just north of Cleveland.

Red-cockaded Woodpecker colonies can be found on FM 2929 about one mile south of US 190 (just east of Huntsville). Early morning is the best time to be sure of success in locating this endangered woodpecker.

To the east of the intersection of FM 2929 and FM 2296 is the Four Notch-Briar Creek Area, which has been proposed as a wilderness area. The Lone Star Trail passes through the proposed section. There is a Red-cockaded Woodpecker colony along Briar Creek about 1.5 miles north of the junction of Forest Road 200 and Forest Road 206. There are also other colonies in the immediate vicinity.

Lake Livingston

Lake Livingston (82,600 surface acres) is a Trinity River Authority impoundment surrounded by pine and hardwood forests approximately 26 miles east of Huntsville on US 190. Nesting species are comparable to those listed for Huntsville and Lake Conroe.

When the water is low and mudflats are exposed, from 10 to 20 migrating shorebird species can be found along the shoreline from mid-July through fall. They are best seen from a boat on the north end of the lake in the SH 19 area near Trinity, the Robb's Lake area just west of Sebastopol, and along FM 356.

In winter check from the two-mile US 190 causeway for Herring, Ring-billed, and Bonaparte's Gulls, Forster's and Caspian Terns, and waterfowl. It is possible to stop and park along the two-mile span. Also, in winter Double-crested Cormorant fly over the causeway—south in the morning to their feeding area, and north in the evening to the roosting area. Flights of more than 10,000 birds are not unusual.

Lake Livingston State Recreation Area (635 acres) is located near the southeast corner of the lake on FM 3216. A bird check-list for the park is being compiled. The park has camping, picnicking, restrooms with hot showers, fishing, swimming, and boat ramps. The park address is Route 9, Box 1300, Livingston, Texas 77351 (713) 365–2201.

McCardell's Lake

One highlight of the Pineywoods region is the exceptionally large nesting colony of wading birds at a natural oxbow swamp just east of US 59 (eight miles south of Livingston, or one mile south of Goodrich). Between 5000 and 10,000 birds nest in this swamp. Most are Cattle Egret, but Little Blue Heron, Black-crowned Night

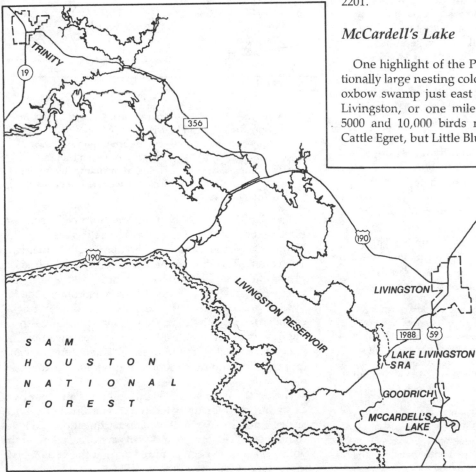

Lake Livingston

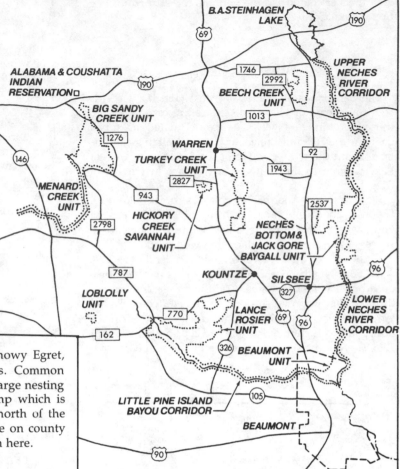

Heron, Great Egret, Great Blue Heron, Snowy Egret, Louisiana Heron, Anhinga and White Ibis. Common and Purple Gallinules nest also. There is a large nesting site at the extreme west end of the swamp which is visible from the highway. The swamp is north of the Trinity River and is called McCardell's Lake on county maps. American alligator are also often seen here.

Big Thicket National Preserve

Big Thicket National Preserve (84,500 acres), the first national preserve in the national park system, is to be managed in such a way that the unique mixture of ecosystems which occur are protected. However, because of the vast energy resources concentrated here, the controlled extraction of minerals and other uses (such as hunting) will be permitted—activities not usually allowed in a national park.

There are as many descriptions of the Big Thicket as there are describers, but the paragraph below from *Biological Survey of the East Texas Big Thicket Area* (1936) by H. B. Parks, V. L. Cory, and others sums it up well:

> The question now comes, is the Big Thicket to pass into legend as have the other areas, or is this area to be protected and made available to those who enjoy the study of animate nature; who enjoy the beauty of the primeval forest with its age old trees, its undergrowth of flowering shrubs, the delicately colored flowers and moss ground cover that bespeaks an age in making; who enjoy to study the wood warblers as high in the forest ceiling they call as they seek their food among the tree tops, or listen to the call of some large birds who far away are employed in nest building; who enjoy to seek out the mammals of such a place and become acquainted with them from the tiny shrew to the huge black bear; who enjoy a long quiet

day in the thick shade along the banks of the creek attempting to lure from its water a selection of choice fish or enjoy in the fall of the year to garner the various kinds of fruits and nuts that grow within the Thicket, and as winter comes, per chance bring from among the numerous inhabitants of the Thicket a whitetail deer, as the prize of a long day's hunt.

The Big Thicket has been divided into eight separate plant associations; six of these are in the Preserve. The Nature Conservancy has land holdings in the other two. The coming together of the hundreds and hundreds of plants and other life forms from north, east, south, and west—"a biological crossroads"—is what makes the Big Thicket unique. The tall pines, about 20 different oaks, orchids, four carnivorous plants, climax forest with no understory vegetation, bald cypress-tupelo swamps, impenetrable tangles, wildflowers in all seasons, streams for canoeing, and much more contribute to the diversity of the area.

The preserve consists of eight land units and four river or stream corridor units located in Hardin, Polk, Tyler, Jasper, and Liberty counties. Land acquisition is not yet complete. Development and plans are proceeding in the units which have been acquired and, at the end of 1980, three units were open to the public.

Turkey Creek Unit. Turkey Creek Unit (7800 acres) has a visitor information station at the south end of FM 420, 2.5 miles east of US 69. There is a nine-mile hiking trail open; 15 miles of trails are planned. This unit contains the greatest concentration of plant diversity in the preserve, with magnificent stands of forest. Although probably not "virgin," the mature stands of bald cypress, sweetgum, and loblolly pine found in the southern portion of this unit between Village Creek and FM 420 are among the highlights of the Big Thicket Nature Preserve.

Beech Creek Unit. Beech Creek Unit (4856 acres) has a short loop trail and a beech-magnolia-loblolly pine plant community. It is in this unit that so much forest was destroyed by pine bark beetles in the summer of 1975. One infestation covered more than 500 acres. Many beautiful magnolia and beech trees were destroyed in the effort to stop the spread of the infestation and in salvage operations to harvest the dead pines. It will be many years before the forest recovers.

Hickory Creek Savannah Unit. Hickory Creek Savannah Unit (660 acres) has longleaf pine savannah forest and acid bog-baygall wetlands. Red-cockaded Woodpecker have been reported in this unit.

I have visited the Big Thicket National Preserve many times to study its great diversity of plants and birds. The Big Thicket grows on a person; the more times I visit, the better I like it.

Nesting birds include Barred Owl, Red-shouldered Hawk, Pileated, Hairy, Downy, Red-bellied, and Red-headed Woodpeckers, White-eyed, Yellow-throated, and Red-eyed Vireos, and 14 species of warblers. Look for Black-and-white, Yellow-throated, Kentucky, and Hooded Warblers throughout. Prothonotary, Swainson's, Northern Parula, and American Redstart are found in the bottomlands, Louisiana Waterthrush along upland sandy bottom streams, Yellow-breasted Chat in beetle spots, Worm-eating in ti-ti thickets or acid bog-baygall wetlands, Common Yellowthroat in pitcher plant bogs, Prairie in longleaf pine-savannah areas, and Pine in upland forests. Brown-headed and White-breasted Nuthatches and Bachman's Sparrow can be common locally. Wintering species include American Woodcock, Purple Finch, American Goldfinch, and woodland sparrows. Look in the uplands portion of the Big Sandy Creek Unit for Red-cockaded Woodpecker.

Units still being acquired and/or developed include:

1. The Lance Rosier Unit (25,024 acres) south and east of Saratoga.

2. The Loblolly Unit (550 acres), a pine-hardwood forest north of Batson.

3. The Beaumont Unit (6218 acres) at the confluence of Pine Island Bayou and the Neches River. This unit is at the northern Beaumont city limits and is the wettest land unit with 80% bald cypress-tupelo swamps. It is subject to periodic flooding, saltwater intrusion, and is accessible by water only.

4. The Neches Bottom and Jack Gore Baygall Unit (13,300 acres). This unit is an ancient flood plain of the Neches River. A primitive campground is planned for the future.

5. The Big Sandy Creek Unit (14,300 acres), mostly upland mixed pine-hardwood forest. Backpack camping, hiking trails, and a horse trail are planned.

Four waterway corridor units are also in the acquisition/development stage:

1. The Little Pine Island Bayou Corridor to connect the Lance Rosier Unit to the Beaumont Unit.

2. The Menard Creek Corridor to connect the Big Sandy Unit to the Trinity River.

3. The Upper Neches River Corridor to connect B.A. Steinhagen Lake below the dam to Neches Bottom and the Jack Gore Baygall Unit.

4. The Lower Neches River Corridor to connect the Neches River and the Jack Gore Baygall Unit to the Beaumont Unit.

A time schedule for the opening of these areas is not available at this writing. The address of the Preserve Superintendent is Big Thicket National Preserve, P.O. Box 7408, Beaumont, Texas 77706.

In addition to the National Preserve, there are several other places in the immediate area well worth a visit. The Alabama-Coushatta Indian Reservation on US 190 between Livingston and Woodville is open March through December. Here are excellent stands of virgin forest. There are tours, displays, demonstrations, and a campground.

The Roy E. Larsen Sandyland Sanctuary (2138 acres), owned and managed by The Nature Conservancy, preserves an excellent example of Arid Sandyland ecosystem—an ecosystem not included in the Big Thicket National Preserve. The sanctuary is between Kountze and Silsbee on SH 327 bordering on and east of Village Creek. Guided hikes are conducted regularly. Contact the manager for the schedule at P.O. Box 909, Silsbee, TX, 77656 (713) 385-4135.

The John K. Kirby State Forest (626 acres) is two miles south of Warren on US 69 and has a picnic area and self-guided nature trail.

In addition, the Texas Parks and Wildlife Department has acquired 942 acres of hardwood forest along Village Creek and the Neches River about five miles south of Silsbee on US 96. This area will be developed into a state recreation park. Camping, picnicking, nature trails, and restrooms with hot showers are planned. The park is scheduled for opening in 1982 or 1983.

Gulf Coast

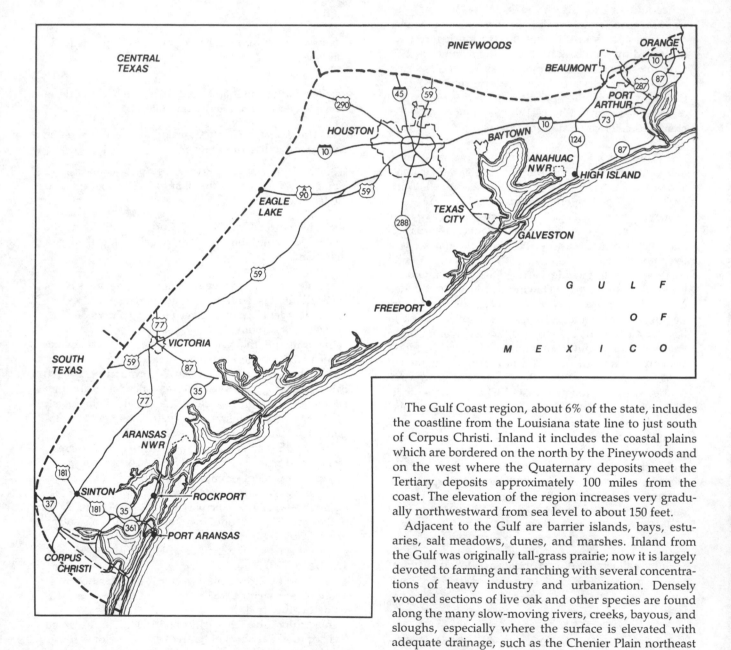

The Gulf Coast region, about 6% of the state, includes the coastline from the Louisiana state line to just south of Corpus Christi. Inland it includes the coastal plains which are bordered on the north by the Pineywoods and on the west where the Quaternary deposits meet the Tertiary deposits approximately 100 miles from the coast. The elevation of the region increases very gradually northwestward from sea level to about 150 feet.

Adjacent to the Gulf are barrier islands, bays, estuaries, salt meadows, dunes, and marshes. Inland from the Gulf was originally tall-grass prairie; now it is largely devoted to farming and ranching with several concentrations of heavy industry and urbanization. Densely wooded sections of live oak and other species are found along the many slow-moving rivers, creeks, bayous, and sloughs, especially where the surface is elevated with adequate drainage, such as the Chenier Plain northeast of Sea Rim State Park, High Island, and Galveston Island.

As might be expected, the region has many nesting birds not found in other sections of the state. Among them are Mottled Duck, Willet, White-faced and White

Ibises, Roseate Spoonbill, Brown and White Pelicans, Reddish Egret, American Oystercatcher, Clapper Rail, Sanderling, Ruddy Turnstone, Wilson's Plover, Laughing Gull, Gull-billed, Forster's, Royal, Sandwich, and Caspian Terns, Black Skimmer, Boat-tailed Grackle, Seaside and Sharp-tailed Sparrows. Inland are Greater Prairie Chicken, White-tailed Hawk, and White-tailed Kite. The latter two are also found in South Texas. Herons, egrets, shorebirds, and waterfowl are very common most of the year. Sandhill Crane, Canada, Snow, and White-fronted Geese winter on the inland prairies in large numbers.

Snow Geese

Sea Rim National Wildlife Refuge

Sea Rim National Wildlife Refuge (8966 acres of marshlands) is approximately 17 miles south of Port Arthur, adjacent to Sabine Pass and south of SH 87. There are no roads for vehicles on the refuge. For a fee, shallow-water boats can be launched into Texas Bayou from a private boat launch located on the east side of the refuge. A cattle path located at the refuge parking lot on SH 87 provides access by foot into the refuge. It is usually very muddy. Hunting is allowed in the morning on certain days of the week during hunting season. The refuge is open 24 hours a day, seven days a week. The birds found here should be the same as those in Sea Rim State Park.

Sea Rim State Park

Sea Rim State Park (15,109 acres of beach and marshlands) is approximately five miles south of Sea Rim National Wildlife Refuge. About 90% of this park is accessible only by boat. The park is divided into two units: the beach south of the highway, and the marshlands north of the highway. The beach unit includes the headquarters, natural history interpretive center, camping on three miles of beach, trailer sites, and 2.2 miles of sea rim marsh, for which the park is named. The sea rim marsh is where marsh grasses extend into the surf, a fertile nursery ground for marine life. In addition, there is the "Gambusia Trail," a boardwalk two feet above the marsh and 3640 feet long, enabling one to observe the marsh life from above. A booklet is available at headquarters that explains the marsh ecology of the trail.

The marshlands unit north of the highway has a boat ramp, boat channels, canoe trails, and an air boat concession where canoes can be rented. In the marsh the Texas Parks and Wildlife Department has built six platforms at intervals for overnight camping, and four observation blinds for photography and observation. A canoe is the best way to see the birds of the marshlands. Most of the year, air boat rides are available for a fee to show the non-canoeist the marshlands; however, the noise of the air boat chases the birds away.

Seaside and Sharp-tailed Sparrows, Red-winged Blackbird, Boat-tailed Grackle, Clapper Rail, Great Blue

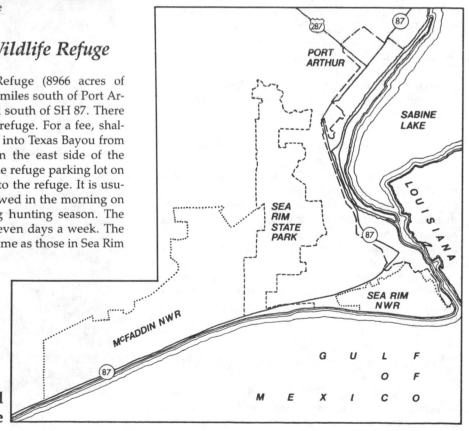

Sea Rim National Wildlife Refuge

Sanderling

Heron, Great, Snowy, and Cattle Egrets, White and White-faced Ibises, Mottled Duck, and Roseate Spoonbill are common year-round. Be on the lookout for Least Bittern in the spring and summer, and American Bittern in the fall, winter, and spring.

All migrants which occur elsewhere on the upper Texas coast should also be here. Thirty-seven warbler species have been recorded in the park.

The upper coast is of great importance to wintering geese and ducks. Numbers of more than 100,000 in winter are not uncommon. Listed in order from abundant to rare are Snow Goose, Green-winged Teal, Lesser Scaup, Mottled Duck, Gadwall, Pintail, American Wigeon, Northern Shoveler, Canvasback, Blue-winged Teal, White-fronted Goose, Ring-necked Duck, Canada Goose, Mallard, Cinnamon Teal, Redhead, Red-breasted Merganser, Black Duck, Wood Duck, Greater Scaup, Common Goldeneye, Bufflehead, Oldsquaw, Surf and Black Scoters, Hooded and Common Mergansers.

Practically all ducks and geese that winter in Texas can be found at Sea Rim State Park, Sea Rim NWR, and McFaddin NWR. The park check-list has 29 waterfowl species.

Other animals seen in the area include river otter, raccoon, nutria, muskrat, striped skunk, oppossum, gray fox, bobcat, and an occasional mink. The red wolf, most of which are now considered hybrids (with coyotes), and river otter have been observed in the marshland unit. Small American alligator are sometimes seen from the boardwalk; the larger ones are in the marshlands unit. Fishing is permitted and certain sections of the park are open to duck hunting in season.

A bird check-list of 289 species recorded in the park is available at park headquarters. The address is Park Superintendent, Sea Rim State Park, P.O. Box 1066, Sabine Pass, Texas 77655 (713) 971-2559.

McFaddin National Wildlife Refuge

McFaddin National Wildlife Refuge (41,682 acres) is adjacent to and southeast of Sea Rim State Park. It includes 12 miles of beach along the Gulf of Mexico for swimming, fishing, camping, picnicking, beachcombing, and birding.

There are eight miles of roads on McFaddin NWR that provide access to the interior and inland lakes and waterways. The inland lakes are usually shallow. The refuge probably has one of the densest populations of American alligator in the state. Birds to be found are the same as in Sea Rim State Park. Visitors must register at the entrance.

Hunting is allowed at certain times during waterfowl season. Check with the refuge manager for further information at P.O. Box 5, Sabine Pass, Texas 77655 (713) 971-2909; or contact the Refuge Manager, Anahuac NWR, P.O. Box 278, Anahuac, Texas 77514 (713) 267-3337 or 267-3131.

Anahuac National Wildlife Refuge

The 11,531-acre Anahuac National Wildlife Refuge is located on the north shore of East Bay, an arm of Galveston Bay 18 miles southeast of Anahuac. This refuge is maintained and managed primarily for migrating and wintering waterfowl, but with extensive coastal marsh and wet prairies, it also provides ideal habitat for many other birds and animals.

The area just east of the refuge, known locally as the Barrow Ranch (12,670 acres), has been acquired as an

Roseate Spoonbill
(courtesy Richard Glasebrook)

addition to Anahuac NWR and will come under the management of the US Fish and Wildlife Service early in 1982.

To reach the refuge from IH 10, drive south on SH 61 from the Anahuac Exit 2.1 miles to FM 562, then continue south on FM 562 8.3 miles to FM 1985. Turn east on FM 1985, and go about four miles to the refuge sign. Turn south and drive three miles to the entrance gate. Or, if approaching from the east, take SH 124 either north from High Island or south from Winnie to FM 1985, then drive west 10 miles to the refuge sign.

Common nesting birds include Black-crowned and Yellow-crowned Night Herons, King and Clapper Rails, Least Bittern, Purple and Common Gallinules, American Coot, Least Tern, Willet, Green Heron, Common Yellowthroat, and Seaside Sparrow. Barn Owl and Long-billed Marsh Wren are less common. Wood Stork are often a summer visitor.

High Island/Galveston

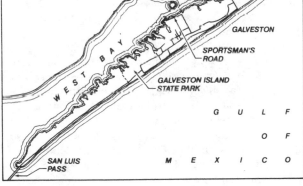

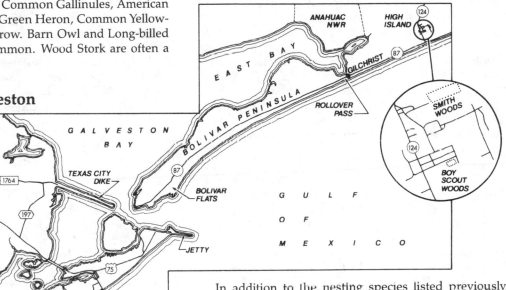

Snow, Canada, and White-fronted Geese roost and loaf on the ponds from late September to March. A few Ross' Goose may be seen also. The geese flights at sunset as the birds are returning from feeding areas can be spectacular in late October and early November. Twenty-two duck species are on the refuge check-list; only five are considered rare. The best time to look for Fulvous Whistling-Ducks on the refuge is in the fall. They are more easily found in rice fields on IH 10 west of Winnie in spring, summer, and fall. Most of the wintering ducks have arrived on the refuge by the middle of November. Short-eared Owl winter in the marsh.

In addition to the nesting species listed previously, year-round visitors include Olivaceous Cormorant, Roseate Spoonbill, White and White-faced Ibises.

In winter watch for Common Loon (on the bay), White Pelican, Double-crested Cormorant, Bald and Golden Eagles, and Sprague's Pipit along the roads.

The place to look for land migrants in spring and fall is among the salt cedars along old fence rows.

The refuge roads are dikes, and using your car as a blind while driving along these roads is an excellent way to view the ponds, particularly Shoveler Pond. After heavy rains, some of the roads of the refuge may be closed to vehicular traffic.

Other animals which reside on the refuge include coyote, coyote/red wolf hybrids, river otter, mink, muskrat, bobcat, swamp rabbit, and American alligator.

A bird check-list of 253 species is available at headquarters. Camping is allowed on the bayshore, mainly to accommodate night fishermen; however, non-fishermen are also welcome. The address is P.O. Box 278, Anahuac, Texas 77514 (713) 267–3337 or 267–3131.

This is THE place in Texas to see rails, and one of the few places where there is a fair chance for Yellow and Black Rails. In some years a farm wagon is pulled through the marsh with a special tractor for the purpose of finding rails. Because of manpower and equipment limitations, the rail marsh buggy is scheduled only for groups of eight or more and only with advance reservations. As of this writing, it runs daily except Sunday, and only in April—the best time for Yellow Rails. The schedule is subject to change without notice.

Within a couple of hours on the refuge I once saw King, Clapper, Virginia, Sora, Yellow, and Black Rails. Seaside Sparrow and Short-billed Marsh Wren are also commonly seen from the farm wagon.

High Island

High Island is 30 miles northeast of Galveston on SH 124, just north of SH 87. It has become the most popular place for bird seekers to visit for spring land bird migration. Mid-April to mid-May is usually the peak time. The town sits atop a salt dome, so it is higher than the surrounding coastal prairie and has thick, live oak groves. The migrants gather in the trees to rest and feed after crossing the Gulf of Mexico. Scarlet Tanager, Indigo Bunting, Rose-breasted Grosbeak, Gray Catbird, orioles, warblers, and vireos can be present in large numbers. Twenty to 30 warbler species in a day is not unusual, including Golden-winged, Blackpoll, and Blue-winged Warblers. The best time is after a shower or the stalling of a cold front—a "fall-out." If possible, plan to spend a whole day to see all the migrants because they can change from hour to hour. Several days is better; several visits for early and late migrants better yet.

There is no way to predict the best day, but whenever I get there on a Saturday, someone always says, "You should have been here on Thursday, it was fantastic."

The first of the two areas is locally called "Boy Scout Woods." Driving north on SH 124, take the first right after the ball park, and drive about two blocks to the wooded area on the right side of the road. The property is being acquired by the Houston Audubon Society for a sanctuary.

A second wooded area, known to birders as "Smith Woods," is much larger and visible from a distance in all directions. Drive north on SH 124 past Roadside Park at the north edge of town. Turn right, go one block, turn right again and go one block, then turn left and drive to the end of the lane, which leads to an old house and barn. This is private property, but birders have always been welcome. Please help to keep us welcome. DO NOT CROSS FENCES OR BLOCK DRIVEWAYS. Here I have seen Black-throated Blue, Cape May and Cerulean Warblers, and Black-billed Cuckoo, all difficult to find elsewhere in Texas. In the marshy area behind the woods Boat-tailed Grackle are sometimes present. This brown-eyed grackle is usually found near the coast from the Galveston area to Louisiana.

Bolivar Peninsula

The town of Gilchrist is eight miles south of High Island, or 20 miles north of the Bolivar ferry. There is a channel between the Gulf and the bay called Rollover Pass. A short stop here to see what is on the bay side will usually turn up Reddish Egret, gulls, terns, and Black Skimmer. A scope is very helpful.

From Gilchrist, follow SH 87 south about 20 miles to Bolivar Flats. Along the way the road parallels the beach, with usually only sand dunes in-between. There are many access roads to the beach, and it is possible to drive along the beach most of the way to see shorebirds and other species in the surf. In winter this sometimes results in all three scoter species (Black, White-winged, and Surf). Red-breasted Merganser, Eared Grebe, and

scaup are more likely. The trick is to find the birds close to the beach.

At the south end of Bolivar Penisula, Loop 108 intersects SH 87, both north and south of the town of Port Bolivar. At the northern intersection, turn east to the beach, then right at the beach to Bolivar Flats. Here shorebirds, gulls, terns, egrets, and herons gather, sometimes in incredible numbers. When the tide is in, it is possible to drive quite close to the birds. When the tide is out, beware of soft sand. Be on the lookout for rarities which have been found here in the past, such as Brant, Great Black-backed, Lesser Black-backed, California, Thayer's, and Glaucous Gulls. Tree Swallow are common migrants near the coast in spring and fall. The marsh areas near Port Bolivar should be checked for Clapper Rail year-round, and migrants can be seen in spring and fall.

Back on SH 87, take the free ferry to Galveston. From the ferry, watch among the abundant Laughing Gull for Bonaparte's Gull in winter. Some winters Black-legged Kittiwake have been recorded.

Galveston

Galveston Island is about 30 miles long from northeast to southwest, and from three-quarters of a mile to three miles wide. Galveston Bay is at the northern end. West Bay (a shallow estuary) is to the west, and San Luis Pass is at the southern tip. In-between are a large city; a state park; countless fresh-water, estuarine, and saltwater ponds and sloughs; coastal wetlands; oak mottes; prairies; the beach; and sand dunes—all creating extensive birding opportunities.

Herons, egrets, Roseate Spoonbill, White and White-faced Ibises, sandpipers and plovers, rails, gulls, terns, and waterfowl are present in all seasons. In summer watch for Magnificent Frigatebird flying up and down the shoreline along both the Gulf and West Bay. Sandhill Crane are present in winter.

The numbers of warblers, tanagers, buntings, grosbeaks, thrushes, orioles, vireos, and other land birds in late April and early May can be unbelievable. These birds, which migrate both up the coast and over the Gulf of Mexico, make landfall along this bend in the Texas coast in great concentrations. The ideal time for migrant "fall-out" comes with the arrival of a cold front, especially when the front stalls and is accompanied by a rain storm.

To see dozens of Indigo Bunting, Northern (Baltimore) Oriole, Scarlet Tanager, and warblers by the hundreds is an unforgettable experience.

Kempner Park is the favorite warbler park in the city of Galveston proper. It is located at Avenue O and 27 to 29 streets. After checking the park, walk in the residential area surrounding the park and check the trees for migrants. The island south of the city on the drive to San Luis Pass can be just as productive if one is there at the proper time.

If you are at the northern end of Galveston Island, a drive to the south jetty of the Galveston Ship Channel is always time well spent. Drive north on Seawall Boulevard to the dead end, then turn right to the jetty. Check the flats for Black Skimmer, Laughing, Ring-billed and Herring Gulls, Sandwich, Gull-billed, Caspian, Royal, Least (summer), Forster's, Common, and Black Terns (migrants). Walk the jetty where an occasional Purple Sandpiper has been found in winter. At the end of the jetty, watch for Common Loon, Blue-faced Booby, jaegers, and Gannet in winter. Peregrine Falcon migrate south in late September and early October.

While in the Galveston area, it is worthwhile to check the Texas City Dike, a jetty that juts five miles into Galveston Bay. To reach Texas City from Galveston, take IH 45 toward Houston. Turn right on Loop 197, then right on FM 1764 to the dike. In winter there are usually Common Loon, Eared and Horned Grebes, and occasional Red-throated Loon and Oldsquaw. Black-legged Kittiwake and Lesser Black-backed Gull have also been recorded (rarely) in winter.

West Galveston Island

West Galveston Island is good for birding year-round. Shorebird migration is from the first week of July to the end of May. Thirty-six species of plovers and sandpipers have been recorded. At least 30 of these are present at the margins of marshes and in the fields.

From 61st Street, a drive down Stewart Road is recommended rather than FM 3005 (Seawall Blvd.). All roads off Stewart Road toward West Bay and between 99th Street and 11-mile Road should be checked if time permits. Check the ponds between Stewart Road and FM 3005 on 7- and 7½-mile Roads. My favorite has always been 8-mile Road to West Bay. When nearly at the end of 8-mile Road, turn left on Sportman's Road. Extensive reeds, marshes, and backwater provide a haven for many waterfowl, including herons, egrets, Reddish Egret (sometimes white phase), Roseate Spoonbill, White and White-faced Ibises, Clapper Rail, American Bittern, gulls, terns, sandpipers, and plovers. Least Bittern are present in the spring. An occasional American Oystercatcher, Magnificent Frigatebird, Red-breasted Merganser, Common Goldeneye, or a completely unexpected bird may be found in West Bay at the end of Sprotman's Road.

Galveston Island State Park

Galveston Island State Park (1921 acres) begins at 13-Mile Road where Stewart Road jogs to join FM 3005. The park consists of coastal wetlands, salt meadow or coastal prairie, and 1.5 miles of beach. The park offers campsites on the beach (with shade), restrooms with hot showers, picnicking, a bathhouse, a trailer camping area, screen shelters (inland), nature trails with bird blinds, an observation platform for viewing the marshes, and fishing areas.

Birds found nesting in the park include Pied-billed Grebe, Black-crowned and Yellow-crowned Night Herons, Seaside Sparrow, Horned Lark, Least Bittern, Clapper Rail, Common Gallinule, Wilson's Plover, Black-necked Stilt, Black Skimmer, Long-billed Marsh Wren, Common Yellowthroat, Orchard Oriole, Willet, and Least Tern. In winter look for Palm Warbler, Le Conte's Sparrow, and Long-billed and Short-billed March Wrens.

A bird check-list of 229 species recorded in the park is available at park headquarters. The park address is Route 1, Box 156-A, Galveston, Texas 77550 (713) 737–1222.

San Luis Pass

San Luis Pass is at the southern tip of Galveston Island. A toll bridge connects Galveston Island with the mainland.

Pelagic birds such as Gannet, Blue-faced Booby, Black, White-winged, and Surf Scoters, and jaegers are possible at San Luis Pass in winter. Migrant and resident shorebirds, egrets, herons, American Avocet, Horned Grebe, gulls, and terns are often found on the flats under and near the bridge.

Freeport

The Freeport Christmas Count consistently leads Texas (and often the nation) in total species found on Christmas Counts. The highest number recorded on the Freeport count was 226 species on December 19, 1971, and it is an off year when less than 200 species are found. The secret to finding this many species in a given area is, as always, a variety of habitats. The Freeport area has the Gulf with the beaches and jetties, thick woods, salt marshes, coastal prairie, farmland, the Brazos River bottom, fresh-water ponds, urban areas, and estuarine bays.

The jetties at Surfside (north) and Quintana (south) along the ship channel near Freeport are good for getting out into the Gulf. Some years Purple Sandpiper winter on these jetties. The beach approaches to the jetties have gulls, terns, and shorebirds. Check the nearby marshes and ponds in spring and fall for Long-billed Curlew and Whimbrel.

The woods should be explored near the Lake Jackson-Clute area on SH 332 for Red-shouldered Hawk, Pileated Woodpecker, and other land birds. Many warblers winter or linger into December. For example, the following are the warblers recorded on the last five Freeport Christmas Counts: Black-and-white, Tennessee, Orange-crowned, Nashville, Yellow, Yellow-rumped, Black-throated Green, Blackburnian, Yellow-throated, Bay-breasted, Blackpoll, Pine, Prairie, Palm, Ovenbird, Northern Waterthrush, Common Yellowthroat, Yellow-breasted Chat, Wilson's, and American Redstart.

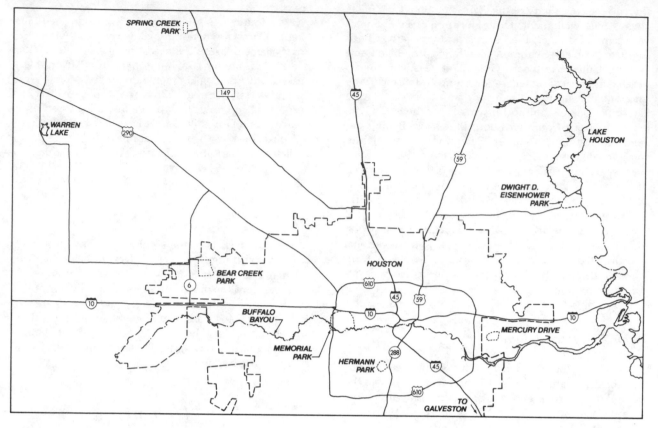

Brazoria and San Bernard National Wildlife Refuges

The Brazoria and San Bernard National Wildlife Refuges are near Freeport. The refuges are not as accessible as Anahuac NWR but have mostly the same birds, including rails. Visitors should check with the Refuge Manager, P.O. Drawer 1088, Angleton, Texas 77515 (713) 849–6062 (same address for both refuges) for the condition of roads, when refuges are open, and what birds are around.

Bird check-lists for both Brazoria and San Bernard National Wildlife Refuges are available at headquarters or at the previous address.

Houston

Houston, the largest city in Texas, is located on the Gulf Coastal Plains approximately 50 miles from the Gulf of Mexico at the southern edge of the Pineywoods. The population of Harris County (Houston is the county seat) has grown from 1,740,000 in 1970 to 2,409,000 in 1980, and the growth continues unabated. In addition to the Port of Houston (the third largest in the nation) and the headquarters for the National Aeronautics and Space

Administration, Houston is a financial, medical, educational, oil and chemical, manufacturing, and transportation center.

The City Parks and Recreation Department oversees some 255 parks totaling nearly 7000 acres. Most are highly developed, but some have extensive natural areas.

Memorial Park

Memorial Park, about 3.5 miles west of downtown on Memorial Drive, has 1468 acres with a golf course, bridle path, arboretum, swimming, picnicking, and playgrounds. A large portion of the park is in a natural condition, especially the area south of Memorial Drive to Buffalo Bayou, the southern boundary. Birding is best in the picnic area, the arboretum, and along the bayou.

Nesting birds include Pine, Swainson's, and Hooded Warblers, Inca Dove, Common Crow, Northern Parula, Barred and Screech Owls, Wood Thrush, Great Crested Flycatcher, American Robin, Acadian Flycatcher, White-eyed Vireo, Yellow-crowned Night Heron, Common and Great-tailed Grackles, Red-bellied, Red-headed, Downy, and Pileated Woodpeckers. Some years Red-eyed Vireo, Common Flicker, and Ruby-throated Hummingbird are summer residents.

In winter look for White-throated Sparrow, Hermit Thrush, Brown Thrasher, Rufous-sided Towhee, Ruby-crowned Kinglet, Solitary Vireo, Brown Creeper, Sharp-shinned Hawk, Yellow-bellied Sapsucker, House and Winter Wrens, Yellow-rumped and Orange-crowned Warblers, Purple Finch, American Goldfinch, and American Woodcock. Some winters there are Pine Siskin and Golden-crowned Kinglet.

Practically all land migrants expected in the area, warblers, vireos, tanagers, grosbeaks, etc., can be found in the picnic area during spring migration, especially April and May. The best birding is during migration "fall-outs" when the birds come down to rest and feed in spring and fall.

Dwight D. Eisenhower Park

Dwight D. Eisenhower Park is at the south end of Lake Houston and has 632 land acres plus the surface of Lake Houston. It is operated by the City of Houston Parks and Recreation Department.

To reach the park, drive north on US 59 about nine miles beyond IH 10, then go east on Mt. Houston Road to Lake Houston Parkway. It is about 12 miles to the park from Lake Houston Parkway. Camping, picnicking, restrooms, and fishing are offered. More than one-half of the park is undeveloped.

Nesting birds include Barred Owl, Blue-gray Gnatcatcher, Hooded and Swainson's Warblers, Orchard Oriole, Red-shouldered Hawk, and Pileated Woodpecker, as well as most of the birds found in Memorial Park. Belted Kingfisher can be found all year.

Hermann Park

Hermann Park is highly developed. The 398-acre park is about four miles south of downtown Houston on Main and/or Fannin Streets. There is a golf course, picnicking and, of particular interest, the Museum of Natural Sci-

Great-tailed Grackle

ence with the Burke Baker Planatarium, and the zoo. The zoo has a representative collection of cracids (curassows, guans, and chachalacas), a large waterfowl pond, flamingos, and the Tropical Bird House. In the Tropical Bird House the visitor enters the flight area of more than 100 tropical bird species. It is well worth a visit.

Mercury Drive

For shorebirds, waterfowl, and long-legged waders, drive east from the intersection of IH 45 and IH 10 about six miles to Mercury Drive exit. Proceed south on Mercury Drive 1.3 miles to a large water impoundment east of the road. Park and look from the road. A scope is highly recommended.

Nesting birds include Black-necked Stilt, Common Gallinule, Mottled Duck, Pied-billed Grebe, Least Tern, Dickcissel, and Red-winged Blackbird.

Ducks are abundant in fall, winter, and spring. Common birds are Northern Shoveler, Lesser Scaup, Green-winged and Blue-winged Teals, Gadwall, Hooded Merganser, and Ruddy Duck. Canvasback and Pintail are less common. Practically all waterfowl on the local check-list will appear here at one time or another. Other common wintering birds are Ring-billed Gull and Water Pipit.

If the water level is low, shorebirds are very common in spring and fall. More than 700 Wilson's Phalarope have been seen in one day. Other regulars are American Avocet, Stilt, Western, Least, Spotted, and White-rumped Sandpipers, Lesser and Greater Yellowlegs, Black-bellied Plover, and Hudsonian Godwit. Barn and Bank Swallows are regular migrants.

This is an excellent location for herons, egrets, gulls, and terns. Reddish Egret has also been seen, but rarely. Late summer is often a good time. Roseate Spoonbill, Black Skimmer, White and White-faced Ibises have all been recorded.

Bear Creek Park

Bear Creek Park, administered by Harris County, is on SH 6 about 2.5 miles north of IH 10. SH 6 intersects IH 10 about 17 miles west of downtown Houston. The park's 2168 acres are about three quarters undeveloped. There are three golf courses, camping, restrooms, picnicking, playgrounds, and a wildlife area.

Nesting birds are comparable to those found in Memorial Park; however, there are more grasslands, making this a favorable area for wintering sparrows. Red-shouldered Hawk are common. Both Golden-crowned Kinglet and Rusty Blackbird are often found in winter.

Spring Creek Park

Spring Creek Park is located northwest of Tomball at the northern edge of Harris County. This county-run park of 114 acres is reached by driving north on IH 45 about 5.1 miles from its intersection with IH 10 to FM

149 (West Mt. Houston Road and West Montgomery Road). Turn northwest on FM 149, and go about 22 miles to the town of Tomball. About one mile north of the intersection with FM 2920, turn left (west) on Brown Road, and follow the signs to the park entrance.

Nesting birds in the woods along Spring Creek include Northern Parula, Hooded, Kentucky, and Swainson's Warblers, White-eyed and Red-eyed Vireos, Eastern Wood Pewee, Pileated, Red-bellied, Red-headed, and Downy Woodpeckers, Wood Thrush, Great Crested Flycatcher, Summer Tanager, American Robin, and Inca Dove. Lark Sparrow nest in the open area at the south end. Other summer residents are Belted Kingfisher and Ruby-throated Hummingbird.

Wintering birds include Dark-eyed Junco, sparrows, Rufous-sided Towhee, Ruby-crowned Kinglet, Yellow-bellied Sapsucker, Brown Creeper, American Woodcock, and Red-tailed Hawk.

A playground, restrooms, and picnicking are offered.

White-tailed Kite

Western Harris County

The Hockley area is located on US 290 approximately 30 miles northwest of Loop 610. It is a favored wintering area for Bald Eagle, Canada, Snow, and White-fronted Geese, Sandhill Crane, ducks, etc. Ross' Goose is also found, but they usually are hard to separate from the abundant Snows.

Warren Lake is reached by driving south from Hockley on Warren Ranch Road (the road with the large "UNITED SALT CORPORATION" sign on US 290). This large private lake is located about four miles down the road on the east side. Waterfowl and Bald Eagle are often present on the lake in winter. Park and bird from the road. A scope is very helpful. The same road north of Hockley will lead to the same birds. In addition, look for wintering sparrows along the county roads, especially in brushy areas. The most numerous are Savannah, Ves-

per, White-crowned, Lincoln's, and Swamp. White-throated, Song, Fox, LeConte's, and Harris' are usually present in smaller numbers. Watch overhead for Red-tailed, Red-shouldered, and Ferruginous Hawks in winter. Short-eared Owl can be found hunting over the fields at dawn and dusk. Shorebirds, including Hudsonian Godwit, are regular in early May in the fields in any direction from the intersection of FM 529 (Clay Road) and Katy-Hockley Cutoff. Dickcissel are abundant at the same time. Permanent residents include Barn and Great Horned Owls, Ground Dove, Eastern Bluebird (more in winter) and King Rail. In late spring and summer look for Fulvous Whistling-Duck and White-tailed Kite in the rice fields. Black-bellied Whistling-Duck are occasionally recorded also.

Brazos Bend State Park

Brazos Bend State Park is 4897 acres on the Brazos River approximately 35 miles south of Houston.

To reach the park, drive southwest on US 59 to the City of Richmond, then go east on FM 762 about 19 miles to the park entrance. The site is being developed, and the scheduled opening is in the spring of 1982.

There are several habitats represented—wooded river bottom, grasslands, creeks, marsh, and lakes.

Facilities are planned for camping, picnicking, restrooms with hot showers, and fishing. White-tailed deer and American alligator are abundant. The development plan calls for most of the site to be left in a natural state.

Nesting birds include Northern Parula, Acadian Flycatcher, Prothonotary Warbler (in willows around the lake), Hooded Warbler, Anhinga, Eastern Kingbird, Red-shouldered Hawk, Barred and Screech Owls, Mottled, Wood, and Black-bellied Whistling-Ducks, Pileated Woodpecker, Yellow-throated Vireo, and Indigo Bunting. American Redstart have also been found in summer and may nest.

Wintering birds include 24 species of waterfowl, Vermilion Flycatcher, American Woodcock, LeConte's, Swamp, Vesper, Fox, Song, Chipping, Field, and White-throated Sparrows, and Rufous-sided Towhee.

Other birds which have been recorded at the park site include Wood Stork, Greater Scaup, Swallow-tailed Kite, Golden and Bald Eagles, Black-billed Cuckoo, Black and Say's Phoebes, Pyrrhuloxia, Rusty Blackbird, and Sharp-tailed Sparrow.

The site will likely become a very popular bird-finding location in all seasons. The park address is Route 1, Needville, Texas 77462 (713) 742–3477.

A *Birder's Checklist of the Upper Texas Coast*, 6th Edition, January, 1980 is available from the Houston Outdoor Club, c/o Mrs. J.M Gillette, 5027 Longmont, Houston, TX 77056, for 10¢ plus stamped, addressed envelope.

Attwater Prairie Chicken National Wildlife Refuge

The Attwater Prairie Chicken National Wildlife Refuge (8000 acres) is located approximately 75 miles from the Gulf of Mexico on the tall-grass coastal plains near the town of Eagle Lake. The refuge is managed to preserve and restore habitat for Attwater's Prairie Chicken, a subspecies of the Greater Prairie Chicken. This subspecies has decreased from more than one million birds to about 1500 as the coastal prairies have been converted from native grasses to cropland and industrial and urban use. In addition, prime prairie chicken habitat has been replaced with the spread of introduced rose hedges and other shrubs. Formerly found on the coastal plains from Corpus Christi into Louisiana, the range of the prairie chicken has been reduced now to only eight Texas counties.

To reach the refuge, drive northeast six miles on FM 3013 from Eagle Lake, or go south from Sealy on SH 36 two miles to FM 3013. Go southwest 10 miles on FM 3013 to the refuge entrance. Sealy is approximately 48 miles west of Houston on IH 10.

The best time to observe the Greater Prairie Chicken is when they are on their "booming grounds," or "leks," from February 15 to April 1. During this period, access is closely regulated so as not to disturb the "booming"; therefore, reservations are necessary and can be made by contacting the refuge manager in advance. The "booming" is part of the mating ritual of the chickens and the reason for the limited visitation. The rest of the year the refuge is open to the public from 8 a.m. to dusk daily.

The San Bernard River is the eastern boundary of the refuge, and there are extensive woodlands near the river. However, most of the refuge is flat grass-lands, some still in pristine condition. The area is managed to provide a diversity of habitat. This diversity will provide the ecological requirement for breeding, nesting, brood-ing, and winter cover—not only for the chickens, but all wildlife of the coastal prairies.

Other common nesting birds include Mottled Duck, Common Nighthawk, Loggerhead Shrike, and Dickcissel. Less common but regular are Fulvous Whistling-Duck, White-tailed Hawk, King Rail, Common Gallinule, American Coot, Black-necked Stilt, Barn, Great Horned, and Barred Owls.

Many birds spend the winter on the refuge. Cattle Egret, Mallard, Gadwall, Pintail, Green-winged Teal, Sandhill Crane, Common Flicker, Short-billed Marsh Wren (in the grasslands), Brewer's Blackbird, LeConte's, Vesper, and White-throated Sparrows are common. Caracara are permanent residents.

There are 22 warbler species recorded on the refuge as migrants (mostly in spring) as well as 28 shorebird species. American Golden Plover, Upland and Buff-breasted Sandpipers, and Hudsonian Godwit are common spring migrants. Eleven duck species winter on the refuge.

Eagle Lake is known as "The Goose Hunting Capital of the World." Canada, White-fronted, and Snow Geese are very abundant in the area from October to March, with a few Ross' Goose usually present with the Snows. The geese can be seen on the refuge but are usually more common on the county roads around Eagle Lake. Fulvous Whistling-Duck nest in the rice fields of the area and are most easily found from April to September.

A check-list, *Birds of Attwater Prairie Chicken National Wildlife Refuge*, is available at the headquarters. The address of the refuge manager is P.O. Box 518, Eagle Lake, Texas 77434 (713) 234–3021. There is no camping or picnicking allowed on the refuge.

Eagle Lake

Eagle Lake (1200 surface acres) is owned and operated by the Lakeside Irrigation Company to supply irrigation water to area rice farmers. The lake is about two miles south of the City of Eagle Lake on FM 102. Wintering and migrating birds include White Pelican, numerous waterfowl, egrets, herons, hawks (including Bald and Golden Eagles), roosting geese in uncountable numbers, rails, as well as many land birds. Black-bellied Whistling-Duck are summer visitors, and Roseate Spoonbill are frequently recorded.

My first organized field trip with the Travis Audubon Society was to Eagle Lake, and it remains one of my most memorable birding experiences. A Least Grebe, Fulvous Whistling-Ducks, and 18 other "life" birds were recorded on that first bird adventure with other bird seekers.

Permission to enter must be obtained from the Lakeside Irrigation Company, P.O. Pox 337, Eagle Lake, TX 77434 (713) 234–5551.

Aransas National Wildlife Refuge

The Aransas National Wildlife Refuge is approximately 70 miles north of Corpus Christi or seven miles

American Coot

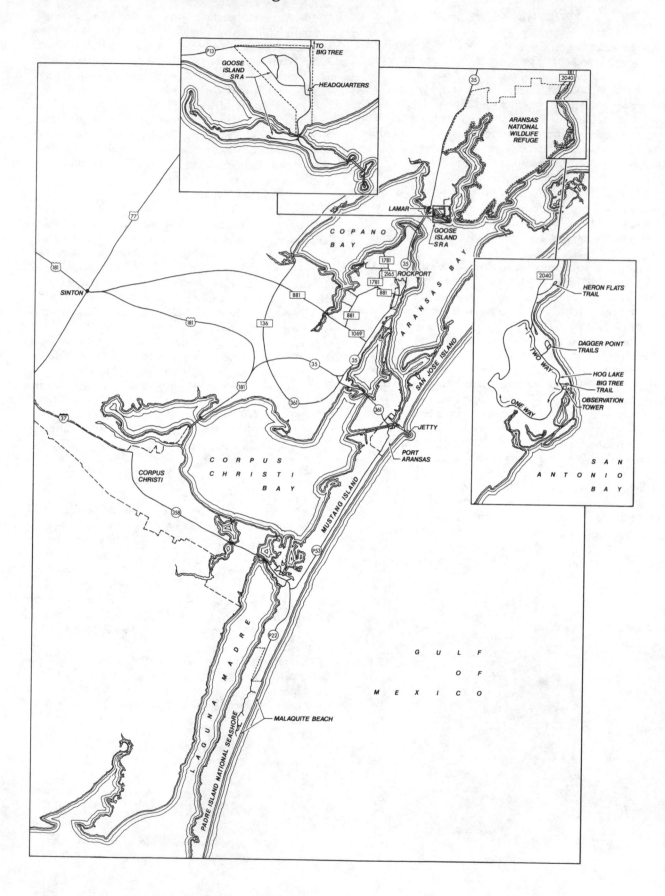

southeast of Austwell. It is another "must" birding location in Texas. The refuge is the wintering ground for the relict wild flock of Whooping Cranes, now about 80 birds from a low of 15 in 1941.

To reach the refuge, drive north from Rockport on SH 35 to FM 774. Turn right (east) and follow signs to the entrance. Lodging is available in Rockport, Refugio, or Port Lavaca, all about 35 miles distant. Camping is available at Goose Island State Park, 30 miles south of the refuge.

In the new Visitor Center there are excellent exhibits, slide shows, and literature that describe the history of the area and the wildlife found on the refuge. Particular emphasis is placed on the efforts to save the Whooping Crane from extinction.

Whooping Crane

The refuge (54,829 acres) is on the Blackjack Peninsula (once a barrier island) with many different habitats: wooded sand dunes, brushlands, oak mottes, grass meadows, cordgrass prairies, tidal marshes, fresh-water ponds, and marine bays.

Whooping Cranes usually begin arriving about the middle of October and stay until the first part of April. The wild flock of Whooping Cranes nest in Wood Buffalo Park, Northwest Territories, Canada, some 2500 miles northwest of Aransas NWR. They make this migration twice each year. In March the cranes begin their courtship dance. Count yourself very lucky if you are fortunate enough to be a witness to this unique display.

An observation tower at the refuge gives an excellent overview of a tidal marsh. Sometimes cranes can be seen from the tower, but usually at a great distance.

To get a better look at the cranes, take a four-hour ride on the *Whooping Crane* from the Sea Gun Resort Hotel at Lamar (just north of Copano Bay causeway on SH 35). The boat makes three or four trips weekly (including Saturday and Sunday) up the intercoastal waterway and through the eastern section of the refuge when the cranes are present. Many other birds can be seen from the boat: American Oystercatcher, White-tailed Hawk, Common Loon, White Pelican, waterfowl, wading birds in large numbers, and more.

Only a small section of the refuge is open to the public, but it is easy to spend a whole day. There is a 16-mile auto road, a loop along which it is not unusual to see 50 or more bird species, especially during migration or during the winter. The observation tower, several trails, a section of the bay, and a picnic area are along the road. Turkey and Roadrunner are common along the drive, but some of the trails need to be walked to find the land birds. Waterfowl and shorebirds can be seen in the bay from the road. Tree, Bank, Rough-winged, Barn, and Cliff Swallows are common migrants.

Nesting birds of the refuge include Pauraque, White-tailed Hawk, Caracara, Purple and Common Gallinules, Wilson's Plover, Greater Prairie Chicken, Groove-billed Ani, and Seaside and Cassin's Sparrows.

In addition to birds, watch for American alligator, white-tailed deer, javelina, armadillo and with luck, a coyote. The interior of the refuge has a population of wild pigs, a cross between local wild domestic hogs and the introduced European boar.

A bird check-list is available at the Visitor Center that lists 35 warblers in migration and 21 sparrows in winter, a total of 328 species with an additional 33 accidentals.

The refuge address is P.O. Box 100, Austwell, TX 77950 (512) 286-3559. No camping is allowed, except to organized youth groups.

Goose Island State Recreation Area

Goose Island State Recreation Area is approximately 12 miles northeast of Rockport at the southern tip of Lamar Peninsula. From Rockport, drive north on SH 35 to the north end of the Copano Bay causeway. Turn east on PR 13, and follow signs to the entrance.

The park has 307 acres of shell beach (Goose Island), marshes, meadows, and live oak groves. There are two campgrounds, one on the beach and one in the oaks, with picnicking, restrooms with hot showers, saltwater fishing, a boat ramp, and swimming.

The National Co-champion live oak is in the northern section of the park. "Big Tree" is estimated to be more than 1000 years old.

The birding at this small park can be outstanding. Year-round resident birds include Reddish Egret, Black-crowned Night Heron, Roseate Spoonbill, Clapper Rail, American Oystercatcher, Forster's, Royal, and Caspian Terns, Black Skimmer, and Seaside Sparrow.

Summer residents are Least Bittern, Black-bellied Whistling-Duck, Gull-billed, Least, and Sandwich Terns. Olivaceous Cormorant, Magnificent Frigatebird, and White-tailed Hawk are occasionally seen flying over.

In migration look for Sora, Virginia, and King Rails in the marshes; warblers in the oaks (33 have been recorded); and shorebirds at the water's edge.

Some of the birds which winter in the area are Common Loon, White Pelican, Common Goldeneye, Red-breasted Merganser—all in the bay along with about 10 other duck species. Lamar Peninsula is just across the bay from Blackjack Peninsula, the wintering home of the Whooping Crane, which can be seen occasionally from Goose Island. Sandhill Crane also winter in the area as well as 15 shorebird species.

A bird check-list is available at park headquarters that lists 278 species. The address of the Park Superintendent is Route 1, Rockport, TX 78382 (512) 729–2858.

Rockport

Rockport has been a "must" birding location in Texas since it was made famous by the late Connie Hagar. It is located on Live Oak Peninsula, 32 miles northeast of Corpus Christi on SH 35. Mrs. Hagar made twice-daily bird excursions on the peninsula for many years and kept detailed records of her findings. Her check-list for the Central Coast, now out of print, lists 413 species (using current nomenclature) plus another 50 subspecies. In her memory a portion of Little Bay in the north section of Rockport has been set aside as the "Connie Hagar Wildlife Sanctuary."

Live Oak Peninsula, roughly four miles by eight miles, offers a wide variety of bird habitats: live oak mottes with very large trees, grasslands, and fresh-water ponds with marshes. Aransas Bay is on the east, and Copano Bay is on the west.

A drive which includes at least Fulton Beach Road and FM 1781, in all seasons, has always been a very rewarding experience for me.

As is true in this section of the state, large concentrations of land birds in migration are common. Mid-April to mid-May is the peak time. In Little Bay herons and egrets are common all year. In migration and winter there are usually Long-billed Curlew, Marbled Godwit, Snowy and Piping Plovers, Whimbrel (rare), Redhead, Canvasback, Red-breasted Merganser, and other waterfowl. Roseate Spoonbill and shorebirds can often be found at Rattlesnake Point on Copano Bay (on the west side of Live Oak Peninsula).

Between Gregory and Bayside, FM 136 crosses the western edge of Copano Bay where there are extensive mud flats with many shorebird species. Wood Stork can be seen here in late summer, and numerous waterfowl in fall, winter, and spring. In the cultivated fields along FM 136 between Gregory and Bayside and along FM 881 between Rockport and Sinton look for wintering Sandhill Crane, Snow, White-fronted, and Canada Geese. The inland ponds of the peninsula should be checked for Olivaceous Cormorant, which are permanent residents.

Mustang Island

Port Aransas

The town of Port Aransas is at the north end of Mustang Island where ocean-going vessels enter Corpus Christi Bay on their way to the Port of Corpus Christi. Brown Pelican can often be seen flying back and forth along the ship channel, especially on the north side near the town of Ingleside. Sometimes they can also be seen from the ferry which crosses the channel. They nest on islands in the channel.

The jetties into the Gulf at the mouth of the ship channel attract many fishermen, but they also provide an opportunity for the bird seeker to get a few hundred yards into the Gulf to see which pelagic or other birds are flying by. From this jetty, I have seen Magnificent Frigatebird, Blue-faced Booby, Peregrine Falcon, and Bonaparte's Gull in addition to abundant terns, gulls, and shorebirds. Other reported rarities from the jetty include Sooty Tern, Brown Booby, and Long-tailed, Parasitic, and Pomarine Jaegers. Birding is excellent for shorebirds, gulls, and terns along the beach south of the jetty and on the drive between Port Aransas and the jetty.

It is possible to reach San Jose Island and the north jetty by boat for a fee. San Jose Island has much less human visitation than Mustang Island. The boat leaves and returns from Fishermen's Wharf at least hourly from 6:30 a.m. to 8 p.m. daily. For exact information, call (512) 749–5760.

Port Aransas Park offers campsites with tables and electricity, restrooms with showers, and primitive camping on the beach. It is operated by Nueces County and is just south of the jetty on the beach.

Probably the least-known bird habitat in Texas is the Gulf of Mexico. From Fishermen's Wharf, the *Scat Cat*, a fast fishing boat, makes regular trips some 50 miles into the Gulf for deep-sea fishing. Food and drinks are available aboard. Non-fishing bird seekers have been welcome at a reduced fee. Contact Box 387, Port Aransas, TX (512) 749–5448 for reservations. The trip usually lasts from 6:30 a.m. to 6:00 p.m.

From the *Scat Cat*, I have seen Cory's Shearwater, Blue-faced Booby, Pomarine and Long-tailed Jaegers, and Magnificent Frigatebird. Birds found by others include Audubon's and Greater Shearwaters, Wilson's Storm-petrel, Parasitic Jaeger, Gannet, and Brown Booby. But on some trips no pelagic birds are seen. On such occasions seeing flying fish, Bottlenose and Dorado Dolphins, and the creatures the fishermen pull out of the water make the trip worthwhile.

Mustang Island State Park

Mustang Island State Park (3704 acres) is 14 miles south of Port Aransas on PR 53. It has picnicking, swimming, camping, restrooms with hot showers, and beachcombing. The park has extensive sand dunes, mud flats, and five miles of frontage on both the Gulf of Mexico and Corpus Christi Bay. Birding should be the same as Padre Island National Seashore 13 miles south.

The park address is Box 326, Port Aransas, TX 78373 (512) 749–5247.

Padre Island National Seashore

Padre Island National Seashore (133,918 acres) is east of Corpus Christi between the Gulf of Mexico and Laguna Madre. The seashore preserves approximately 80% of Padre Island.

To reach the seashore, drive east from Corpus Christi on SH 358 (Padre Island Drive) to Park Road 22. Cross the Kennedy Causeway, and continue south on Park Road 22 for about 13 miles to the seashore entrance.

At Malaquite Beach, there is a visitor's center, swimming in the surf, free showers, restrooms, locker rooms, and paved campground for trailer and recreational vehicles. However, there are no hookups. Primitive camping is permitted on the beach.

Padre Island and Mustang Island (adjacent to and just north of Padre Island) are the longest of the Texas barrier islands. They act as a buffer against wind and wave action between the Gulf of Mexico and the mainland. Laguna Madre and Corpus Christi Bay are very shallow estuaries between the mainland and the islands. The bays are a nursery for many fish and other life forms. The gulf beach, sand dunes, and fresh-water ponds of the islands, estuaries, and islands in the estuaries (both natural and man-made) each create a separate feeding, resting, and nesting habitat for the great variety of birds and other wildlife found in the area.

Nesting birds on or near the National Seashore include Least, Royal, Sandwich, Gull-billed, Forster's, and Caspian Terns, a small flock of White Pelican, Reddish, Great, Snowy, and Cattle Egrets, Snowy and Wilson's Plovers, Roseate Spoonbill, American Oystercatcher, Willet, Mottled Duck, Clapper Rail, and White-tailed Hawk.

Land bird migration can be spectacular. There are 38 species of warblers on the check-list. Twenty-eight were recorded in two days in April, 1980, at Packery Channel County Park, eight miles north of the Seashore. Late September and early October is the best time for migrating Peregrine Falcon.

Shorebirds, gulls, and terns are abundant along the beach; waterfowl are plentiful on the inland ponds in fall, winter, and spring.

Some of the rarities which have been reported are Audubon's and Sooty Shearwaters, Brown and Blue-faced Boobies, Gannet, Harcourt's and Leach's Storm-Petrels, White-tailed Tropicbird, Masked Duck, Long-tailed Jaeger, Glaucous, Great Black-backed, and Sabine's Gulls, Sooty and Roseate Terns. For the past three or four years, an American Flamingo has been a summer visitor on an island in Laguna Madre near the northern boundary of the National Seashore.

While the seashore is more than 80 miles long from north to south, only the northern 14 miles can be driven with a passenger car. Farther south, a four-wheel drive vehicle is needed.

A bird check-list with 345 species is available at the Visitor's Center with other literature about the area. The seashore address is 9405 South Padre Island Drive, Corpus Christi, TX 78418 (512) 937–2621.

Corpus Christi

Oso Bay, or Cayo del Oso, is a very large inlet just south of Corpus Christi Bay between the City of Corpus Christi and the Corpus Christi Naval Air Station. With the extensive mud flats, some of the largest and most diverse concentrations of shorebirds in the state can be found here. Two of the best locations to see these concentrations are from the north end of Ennis Joslin Road near its junction with Ocean Drive, or from Ocean Drive at the western approach to the campus of Corpus Christi State University. Ennis Joslin Road follows the western shoreline of Oso Bay between Ocean Drive and Padre Island Drive (SH 358). Along with the many shorebirds, waterfowl and wading birds are also abundant in fall, winter, and spring. This is the only place in Texas where I have seen a Ruff and a Jabiru. California Gull has been recorded here.

A check-list of the Birds of Nueces County, Texas, is available from the Audubon Outdoor Club of Corpus Christi, Box 3352, Corpus Christi, TX 78401, for 25¢ plus stamped, addressed envelope.

In addition, there is a *Check-list of Birds of the Central Coast of Texas*, 1976, available from Corpus Christi Museum, 1919 W. Water St., Corpus Christi, TX 78401, for 25¢ plus stamped, addressed envelope.

Welder Wildlife Foundation

The Rob and Bessie Welder Wildlife Foundation is approximately eight miles north of Sinton, or 35 miles north of Corpus Christi on US 77. With approximately 7800 acres, the refuge preserves portions of both the Coastal Plains and South Texas.

The foundation is unique in many respects. It was established to be managed as a place where "wildlife could live, forage and propagate. . . ." and "to provide the means and opportunity for research and education in wildlife, in conservation and in related fields." It is probably the largest privately owned nature preserve of its type in existence. There is an extensive natural history library, 2500 bird study skins, 4000 bird egg sets, a laboratory, living quarters for graduate students, and classes for area students and teachers.

Habitats represented are extensive woodlands along the 12 miles of the Aransas River, live oak-savannah and brushlands (chaparral) in the uplands, along with ponds, lakes, and marshes. The refuge has never been cultivated, but cattle graze under a carefully managed program.

More than 1300 plants, 55 mammals, 55 reptiles and amphibians, and 372 birds (96 of which nest or have nested) have been recorded on the refuge.

Common typical South Texas nesting birds include Turkey, Ground and Inca Doves, Roadrunner, Pauraque, Golden-fronted and Ladder-backed Woodpeckers, Ash-throated Flycatcher, Bewick's Wren, Long-billed Thrasher, and Cassin's Sparrow.

Less common nesters are White-tailed Hawk, Caracara, Wied's Crested Flycatcher, Cactus Wren, Curve-billed Thrasher, Bell's Vireo, Pyrrhuloxia, Verdin, and Olive Sparrow. The latter two species seem to be decreasing, perhaps because of weather variations.

Birds which nest near the ponds and lakes include Black-crowned Night Heron, Least Bittern, Black-bellied Whistling-Duck, Purple and Common Gallinules. Least Grebe, Anhinga, White-faced Ibis, Roseate Spoonbill, Fulvous Whistling-Duck, and Black-necked Stilt also nest, but in fewer numbers.

Migration can be outstanding. Twenty-three hawks, 39 warblers, and 38 shorebirds are on the refuge check-list.

The refuge is open to the public at 3 p.m. each Thursday (holidays excluded) with tours and lectures to acquaint the visitor with the workings of the foundation. Visits for organized groups at other times can be made by contacting the office in advance of time of visit.

A bird check-list and other literature about the natural history of South Texas and the Coastal Bend area are available at headquarters. The address is P.O. Drawer 1400, Sinton, TX 78387 (512) 364–2643.

South Texas

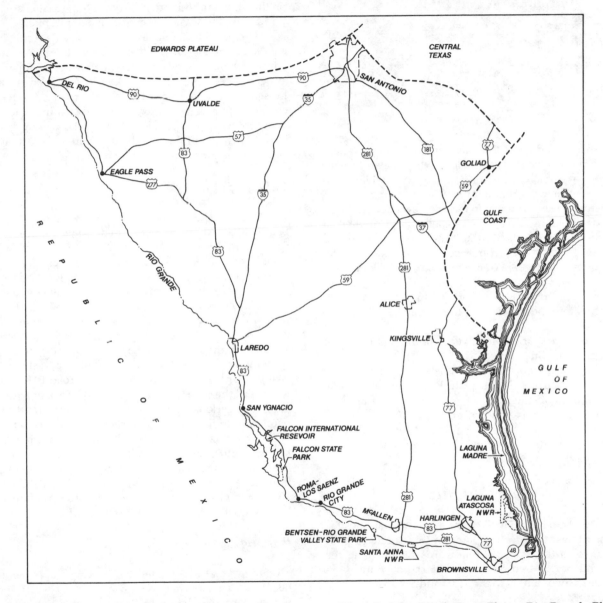

For the purposes of this book, South Texas is approximately 12% of the state. Its northern limit is the Balcones Escarpment from Del Rio to San Antonio and continuing along the San Antonio and Guadalupe Rivers southeast to near Goliad. The demarcation between Central Texas and South Texas (from San Antonio to Goliad) is gradual, wide, and indistinct. The boundary line then proceeds south along the western limit of the Coastal Plains to near Kingsville and eastward to the Gulf.

Also called the South Texas Plains, Rio Grande Plains, Tamaulipan Brushlands, or Mesquite Grasslands, most of the region consists of large ranches. Almost no lands have been set aside as parks or refuges, except on the eastern and southern perimeters. The major drainage is the Nueces River plus the tributaries of the Rio Grande. Quaternary and Tertiary deposits predominate and are mostly level to slightly rolling, with sandy and loamy soils. The dominant vegetation on natural sites is head-

White-winged Dove

high shrubs and extensive grasslands. The shrubs represent many species, nearly all of which seem to have thorns. Javelina, coyote, rattlesnake, and white-tailed deer are common throughout.

Nesting birds of the region include Least Grebe, Black-bellied Whistling-Duck, Long-billed and Curve-billed Thrashers, Harris' Hawk, Caracara, White-winged and Ground Doves, Golden-fronted Woodpecker, White-necked Raven, Cactus Wren, Pyrrhuloxia, Black-throated and Cassin's Sparrows, Scaled Quail, Pauraque, Lesser Nighthawk, Turkey, Roadrunner, Bronzed Cowbird, Ash-throated and Wied's Crested Flycatchers, and Verdin.

Hawks and sparrows are very common throughout the region in winter.

Birding locations with check-lists are Goliad State Park, Lake Corpus Christi State Park, Welder Wildlife Foundation, and the City of San Antonio. The extreme southern portion is the Lower Rio Grande Valley, a subregion with many public parks and refuges that are all excellent birding locations.

San Antonio

San Antonio (pop. 785,000) is astride the Balcones Escarpment near the meeting point for three of the regions presented in this book. The Edwards Plateau is to the west and north, Central Texas (Blackland Prairies and Post Oak Savannah) is to the east, and South Texas is to the south.

Mitchell Lake

Mitchell Lake (660 surface acres) is one of three large lakes favored by local birders for migrating shorebirds, waterfowl in winter, and visiting herons and egrets in late summer and fall. The lake is located south of San Antonio and is part of the sewage disposal system for the city. To reach Mitchell Lake from Loop 410, drive south on Moursund Boulevard between SH 16 and US 281. From there, it is about 0.6 of a mile to the entrance. Birders are authorized to proceed where the sign says, "Authorized Vehicles Only." It is possible to view many birds from a car on a drive around the lake. The lake can also be reached a short distance south of the main gate through the dump and/or the rifle or skeet range (when the gates are open). From the latter two locations, some parts of the lake are accessible which cannot be reached on the drive around the lake through the main gate.

Migrating and wintering birds include White Pelican, Double-crested and Olivaceous Cormorants, Little Blue and Louisiana Herons, Mallard, Gadwall, Pintail, Green-winged, Blue-winged and Cinnamon Teals, American Wigeon, Redhead, Ring-necked Duck, Canvasback, Lesser Scaup, and Ruddy Duck. More than a dozen species of shorebirds can be expected regularly in migration, and another dozen species are irregular or rare in the area. March, April, July, and August are the most favorable months for migrating shorebirds.

Calaveras Lake

Calaveras Lake is operated by the City Public Service Board of San Antonio. It is located 15 miles southeast of San Antonio and has 3450 surface acres. Drive southeast from Loop 410 on US 181 for approximately 8.5 miles. Turn left on Loop 1604 to the sign leading to the picnic area. There is an entrance fee, which is also good for same-day entry to Braunig Lake. About one mile before Loop 1604, two roads lead to the lake on the south side of the dam. Here the lake shore has not been cleared. There is high grass for sparrows in winter, trees for perching birds, and the possibility of approaching the lake unseen to view water birds. One road is Kilowatt Road, and the other is Adkins-Elmendorf Road. Both are good for overlooking the lake with a minimum of competition from fishermen, picnickers, and other visitors.

The brushy sections around the lakes are nesting habitat for South Texas birds: White-winged Dove, Curve-billed and Long-billed Thrashers, Pyrrhuloxia, Black-throated Sparrow, Lesser Nighthawk, Wied's Crested Flycatcher, Ground Dove, Golden-fronted Woodpecker, Verdin, Cactus Wren, and Bronzed Cowbird.

Braunig Lake

Braunig Lake is operated by the City Public Service Board of San Antonio to provide cooling water for a power plant. The lake's 1350 surface acres are 15 miles southeast of downtown on IH 37. Access to Braunig and Calaveras lakes is contolled by the San Antonio River Authority. The principal access is for fishing, but there are also picnic tables for picnickers. An entrance fee is charged which is also good for same-day entry to Calaveras Lake. The bird life is much the same for all three lakes, although some species might be found at one and not the others.

Emilie and Albert Friedrich Park

Emilie and Albert Friedrich Park is 232 acres of typical Edwards Plateau (Hill Country) habitat preserved in a near-natural state by the San Antonio Department of Parks and Recreation.

To reach the park, drive about 12 miles north of Loop 410 on IH 10. Take the Camp Bullis exit, and turn left under IH 10 at the underpass. Then drive north on the west side access road one mile to the sign "Friedrich Wilderness Park." Turn left, drive one-half mile to a dead end, and turn right to the entrance.

Located in the northwest section of Bexar County, the park provides the nearest location to the city for nesting Golden-cheeked Warbler and Black-capped Vireo, both of which nest in the canyonlands along the southeastern edge of the Edwards Plateau. There are seven trails within the park, each depicting a different habitat or feature of the park. All but one of the trails branch off the Main Loop Trail. The nesting site of the Golden-cheeked Warbler is along the west side of the Main Loop Trail. Concentrate on the shaded side of the hill where mature Ashe Junipers are present.

The Black-capped Vireo nesting site is on the east side of the Main Loop Trail. Look toward the top of the hill in the sumac thicket. Other nesting species include Ash-throated Flycatcher, Bewick's Wren, Painted Bunting, Northern (Bullock's) Oriole, Black-chinned Humming-bird, Golden-fronted Woodpecker, Bobwhite, Turkey, Roadrunner, Ladder-backed Woodpecker, Verdin, Bush-tit, White-eyed and Bell's Vireos, Yellow-breasted Chat, Orchard Oriole, House Finch, and Lesser Goldfinch.

A brochure is available at headquarters listing some of the animals of the area, a list of "Hill Country" plants in the park, and archeological highlights.

The park is open from 9 a.m. to 5 p.m. Wednesday through Sunday, but there is no admission after 4 p.m.

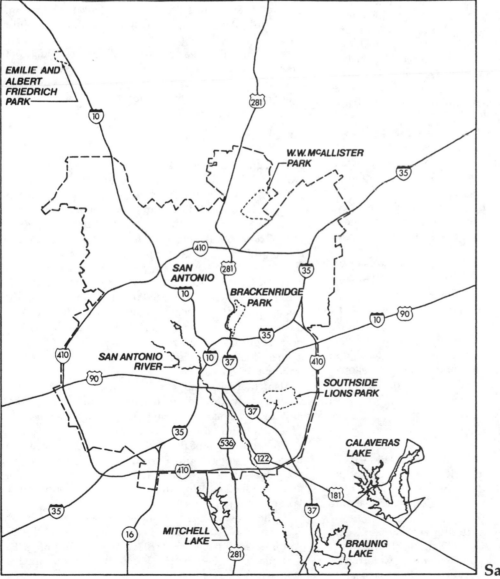

San Antonio

Bobwhite

Jack Judson Nature Trail

The Jack Judson Nature Trail is located within the Olmos Flood Basin along Hondondo and Olmos Creeks. The trail is rich in native trees and shrubs within the ten-acre area.

Drive north on Broadway about two blocks past the intersection with US 81 Business (Austin Highway). Turn left on Ogden Lane, continue past two stop signs, and turn left on Greely. Take the first right to the Nature Trail parking lot on the left.

Birds which nest include Yellow-crowned Night Heron, Inca Dove, Chuck-will's-widow, Black-chinned Hummingbird, Golden-fronted Woodpecker, Great Crested Flycatcher, Carolina Wren, Verdin, White-eyed Vireo, and House Finch.

During spring and fall, the Nature Trail is a good location for migrating land birds, warblers (the checklist has 37 species), vireos, tanagers, thrushes, grosbeaks, etc.

In winter look for Common Flicker, Yellow-bellied Sapsucker, Brown Creeper, House Wren, Hermit Thrush, Blue-gray Gnatcatcher, Cedar Waxwing, Solitary Vireo, Brewer's Blackbird, Common Grackle, American Goldfinch, Rufous-sided Towhee, Dark-eyed Junco, White-throated, Fox, Lincoln's, and Song Sparrows. Also, watch for these less common birds: Red-breasted Nuthatch, Winter Wren, Black-and-white Warbler, Yellow-rumped (Audubon's) Warbler, Purple Finch, and Pine Siskin.

Southside Lions Park

Southside Lions Park is 500 acres along Salado Creek in the southeast section of the city. Take IH 37 south about three miles beyond IH 10 to the Pecan Valley Drive exit. Turn east on Pecan Valley Drive, and drive about two miles to the park.

A lake in the park is the wintering area for Gadwall, American Wigeon, Green-winged Teal, Northern Shoveler, Canvasback, Lesser Scaup, and other waterfowl. The bottomland along Salado Creek has the typical land birds of the area as permanent residents: Cardinal, Carolina Chickadee, and Tufted Titmouse. In the mesquite shrub, about one-quarter of the park, look for typical South Texas birds: Curve-billed and Long-billed Thrashers, Cactus Wren, and Pyrrhuloxia. In winter, watch for Harris', White-crowned, Vesper, and Savannah Sparrows.

W.W. McAllister Park

W.W. McAllister Park is north of the airport in the northern part of the city. The 856 acres of the park are operated by the San Antonio Department of Parks and Recreation. From Loop 410 (just east of the airport), take Broadway north 1.4 miles to Bitters Road. Turn left onto Bitters Road to the dead end at Wetmore, turn right on Wetmore, and go about one mile to Starcrest. Turn left (west) on Starcrest for 2.0 miles to Jones-Maltsberger. Turn right (north) on Jones-Maltsberger for the one-half mile to the entrance.

When there is water in the lake, look for shorebirds during July, August, April and May, and ducks in winter. Golden-crowned Kinglet, American Woodcock, Brown Creeper, and Fox Sparrow have all been recorded here in winter. This is a good place for wintering sparrows.

The park is subject to large crowds on weekends; other times are better for birding.

Brackenridge Park

Brackenridge Park (343 acres) is located on the San Antonio River about two miles north of downtown. It includes a large zoo, concessions, golf course, picnicking, playground, and the Sunken Gardens. From downtown, take either North St. Mary's or Broadway to the park. The zoo has approximately 700 bird species from around the world, including a male and female Whooping Crane.

The F. C. Hixon Tropical Bird House has a free-flying area in the center surrounded by 14 dioramas. Each diorama represents a specific habitat from a different part of the world. The scenes are changed periodically. The African Flight Cage features many birds from Africa in a large enclosed area. Visitors can enter and view the birds from within the cage.

Also, there is a large collection of waterbirds from around the world. These are joined in summer by Wood and Black-bellied Whistling-Ducks, and in winter by other wintering ducks.

The woodlands of the park can be very good for land birds during migration. The San Antonio Botanical Center is just east of the park at 555 Funston Place. Wood and Black-bellied Whistling-Ducks can be found on the lake in summer.

A check-list of Bexar County birds prepared by the San Antonio Audubon Society is available at the San Antonio Garden Center, 3310 North New Braunfels, San Antonio, TX 78209, for 15¢ plus addressed, stamped envelope.

Lower Rio Grande Valley

The Lower Rio Grande Valley, a subregion of South Texas, is generally considered to be that part of Texas which was formerly the flood plain of the Rio Grande. The river has changed courses several times as it neared the Gulf, leaving resacas (oxbows) and alluvial deposits which are very fertile. The area has been almost completely cleared for agriculture. Citrus and vegetables are the principal crops, and much of the land is irrigated from the river. The traditional valley is an irregular line from just north of Mission to just south of Raymondville but birdwise could be considered to include the lands adjacent to the river up to and including International Falcon Reservoir. The vegetation is the same as the South Plains, except for a few Mexican species which reach their northern limit along the Rio Grande. These plants include Montezuma Bald Cypress, Texas Palmetto (also called Sabal Palm), ebony, and others.

Before clearing, the Valley was composed of dense brush, a small portion of which is preserved at Santa Ana National Wildlife Refuge, Bentsen-Rio Grande Valley State Park, and a few other locations.

Some of the nesting species include Chachalaca, White-fronted Dove, Groove-billed Ani, Buff-bellied Hummingbird, Green and Ringed Kingfishers, Tropical Kingbird, Kiskadee Flycatcher, Green Jay, Black-headed and Lichtenstein's Orioles, and Olive Sparrow.

White-collared Seedeater were formerly more common in the Valley than now, but they have been found recently in winter in the village of San Ygnacio, which is 14 miles northwest of Zapata on US 83.

Santa Ana National Wildlife Refuge

Referred to as the "Gem of the National Wildlife Refuge System," Santa Ana NWR is generally considered one of the "must" places to look for birds in Texas, and indeed, in the nation. The refuge is located on the Rio Grande between the flood control levee of the International Boundary and Water Commission and the river between McAllen and Brownsville.

To reach the refuge from McAllen, drive six miles east on US 83 to Alamo, then turn south on FM 907 to US 281. Go east one-half mile to the entrance sign.

Santa Ana NWR contains nearly 5000 acres in several units (2065 in the main unit) which preserve a small remnant of the native subtropical vegetation that made up much of the Lower Valley before land clearing for farming and development. At present, only the main unit is open to the public. There is a one-way loop road through the refuge for those who wish to drive through,

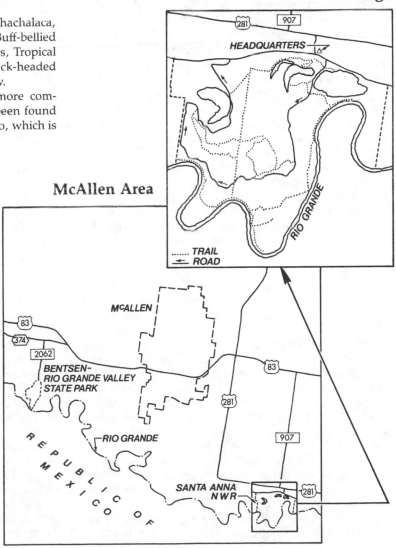

Green Jay

and a dozen or more trails which crisscross around the lakes, woodlands, and thick brush which comprise the refuge. The river is the southern boundary. Plan to walk some trails and the edges of some of the lakes to realize the maximum number of bird possibilities available.

Many Mexican species occur which are near their northern limit. Of course, the same can be said for the other birding locations in the Lower Valley, such as Bentsen-Rio Grande Valley State Park, Laguna-Atascosa NWR, and the Falcon Dam area.

Nesting birds include Least Grebe, Black-bellied Whistling Duck, Harris' Hawk, Chachalaca, White-winged and White-fronted Doves, Groove-billed Ani, Pauraque, Lesser Nighthawk, Buff-bellied Hummingbird, Tropical Kingbird, Kiskadee Flycatcher, Wied's Crested Flycatcher, Green Jay, Long-billed Thrasher, Tropical Parula, Black-headed and Lichtenstein's Orioles, Olive Sparrow, and a new addition to the nesting list, the Hook-billed Kite.

Masked Duck, Gray Hawk, Jaçana, Red-billed Pigeon, Rose-throated Becard, Beardless Flycatcher, Clay-colored Robin, Rufous-backed Robin, and Yellow-green Vireo are not easy to find but have been recorded. Many migrants funnel up and down the southern tip of Texas. Their concentrations at the refuge can be spectacular. Broad-winged Hawk have been reported in the thousands. Thirty-six warbler species, most in migration, are on the refuge check-list.

Black-and-white, Nashville, Northern Parula, and Tropical Parula (rare nester), Black-throated Gray, Yellow-throated, Prairie, Common Yellowthroat, Yellow-breasted Chat, and Wilson's Warblers are common-to-occasional winter residents.

As this was being written, the refuge was undergoing some changes. Previously, as good a place to look for birds as any was within a few hundred yards of the old headquarters building in all directions. Now the headquarters will be north of the levee. The trees around the headquarters (previous) are very good for land birds; the photography blinds are excellent for observing and taking photographs of Lichtenstein's and Black-headed Orioles, Green Jay, Chachalaca, and White-fronted Dove. The Turk's Cap (*Malvaviscus* sp.) should be watched for hummingbirds and the ponds checked for waterfowl in winter.

I have many fond memories of birding experiences at Santa Ana NWR. With no diary of all my trips, I don't know exactly how many times I have been there, but the first time was April 1966, and I have probably averaged about one trip per year since then. Masked Duck, Jaçana, Hook-billed Kite, Gray Hawk, Beardless Flycatcher, Yellow-green Vireo, Tropical Parula, and Buff-bellied Hummingbird come to mind as some of the highlights.

In particular I remember the Hook-billed Kite. The plan was for a one-day trip—to leave Austin early, see the bird, and return late. It is about a six-hour drive from my home to the refuge. On the way there was car trouble, which cost us two or three hours, but eventually the car was made whole again, and we were on our way.

The grapevine said the birds came to a certain grove of trees just west of the refuge and so shouldn't be hard to see, but no one passed this information on to the birds.

We stayed all afternoon until nearly dark. Then the word was that they are very easy to see first thing in the morning. So with not even a toothbrush for an overnight stay, it was decided we should give the kites a chance in the morning, and we spent the night. Sure enough, about 7 a.m. the kites made their appearance and were duly recorded on our lists. With their bulky body and rounded wings, they looked nothing like a White-tailed or Mississippi Kite. Satisfied we had recorded a very rare bird in Texas, we returned to Austin, 300 miles north.

There is not only a chance to see many unique bird species but also the other animals and plants which were common in the Lower Valley before the land was cleared. The refuge brochure states that more than 450 species of plants and 29 species of mammals have been recorded.

A bird check-list is available at headquarters with more than 320 species, a great number for only 2065 acres.

To contact the Refuge Manager, write Route 1, Box 202-A, Alamo, TX 78516, or call (512) 787–3079. There is no camping on the refuge.

Bentsen-Rio Grande Valley State Park

Bentsen-Rio Grande Valley State Park is located about 20 miles up the Rio Grande from Santa Ana NWR. To reach the 588-acre park, drive west from Mission for five miles on US 83 to Loop 374. Continue west 1.5 miles to FM 2062, then turn south to the park. The park has camping, picnicking, fishing, hiking, and restrooms with hot showers.

The park bird list is very similar to that of the Santa Ana NWR, but some species have been easier for me to find at Bentsen than at Santa Ana. These include Red-billed Pigeon, and Elf, Barn, and Screech Owls. In summer Groove-billed Ani are very common. Hook-billed Kite have occurred here also.

An advantage of Bentsen over Santa Ana is that you can camp and do some night and early morning birding. A favorite activity of some observers is to drive or walk the park roads after dark to look for Pauraque on the road, Barn Owl perched in the trees near the road, to listen to Screech Owl calling, and to listen and look for Elf Owl. The Singing Chaparral Trail, which starts just south of the headquarters, will acquaint the visitor with the vegetation of the Lower Valley, especially if you pick up one of the brochures available at headquarters. Another hiking trail in the park leads through dense trees from the loop road south to the Rio Grande.

The park bird check-list has 272 species recorded within the park and adjoining land. The park list of reptiles and amphibians has 28 species.

The address is P.O. Box 988, Mission, TX 78572 (512) 585–1107.

Falcon Reservoir Area

Santa Margarita Ranch

The Santa Margarita Ranch has been the best place in the United States to find the Brown Jay, a bird which has been regular north of Mexico for only about 10 years. The ranch is located on the Rio Grande off old US 83 between Falcon Dam and Roma-Los Saenz. Approximately eight miles north of Roma-Los Saenz (or six miles south of Falcon Dam), the old highway jogs west from US 83. There are three gravel roads which lead from the old highway toward the river: take the middle one at the top of the hill, and drive to the ranch where there are several houses. This is private property, and a fee is charged for entry. Stop at the houses until someone comes out to collect the fee. Drive straight toward the river, park at the top of the bluff, and walk to the river.

Though the jays are sometimes seen at Falcon Dam, this site has been the most reliable location. They are usually found along the river below the bluff. In addition to Brown Jay, Santa Margarita Ranch is also an excellent place for most of the other Valley specialities, including Green and Ringed Kingfishers, Olive Sparrow, Green Jay, and Kiskadee Flycatcher.

Falcon State Recreation Area

Falcon State Recreation Area is located on the Rio Grande just off US 83, 29 miles northwest of Rio Grande City, or 25 miles southeast of Zapata. The 573-acre park includes about four miles of shoreline on International Falcon Reservoir and offers camping, picnicking, an airstrip, fishing, and restrooms with hot showers.

The reservoir is owned by the United States and Mexico and is operated by the International Boundary and Water Commission for power generation, flood control, municipal and irrigation water supply, and recrea-

Ferruginous Owl

tion. The lake has 87,210 surface acres at conservation storage level.

In the park most of the birds are those expected in the South Texas region: Scaled Quail, Roadrunner, Black-throated Sparrow, Pyrrhuloxia, and White-necked Raven. However, most bird seekers come to Falcon Dam to bird the area just below and east of the dam on the Texas side. The best place in the United States to find three kingfisher species—Ringed, Belted, and Green; sometimes all three at the same time—is along the river from the dam to the town of Roma-Los Saenz. If not found near the dam, try Chapeno Falls, Salineño, Santa Margarita Ranch, or Fronton.

A walk in the woods below the dam can be very rewarding. Many strays from Mexico have been found, such as Brown Jay, Beardless Flycatcher, White-collared Seedeater, Ferruginous Owl (a very rare species in Texas, especially in areas accessible to the public), and Rufous-capped Warbler. In addition, most of the species of the Lower Valley occur in these woods, including Lichtenstein's and Black-headed Orioles, Kiskadee Flycatcher, Green Jay, and Olive Sparrow.

Look for Caracara, Harris' Hawk, and White-tailed Kite in the open country north of the park and the river. Olivaceous Cormorant and Vermilion Flycatcher are found along the river and lake, and Ring-billed Gull are very common in winter.

This is rattlesnake country, so walk carefully, especially at night. A bird check-list with 233 species is available at park headquarters.

The park address is P.O. Box 2, Falcon Heights, TX 78545 (512) 848–5327.

Laguna Atascosa National Wildlife Refuge

Laguna Atascosa National Wildlife Refuge is about 25 miles east of Harlingen on Laguna Madre. From Harlin-

Laguna Atascosa National Wildlife Reservior

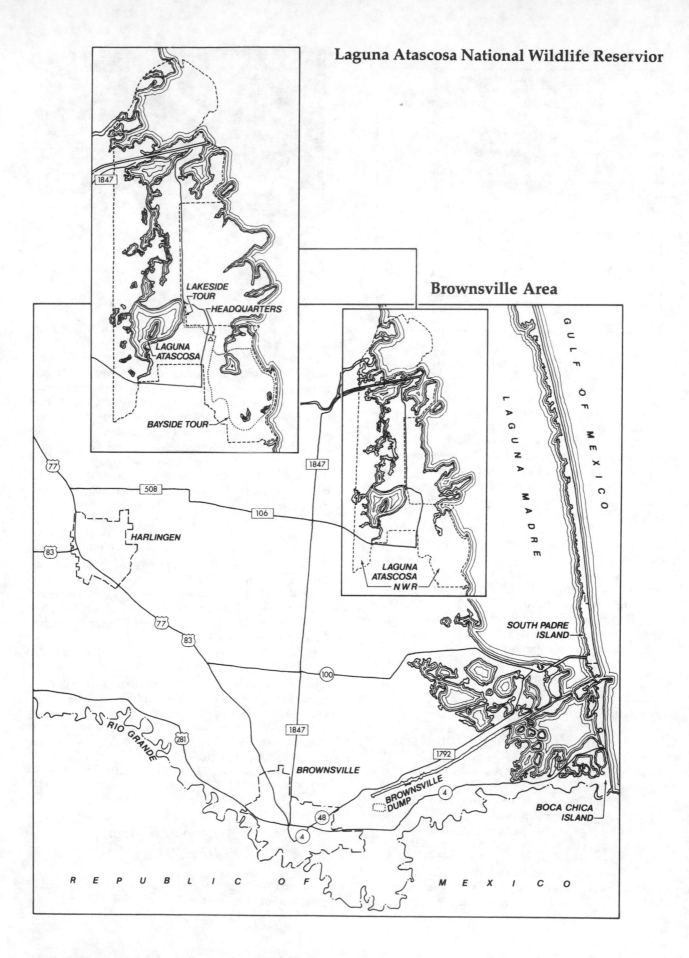

Brownsville Area

LAKESIDE
TOUR

HEADQUARTERS

LAGUNA
ATASCOSA

BAYSIDE TOUR

1847

508

106

HARLINGEN

77

83

77

83

100

1847

281

RIO GRANDE

BROWNSVILLE

48

4

BROWNSVILLE
DUMP

4

1792

1847

LAGUNA
ATASCOSA
N W R

GULF OF MEXICO

LAGUNA MADRE

SOUTH PADRE
ISLAND

BOCA CHICA
ISLAND

R E P U B L I C   O F   M E X I C O

gen drive east on FM 106 to the intersection with FM 1847. Continue east on the county road to the refuge entrance. From north of Harlingen, go east on FM 508 until it joins FM 106. From Brownsville, drive north on FM 1847 to the intersection with FM 106, then east on the county road.

The 45,190-acre refuge is typical coastal prairie, with grass and cacti in the low places, and thick brush on the higher ground. Practically all of the brush seems to have thorns. For contrast, there are 7000 acres of ponds and marshes as well as about 12 miles of shoreline frontage on Laguna Madre. Each offers different animal and plant habitats.

Canada, Snow, and White-fronted Geese and Sandhill Crane are plentiful in winter and should be looked for in cultivated fields along the roads leading to the refuge as well as within its boundaries.

Laguna Madre, Laguna Atascosa, and the ponds of the refuge support 24 species of ducks. Black-bellied Whistling and Mottled Ducks are the only regular nesters. Large numbers of Redhead winter on Laguna Madre.

The Bayside Tour (a 15-mile, one-way drive through the southern section of the refuge) leads through marshlands, ponds, several miles of Laguna Madre, and through the dry uplands on the west side. Shorebirds, waterfowl, herons, and egrets, including the Reddish Egret, are plentiful in the marshlands.

Most of the specialty species of the Lower Valley can be found, such as Harris' Hawk, Pauraque, Wied's Crested Flycatcher, Bronzed Cowbird, Olive Sparrow, Tropical Kingbird, Kiskadee Flycatcher, Groove-billed Ani, Chachalaca, Green Jay, and Long-billed Thrasher.

In spring listen and look for the Varied Bunting and Botteri's Sparrow in the open brush country along the west side of the Bayside Tour. Both nest regularly on the refuge. Other regular nesters include the Caracara, White-tailed Kite, Cassin's Sparrow, and Lesser Nighthawk.

Laguna Atascosa NWR is also a great place to be during spring migration. Many species stop here to feed and rest on their journey north: Northern Oriole, Blue Grosbeak, Indigo Bunting, Rose-breasted Grosbeak. Vireos, and 28 warbler species are sometimes present in large numbers.

Nesting species of the marshes and Laguna Madre are Wilson's Plover, Black-necked Stilt, Least Grebe, King Rail, Common Gallinule, and Purple Gallinule (rarely).

Nesting in dry uplands are Cactus Wren, Curve-billed Thrasher, Verdin, and the occasional White-necked Raven and Black-throated Sparrow.

The 2.5-mile Lakeside Tour leads to Laguna Atascosa, the 3100-acre lake which gives the refuge its name and usually provides a winter home for a Western Grebe or two.

I remember a field trip in November when it was cold, raining, and muddy. We tallied 93 species in about six hours, mostly without getting out of the car. This is the only place in Texas I have seen a wild long-tailed weasel.

A bird check-list is available at headquarters with 313 species, but it does not include a Bahama Duck which spent the winter of 1978–79. The address of the Refuge Manager is P.O. Box 2683, Harlingen, TX 78550 (512) 748–2426. There is no camping on the refuge.

Brownsville

Birds of the Valley can be found in all directions from Brownsville. The surrounding area has many resacas replenished by rainfall and periodic floods. Hurricanes are another water source which strike the Lower Valley from time to time, often with torrential rain. In addition to the resacas, hurricane water collects in numerous low places and will sometimes remain for several years. This casual water attracts wintering and migrating waterfowl and shorebirds, and from the south, an occasional Masked Duck and Jaçana.

Boca Chica is on the Gulf of Mexico about 25 miles east of Brownsville on SH 4. After reaching the end of SH 4, a drive south along the beach will lead to the mouth of the Rio Grande. Laughing, Ring-billed, and Herring Gulls, Sanderling, Black-bellied, Snowy, and Piping Plovers, and Ruddy Turnstones are regulars along the beach in winter.

Rarities which have been found in winter include Lesser Black-backed, Thayer's, and Glaucous Gulls, and Gannet. In summer Wilson's Plover, Least, Sandwich, Royal, and Caspian Terns are common.

South Padre Island is reached by driving northeast from Brownsville on SH 48 about 23 miles to Port Isabel, then east over the causeway to South Padre Island. Drive north on PR 100 and then on to the beach for the same birds listed previously. Here the white phase of the Reddish Egret is often found.

Port Isabel can be reached from Harlingen by driving south on US 77 and 83 for six miles, then east on SH 100 for 24 miles.

The Brownsville dump has been an excellent location in recent years for Mexican Crow, November through March, along with White-necked Raven and the numerous Great-tailed Grackle. The dump is just south of the Port of Brownsville on FM 511, 1.5 miles north of SH 4, or one-half mile south of SH 48.

Appendix

A Check-list of Texas Birds

This appendix is a list of all birds recorded in Texas as compiled by the Texas Bird Records Committee of the Texas Ornithological Society. The list will be published by the Texas Parks and Wildlife Department as a work sheet for recording observations by location and to provide an accurate reference and inventory for conservation or environmental workers, students, educators, and ecologists.

There are 604 birds listed. Two are extinct, two are extirpated, and 45 are hypothetical. This tabulation leaves 555 as documented, but 85 of these are accidentals.

I have revised the list slightly so that the common name in the first column agrees with the *Check-list of North American Birds, Fifth Edition*, 1957, American Ornithologists' Union, as amended by the 32nd Supplement, 1973, and the 33rd Supplement, 1976. The 1957 check-list name is shown in quotation marks where the name was changed by the supplements, and "new" names which may be adopted in the anticipated check-

list revision are shown in parenthesis. I have also added the nesting symbol for those species I believe nest in Texas at least occasionally.

The following symbols are used:

(X) Extinct
(E) Extirpated
(A) Accidental
(H) Hypothetical
(*) Nests (at least occasionally)
(†) A.O.U. sequence not known

Any bird species found with the symbol (A) or (H) should be reported with as many details as possible, such as time, place, observers, photographs, recordings, etc., to the Texas Bird Records Committee, c/o Dr. Keith A. Arnold, Department of Wildlife and Fisheries Sciences, Texas A & M University, College Station TX 77843 (713) 845–6751.

Class: Aves, Birds

GAVIIFORMES: Loons
GAVIIDAE: Loons
 Common Loon
 Gavia immer
 Arctic Loon (A)
 G. arctica
 Red-throated Loon
 G. stellata
PODICIPEDIFORMES: Grebes
PODICIPEDIDAE: Grebes
 Red-necked Grebe
 Podiceps grisegena
 Horned Grebe
 P. auritus
 Eared Grebe
 P. nigricollis
 Least Grebe*
 P. dominicus
 Western Grebe
 Aechmophorus occidentalis
 Pied-billed Grebe*
 Podilymbus podiceps

PROCELLARIIFORMES: Albatrosses, Shearwaters, Petrels, and Allies
DIOMEDEIDAE: Albatrosses
 Yellow-nosed Albatross (A)
 Diomedea chlororhynchos
PROCELLARIIDAE: Shearwaters
 Cory's Shearwater
 Puffinus diomedea
 Greater Shearwater (A)
 P. gravis
 Sooty Shearwater (A)
 P. griseus
 Manx Shearwater (A)
 P. puffinus
 Audubon's Shearwater (A)
 (Dusky-backed Shearwater)
 P. lherminieri
HYDROBATIDAE: Storm Petrels
 Leach's Storm-petrel (A)
 "Leach's Petrel"
 Oceanodroma leucorhoa
 Harcourt's Storm-petrel (A)

 "Harcourt's Petrel" (Band-rumped Storm-Petrel)
 O. castro
 Wilson's Storm-petrel (A)
 "Wilson's Petrel"
 Oceanites oceanicus
PELECANIFORMES: Tropicbirds, Pelicans, Frigatebirds, and Allies
PHAETHONTIDAE: Tropicbirds
 White-tailed Tropicbird (H)
 Phaethon lepturus
PELECANIDAE: Pelicans
 White Pelican*
 Pelicanus erythrorhynchos
 Brown Pelican*
 P. occidentalis
SULIDAE: Boobies and Gannets
 Blue-faced Booby
 (Masked Booby)
 Sula dactylatra
 Blue-footed Booby (A)
 S. nebouxii

Brown Booby (A)
  S. leucogaster
Red-footed Booby (A)
  S. sula
Gannet
(Northern Gannet)
  Morus bassanus
PHALACROCORACIDAE: Cormorants
Double-crested Cormorant*
  Phalacrocorax auritus
Olivaceous Cormorant*
(Neotropic Cormorant)
  P. olivaceus
Red-footed Cormorant (H)†
  P. gaimardi
ANHINGIDAE: Darters
Anhinga*
(American Anhinga)
  Anhinga unhinga
FREGATIDAE: Frigatebirds
Magnificent Frigatebird
  Fregata magnificens

CICONIIFORMES: Herons, Storks, Ibises, Flamingos, and Allies
ARDEIDAE: Herons and Bitterns
Great Blue Heron*
  Ardea herodias
Green Heron*
  Butorides striatus
Little Blue Heron*
  Florida caerulea
Cattle Egret*
  Bubulcus ibis
Reddish Egret*
  Dichromanassa rufescens
Great Egret*
"Common Egret"
  Casmerodius albus
Snowy Egret*
  Egretta thula
Louisiana Heron*
(Tricolored Heron)
  Hydranassa tricolor
Black-crowned Night Heron*
  Nycticorax nycticorax
Yellow-crowned Night Heron*
  Nyctanasso violacea
Least Bittern*
  Ixobrychus exilis
American Bittern*
  Botaurus lentiginosus
CICONIIDAE: Storks
Jabiru (A)†
  Jabiru mycteria
Wood Stork
"Wood Ibis"
  Mycteria americana
THRESKIORNITHIDAE: Ibises and Spoonbill
Glossy Ibis (H)
  Plegadis falcinellus
White-faced Ibis*
  P. chihi
White Ibis*
  Eudocimus albus
Scarlet Ibis (A)
  E. ruber

Roseate Spoonbill*
  Ajaia ajaja
PHOENICOPTERIDAE: Flamingos
American Flamingo (A)
  Phoenicopterus ruber

ANSERIFORMES: Swans, Geese, and Ducks
ANATIDAE: Swans, Geese, and Ducks
Whistling Swan
  Olor columbianus
Trumpeter Swan
  O. buccinator
Canada Goose
  Branta canadensis
Brant (A)
  B. bernicla
Barnacle Goose (H)
  B. leucopsis
Red-breasted Goose (H)†
  B. ruficollis
White-fronted Goose
  Anser albifrons
Snow Goose
"Blue Goose," in part.
  Chen caerulescens
Ross' Goose
  C. rossii
Black-bellied Whistling-Duck*
"Black-bellied Tree Duck"
  Dendrocygna autumnalis
Fulvous Whistling-Duck*
"Fulvous Tree Duck"
  D. bicolor
Mallard*
  Anas platyrhynchos
Mexican Duck*
(may be lumped with Mallard)
  A. diazi
Black Duck
(American Black Duck)
  A. rubripes
Mottled Duck*
  A. fulvigula
Gadwall
  A. strepera
Pintail*
(Common Pintail)
(Northern Pintail)
  A. acuta
Bahama Duck (A)
(White-cheeked Pintail or Bahama Pintail)
  A. bahamensis
Green-winged Teal
  A. crecca
Blue-winged Teal*
  A. discors
Cinnamon Teal
  A. cyanoptera
European Wigeon
"European Widgeon" (Eurasian Wigeon)
  A. penelope
American Wigeon
"American Widgeon"
  A. americana

Northern Shoveler
"Shoveler"
  A. clypeata
Wood Duck*
  Aix sponsa
Redhead
  Aythya americana
Ring-necked Duck
  A. collaris
Canvasback
  A. valisineria
Greater Scaup
  A. marila
Lesser Scaup
  A. affinis
Common Goldeneye
  Bucephala clangula
Barrow's Goldeneye (A)
  B. islandica
Bufflehead
  B. albeola
Oldsquaw
  Clangula hyemalis
Harlequin Duck (H)
  Histrionicus histrionicus
King Eider (H)
  Somateria spectabilis
White-winged Scoter
  Melanitta deglandi
Surf Scoter
  M. perspicillata
Black Scoter
"Common Scoter"
  M. nigra
Ruddy Duck
  Oxyura jamaicensis
Masked Duck*
  O. dominica
Hooded Merganser
  Lophodytes cucullatus
Common Merganser
  Mergus merganser
Red-breasted Merganser
  M. serrator

FALCONIFORMES: Vultures, Hawks, and Falcons
CATHARTIDAE: American Vultures
Turkey Vulture*
  Cathartes aura
Black Vulture*
  Coragyps atratus
California Condor (E)
  Gymnogyps californianus [Fossil record only]
ACCIPITRIDAE: Hawks and Harriers
White-tailed Kite*
  Elanus leucurus
Hook-billed Kite* (A)†
  Chondrohierax uncinatus
Swallow-tailed Kite
  Elanoides forficatus
Mississippi Kite*
  Ictinia mississippiensis
Everglade Kite (A)
(Snail Kite)
  Rostrhamus sociabilis

Goshawk (A)
(Northern Goshawk)
Accipiter gentilis
Sharp-shinned Hawk*
A. striatus
Cooper's Hawk*
A. cooperii
Red-tailed Hawk*
"Harlan's Hawk," in part.
Buteo jamaicensis
Red-shouldered Hawk*
B. lineatus
Broad-winged Hawk*
B. platypterus
Swainson's Hawk*
B. swainsoni
Zone-tailed Hawk*
B. albonotatus
White-tailed Hawk*
B. albicaudatus
Short-tailed Hawk (H)
B. brachyurus
Rough-legged Hawk
B. lagopus
Ferruginous Hawk*
B. regalis
Gray Hawk
B. nitidus
Roadside Hawk (A)†
B. magnirostris
Harris' Hawk*
(Bay-winged Hawk)
Parabuteo unicinctus
Black Hawk*
(Lesser Black Hawk) (Common Black Hawk)
Buteogallus anthracinus
Golden Eagle*
Aquila chrysaetos
Bald Eagle*
Haliaeetus leucocephalus
Marsh Hawk*
(Northern Harrier)
Circus cyaneus
PANDIONIDAE: Osprey
Osprey
Pandion haliaetus

FALCONIDAE: Caracara and Falcons
Caracara*
(Crested Caracara)
Caracara cheriway
Prairie Falcon*
Falco mexicanus
Peregrine Falcon*
F. peregrinus
Aplomado Falcon (A)
F. femoralis
Merlin
"Pigeon Hawk"
F. columbarius
American Kestrel*
"Sparrow Hawk"
F. sparverius

GALLIFORMES: Megapodes and Pheasants
CRACIDAE: Chachalacas

Chachalaca*
(Plain Chachalaca)
Ortalis vetula
TETRAONIDAE: Grouse
Greater Prairie Chicken*
Tympanuchus cupido
Lesser Prairie Chicken*
T. pallidicinctus
Sharp-tailed Grouse (E)
Pedioecetes phasianellus

PHASIANIDAE: Quails and Pheasants
Bobwhite*
(Common Bobwhite)
Colinus virginianus
Scaled Quail*
Callipepla squamata
Gambel's Quail*
Lophortyx gambelii
Montezuma Quail*
"Harlequin Quail"
Cyrtonyx montezumae
Ring-necked Pheasant*
Phasianus colchicus
Chukar (H)
Alectoris chukar
MELEAGRIDIDAE: Turkeys
Turkey*
(Wild Turkey) (Common Turkey)
Meleagris gallopavo

GRUIFORMES: Cranes, Rails, and Allies
GRUIDAE: Cranes
Whooping Crane
Grus americana
Sandhill Crane
G. canadensis
ARAMIDAE: Limpkin
Limpkin (A)
Aramus guarauna

RALLIDAE: Rails, Gallinules, and Coots
King Rail*
Rallus elegans
Clapper Rail*
R. longirostris
Virginia Rail
R. limicola
Spotted Rail (A)†
Pardirallus maculatus
Sora
Porzana carolina
Yellow Rail
Coturnicops noveboracensis
Black Rail*
Laterallus jamaicensis
Paint-billed Crake (A)†
Neocrex erythrops
Purple Gallinule*
Porphyrula martinica
Common Gallinule*
Gallinula chloropus
American Coot*
Fulica americana

CHARADRIIFORMES: Shorebirds, Gulls, and Allies
JACANIDAE: Jacanas
Jacana*

(North American Jacana) (Northern Jacana)
Jacana spinosa
HAEMATOPODIDAE: Oystercatchers
American Oystercatcher*
Haematopus palliatus

CHARADRIIDAE: Plovers
Semipalmated Plover*
Charadrius semipalmatus
Piping Plover*
C. melodus
Snowy Plover*
C. alexandrinus
Wilson's Plover*
C. wilsonia
Killdeer*
C. vociferus
Mountain Plover*
C. montanus
American Golden Plover
(Lesser Golden Plover)
Pluvialis dominica
Black-bellied Plover
P. squatarola
Surfbird (A)
Aphriza virgata

SCOLOPACIDAE: Turnstone, Woodcock, Snipe, and Sandpipers
Ruddy Turnstone*
Arenaria interpres
American Woodcock*
Philohela minor
Common Snipe
Capella gallinago
Long-billed Curlew*
Numenius americanus
Whimbrel
N. phaeopus
Eskimo Curlew (A)
N. borealis
Upland Sandpiper
"Upland Plover"
Bartramia longicauda
Spotted Sandpiper
Actitis macularia
Solitary Sandpiper
Tringa solitaria
Wood Sandpiper (H)
T. glareola
Greater Yellowlegs
T. melanoleucus
Lesser Yellowlegs
T. flavipes
Spotted Redshank (H)†
T. erythropus
Willet*
Catoptrophorus semipalmatus
Red Knot
"Knot"
Calidris canutus
Purple Sandpiper
C. maritima
Sharp-tailed Sandpiper (H)
C. acuminata
Pectoral Sandpiper
C. melanotos

White-rumped Sandpiper
  C. fuscicollis
Baird's Sandpiper
  C. bairdii
Least Sandpiper*
  C. minutilla
Curlew Sandpiper (H)
  C. ferruginea
Dunlin
  C. alpina
Semipalmated Sandpiper
  C. pusillus
Western Sandpiper
  C. mauri
Sanderling*
  C. alba
Short-billed Dowitcher
(Common Dowitcher)
  Limnodromus griseus
Long-billed Dowitcher
  L. scolopaceus
Stilt Sandpiper
  Micropalama himantopus
Buff-breasted Sandpiper
  Tryngites subruficollis
Marbled Godwit
  Limosa fedoa
Bar-tailed Godwit (H)
  L. lapponica
Hudsonian Godwit
  L. haemastica
Ruff (A)
  Philomachus pugnax
RECURVIROSTRIDAE: Avocets and Stilts
American Avocet*
  Recurvirostra americana
Black-necked Stilt*
  Himantopus mexicanus
PHALAROPODIDAE: Phalaropes
Red Phalarope (A)
  Phalaropus fulicarius
Wilson's Phalarope
  Steganopus tricolor
Northern Phalarope
  Lobipes lobatus
BURHINIDAE: Thick-Knees
Double-striped Thick-knee (A)†
  Burhinus bistriatus
STERCORARIIDAE: Jaegers
Pomarine Jaeger (A)
  Stercorarius pomarinus
Parasitic Jaeger (A)
  S. parasiticus
Long-tailed Jaeger (A)
  S. longicaudus
LARIDAE: Gulls and Terns
Glaucous Gull (A)
  Larus hyperboreus
Iceland Gull (H)
  L. glaucoides
Great Black-backed Gull (H)
(Greater Black-backed Gull)
  L. marinus
Lesser Black-backed Gull (A)
  L. fuscus
Herring Gull
  L. argentatus

Thayer's Gull (A)
"Herring Gull," in part
  L. thayeri
California Gull (A)
  L. californicus
Ring-billed Gull
  L. delawarensis
Laughing Gull*
  L. articilla
Franklin's Gull
  L. pipixcan
Bonaparte's Gull
  L. philadelphia
Little Gull (A)
  L. minutus
Heermann's Gull (A)
  L. heermanni
Black-legged Kittiwake
  Rissa tridactyla
Sabine's Gull (A)
  Xema sabini
Gull-billed Tern*
  Gelochelidon nilotica
Forster's Tern*
  Sterna forsteri
Common Tern
  S. hirundo
Arctic Tern (A)
  S. paradisaea
Roseate Tern (A)
  S. dougallii
Sooty Tern*
  S. fuscata
Bridled Tern (H)
  S. anaethetus
Least Tern*
(Little Tern)
  S. albifrons
Royal Tern*
  S. maxima
Elegant Tern (A)
  S. elegans
Sandwich Tern*
  S. sandvicensis
Caspian Tern*
  S. caspia
Black Tern
  Chlidonias niger
Noddy Tern (A)
(Brown Noddy)
  Anous stolidus
Black Noddy Tern (A)†
  A. tenuirostris
RYNCHOPIDAE: Skimmers
Black Skimmer*
  Rynchops niger

COLUMBIFORMES: Pigeons and Doves
COLUMBIDAE: Pigeons and Doves
Band-tailed Pigeon*
  Columba fasciata
Red-billed Pigeon*
  C. flavirostris
Rock Dove*
  C. livia
White-winged Dove*
  Zenaida asiatica

Mourning Dove*
  Z. macroura
Passenger Pigeon (X)
  Ectopistes migratorius
Ringed Turtle Dove
  Streptopelia risoria
Ground Dove*
(Common Ground Dove)
  Columbina passerina
Ruddy Ground Dove (H)
  C. talpacoti
Blue Ground Dove (H)†
  Claravis pretiosa
Inca Dove*
  Scardafella inca
White-fronted Dove*
(White-tipped Dove)
  Leptotila verreauxi
PSITTACIDAE: Parrots
Green Parakeet (H)†
  Aratinga holochlora
Carolina Parakeet (X)
  Conuropsis carolinensis
Red-crowned Parrot (H)†
  Amazona viridigenalis
Yellow-headed Parrot (H)†
  A. ochrocephala

CUCULIFORMES: Cuckoos
CUCULIDAE: Cuckoos, Roadrunners, and
Anis
Mangrove Cuckoo (H)
  Coccyzus minor
Yellow-billed Cuckoo*
  C. americanus
Black-billed Cuckoo
  C. erythropthalmus
Roadrunner*
(Greater Roadrunner)
  Geococcyx californianus
Smooth-billed Ani (H)
  Crotophaga ani
Groove-billed Ani*
  C. sulcirostris

STRIGIFORMES: Owls
TYTONIDAE: Barn Owl
Barn Owl*
  Tyto alba
STRIGIDAE: Typical Owls
Screech Owl*
(Common Screech Owl)
  Otus asio
Flammulated Owl*
(Flammulated Screech Owl)
  O. flammeolus
Great Horned Owl*
  Bubo virginianus
Snowy Owl (A)
  Nyctea scandiaca
Pygmy Owl (A)
(Northern Pygmy Owl)
  Glaucidium gnoma
Ferruginous Owl*
(Ferruginous Pygmy Owl)
  G. brasilianum
Elf Owl*
  Micrathene whitneyi

Burrowing Owl*
  Athene cunicularia
Barred Owl*
  Strix varia
Spotted Owl*
  S. occidentalis
Long-eared Owl*
  Asio otus
Short-eared Owl
  A. flammeus
Saw-whet Owl* (A)
(Northern Saw-whet Owl)
  Aegolius acadicus

CAPRIMULGIFORMES: Goatsuckers
CAPRIMULGIDAE: Goatsuckers
Chuck-will's-widow*
  Caprimulgus carolinensis
Whip-poor-will*
  C. vociferus
Poor-will*
(Common Poorwill)
  Phalaenoptilus nuttallii
Pauraque*
  Nyctidromus albicollis
Common Nighthawk*
  Chordeiles minor
Lesser Nighthawk*
  C. acutipennis

APODIFORMES: Swifts and Hummingbirds
APODIDAE: Swifts
White-collared Swift (H)†
  Streptoprocne zonaris
Black Swift (H)
  Cypseloides niger
Chimney Swift*
  Chaetura pelagica
Vaux's Swift (H)
  C. vauxi
White-throated Swift*
  Aeronautes saxatalis

TROCHILIDAE: Hummingbirds
Crested Hummingbird (A)†
  Orthorhyncus cristatus
Green Violet-ear (A)
  Colibri thalassinus
Black-crested Coquette (H)†
  Paphosia helenae
Lucifer Hummingbird*
  Calothorax lucifer
Ruby-throated Hummingbird*
  Archilochus colubris
Black-chinned Hummingbird*
  A. alexandri
Costa's Hummingbird (A)
  Calypte costae
Anna's Hummingbird
  C. anna
Broad-tailed Hummingbird*
  Selasphorus platycercus
Rufous Hummingbird
  S. rufus
Allen's Hummingbird
  S. sasin
Calliope Hummingbird (A)
  Stellula calliope

Rivoli's Hummingbird
(Magnificent Hummingbird)
  Eugenes fulgens
Blue-throated Hummingbird*
  Lampornis clemenciae
Rieffer's Hummingbird (A)
  Amazilia tzacatl
Buff-bellied Hummingbird*
  A. yucatanensis
White-eared Hummingbird (A)
  Hylocharis leucotis
Broad-billed Hummingbird (A)
  Cynanthus latirostris

TROGONIFORMES: Trogons
TROGONIDAE: Trogons
Coppery-tailed Trogon (A)
(Elegant Trogan)
  Trogon elegans

CORACIIFORMES: Kingfishers
ALCEDINIDAE: Kingfishers
Belted Kingfisher*
  Ceryle alcyon
Ringed Kingfisher*
  C. torquata
Green Kingfisher*
  Chloroceryle americana

PICIFORMES: Woodpeckers
PICIDAE: Woodpeckers
Common Flicker*
"Yellow-shafted, Red-shafted and
Gilded Flickers"
  Colaptes auratus
Pileated Woodpecker*
  Dryocopus pileatus
Red-bellied Woodpecker*
  Melanerpes carolinus
Golden-fronted Woodpecker*
  M. aurifrons
Red-headed Woodpecker*
  M. erythrocephalus
Acorn Woodpecker*
  M. formicivorus
Lewis' Woodpecker (A)
  M. lewis
Yellow-bellied Sapsucker
  Sphyrapicus varius
Williamson's Sapsucker
  S. thyroideus
Hairy Woodpecker*
  Picoides villosus
Downy Woodpecker*
  P. pubescens
Ladder-backed Woodpecker*
  P. scalaris
Red-cockaded Woodpecker*
  P. borealis
Ivory-billed Woodpecker (A)
  Campephilus principalis

PASSERIFORMES: Perching Birds
COTINGIDAE: Cotingas
Rufous Mourner (H)†
  Rhytipterna holerythra
Rose-throated Becard*
  Platypsaris aglaiae

Jamaican Becard (H)†
  P. niger

TYRANNIDAE: Tyrant Flycatchers
Eastern Kingbird*
  Tyrannus tyrannus
Gray Kingbird (A)
  T. dominicensis
Tropical Kingbird*
[May be split into *T. melancholus*,
Tropical Kingbird (A) and *T. couchii*,
Thorn-scrub Kingbird]
  T. melancholicus
Western Kingbird*
  T. verticalis
Thick-billed Kingbird†
  T. crassirostris
Cassin's Kingbird*
  T. vociferans
Fork-tailed Flycatcher (A)
  Muscivora tyrannus
Scissor-tailed Flycatcher*
  M. forficata
Kiskadee Flycatcher*
(Kiskadee) (Great Kiskadee)
  Pitangus sulphuratus
Sulphur-bellied Flycatcher (A)
  Myiodynastes luteiventris
Streaked Flycatcher (H)
  M. maculatus
Great Crested Flycatcher*
  Myiarchus crinitus
Wied's Crested Flycatcher*
(Brown-crested Flycatcher)
  M. tyrannulus
Ash-throated Flycatcher*
  M. cinerascens
Olivaceous Flycatcher (A)
(Dusky-capped Flycatcher)
  M. tuberculifer
Eastern Phoebe*
  Sayornis phoebe
Black Phoebe*
  S. nigricans
Say's Phoebe*
  S. saya
Yellow-bellied Flycatcher
  Empidonax flaviventris
Acadian Flycatcher*
  E. virescens

Willow Flycatcher
"Traill's Flycatcher"
  E. traillii
Alder Flycatcher
"Traill's Flycatcher"
  E. alnorum
Least Flycatcher
  E. minimus
Hammond's Flycatcher
  E. hammondii
Dusky Flycatcher
  E. oberholseri
Gray Flycatcher
  E. wrightii
Western Flycatcher*
  E. difficilis

Buff-breasted Flycatcher (H)
E. fulvifrons
Coues' Flycatcher (A)
(Greater Pewee)
Contopus pertinax
Eastern Wood Pewee*
(Eastern Pewee)
C. virens
Western Wood Pewee*
(Western Pewee)
C. sordidulus
Olive-sided Flycatcher*
Nuttallornis borealis
Vermilion Flycatcher*
Pyrocephalus rubinus
Beardless Flycatcher
(Northern Beardless Tyrannulet)
Camptostoma imberbe
ALAUDIDAE: Larks
Horned Lark*
Eremophila alpestris

HIRUNDINIDAE: Swallows
Violet-green Swallow*
Tachycineta thalassina
Tree Swallow
T. bicolor
Bank Swallow
Riparia riparia
Rough-winged Swallow*
Stelgidopteryx ruficollis
Barn Swallow*
Hirundo rustica
Cliff Swallow*
Petrochelidon pyrrhonota
Cave Swallow*
P. fulva
Purple Martin*
Progne subis
Gray-breasted Martin (A)
P. chalybea

CORVIDAE: Jays and Crows
Blue Jay*
Cyanocitta cristata
Steller's Jay*
C. stelleri
Scrub Jay*
Aphelocoma coerulescens
Mexican Jay*
(Gray-breasted Jay)
A. ultramarina
Green Jay*
Cyanocorax yncas
Black-billed Magpie (A)
Pica pica
Common Raven*
(Northern Raven)
Corvus corax
White-necked Raven*
C. cryptoleucus
Common Crow*
(American Crow)
C. brachyrhynchos
Mexican Crow†
C. imparatus
Fish Crow*
C. ossifragus

Piñon Jay
(Pinyon Jay)
Gymnorhinus cyanocephalus
Clark's Nutcracker (A)
Nucifraga columbiana
Brown Jay*†
Psilorhinus morio
PARIDAE: Titmice, Verdins, and Bushtits
Black-capped Chickadee (H)
Parus atricapillus
Carolina Chickadee*
P. carolinensis
Mexican Chickadee (H)
(Gray-sided Chickadee)
P. sclateri
Mountain Chickadee*
P. gambeli
Tufted Titmouse*
"Black-crested Titmouse"
P. bicolor
Plain Titmouse*
P. inornatus
Bridled Titmouse (H)
P. wollweberi
Verdin*
Auriparus flaviceps
Bushtit*
"Common Bushtit"
"Black-eared Bushtit"
Psaltriparus minimus
SITTIDAE: Nuthatches
White-breasted Nuthatch*
Sitta carolinensis
Red-breasted Nuthatch
S. canadensis
Brown-headed Nuthatch*
S. pusilla
Pygmy Nuthatch*
S. pygmaea
CERTHIIDAE: Creepers
Brown Creeper
Certhia familiaris
CINCLIDAE: Dippers
Dipper (A)
(North American Dipper) (American Dipper)
Cinclus mexicanus
TROGLODYTIDAE: Wrens
House Wren*
(Northern House Wren)
Troglodytes aedon
Brown-throated Wren (H)
T. brunneicollis
Winter Wren
T. troglodytes
Bewick's Wren*
Thryomanes bewickii
Carolina Wren*
Thryothorus ludovicianus
Cactus Wren*
Campylorhynchus brunneicapillus
Long-billed Marsh Wren
(Marsh Wren)
Cistothorus palustris
Short-billed Marsh Wren
(Sedge Wren)
C. platensis

Cañon Wren*
(Canyon Wren)
Catherpes mexicanus
Rock Wren*
Salpinctes obsoletus

MIMIDAE: Mockingbirds and Thrashers
Mockingbird*
(Northern Mockingbird)
Mimus polyglottos
Black Catbird (H)†
Melanoptila glabrirostris
Gray Catbird*
"Catbird"
Dumetella carolinensis
Brown Thrasher*
Toxostoma rufum
Long-billed Thrasher*
T. longirostre
Bendire's Thrasher (H)
T. bendirei
Curve-billed Thrasher*
T. curvirostre
Crissal Thrasher*
T. dorsale
Sage Thrasher
Oreoscoptes montanus

TURDIDAE: Thrushes, Solitaires, and Bluebirds
American Robin*
"Robin"
Turdus migratorius
Rufous-backed Robin (A)†
T. rufopalliatus
Clay-colored Robin (A)†
T. grayi
Varied Thrush (A)
Ixoreus naevius
Aztec Thrush (A)†
Ridgwayia pinicola
Wood Thrush*
Hylocichla mustelina
Hermit Thrush*
Catharus guttatus
Swainson's Thrush
C. ustulatus
Gray-cheeked Thrush
C. minimus
Veery
C. fuscescens
Eastern Bluebird*
Sialia sialis
Western Bluebird*
S. mexicana
Mountain Bluebird
S. currucoides
Townsend's Solitaire
Myadestes townsendi

SYLVIIDAE: Gnatcatchers and Kinglets
Blue-gray Gnatcatcher*
Polioptila caerulea
Black-tailed Gnatcatcher*
P. melanura
Golden-crowned Kinglet
Regulus satrapa
Ruby-crowned Kinglet
R. calendula

MOTACILLIDAE: Pipits
  Water Pipit
    Anthus spinoletta

PTILOGONATIDAE: Silky Flycatchers
  Phainopepla*
    Phainopepla nitens
LANIIDAE: Shrikes
  Northern Shrike (A)
    Lanius excubitor
  Loggerhead Shrike*
    L. ludovicianus
STURNIDAE: Starlings
  Starling*
  (European Starling) (Common
  Starling)
    Sturnus vulgaris
VIREONIDAE: Vireos
  Black-capped Vireo*
    Vireo atricapilla
  White-eyed Vireo*
    V. griseus
  Hutton's Vireo*
    V. huttoni
  Bell's Vireo*
    V. bellii
  Gray Vireo*
    V. vicinior
  Yellow-throated Vireo*
    V. flavifrons
  Solitary Vireo*
    V. solitarius
  Black-whiskered Vireo (A)
    V. altiloquus
  Yellow-green Vireo (A)
    V. flavoviridis
  Red-eyed Vireo*
    V. olivaceus
  Philadelphia Vireo
    V. philadelphicus
  Warbling Vireo*
    V. gilvus

PARULIDAE: Wood Warblers
  Black-and-white Warbler*
    Mniotilta varia
  Prothonotary Warbler*
    Protonotaria citrea
  Swainson's Warbler*
    Limnothlypis swainsonii
  Worm-eating Warbler
    Helmitheros vermivorus
  Golden-winged Warbler
    Vermivora chrysoptera
  Blue-winged Warbler
    V. pinus
  Bachman's Warbler (H)
    V. bachmanii
  Tennessee Warbler
    V. peregrina
  Orange-crowned Warbler
    V. celata
  Nashville Warbler
    V. ruficapilla
  Sprague's Pipit
    A. spragueii

BOMBYCILLIDAE: Waxwings
  Bohemian Waxwing (A)
    Bombycilla garrulus
  Cedar Waxwing
    B. cedrorum
  Virginia's Warbler*
    V. virginiae
  Colima Warbler*
    V. crissalis
  Lucy's Warbler*
    V. luciae
  Northern Parula*
  "Parula Warbler" (Northern Parula
  Warbler)
    Parula americana
  Tropical Parula*
  "Olive-backed Warbler"
    P. pitiayumi
  Olive Warbler (H)
    Peucedramus taeniatus
  Yellow Warbler*
    Dendroica petechia
  Mangrove Warbler (A)†
    D. erithachorides
  Magnolia Warbler
    D. magnolia
  Cape May Warbler
    D. tigrina
  Black-throated Blue Warbler
    D. caerulescens
  Yellow-rumped Warbler*
  "Myrtle Warbler" "Audubon's
  Warbler"
    D. coronata
  Black-throated Gray Warbler
    D. nigrescens
  Townsend's Warbler
    D. townsendi
  Black-throated Green Warbler
    D. virens
  Golden-cheeked Warbler*
    D. chrysoparia
  Hermit Warbler
    D. occidentalis
  Cerulean Warbler
    D. cerulea
  Blackburnian Warbler
    D. fusca
  Yellow-throated Warbler*
    D. dominica
  Grace's Warbler*
    D. graciae
  Chestnut-sided Warbler
    D. pensylvanica
  Bay-breasted Warbler
    D. castanea

  Blackpoll Warbler
    D. striata
  Pine Warbler*
    D. pinus
  Prairie Warbler*
    D. discolor
  Palm Warbler
    D. palmarum

  Ovenbird
    Seiurus aurocapillus
  Northern Waterthrush
    S. noveboracensis
  Louisiana Waterthrush*
    S. motacilla
  Kentucky Warbler*
    Oporornis formosus
  Connecticut Warbler
    O. agilis
  Mourning Warbler
    O. philadelphia
  MacGillivray's Warbler
    O. tolmiei
  Common Yellowthroat*
  "Yellowthroat"
    Geothlypis trichas
  Ground-chat (A)
    G. poliocephala
  Yellow-breasted Chat*
    Icteria virens
  Red-faced Warbler (H)
    Cardellina rubrifrons
  Hooded Warbler*
    Wilsonia citrina
  Wilson's Warbler
    W. pusilla
  Canada Warbler
    W. canadensis
  American Redstart*
    Setophaga ruticilla
  Painted Redstart*
    Myioborus pictus
  Golden-crowned Warbler (A)†
    Basileuterus culicivorus
  Rufous-capped Warbler (A)†
    B. rufifrons
PLOCEIDAE: Weaver Finches
  House Sparrow*
    Passer domesticus

ICTERIDAE: Meadowlarks, Blackbirds,
and Orioles
  Bobolink
    Dolichonyx oryzivorus
  Eastern Meadowlark*
    Sturnella magna
  Western Meadowlark*
    S. neglecta
  Yellow-headed Blackbird
    Xanthocephalus xanthocephalus
  Red-winged Blackbird*
    Agelaius phoeniceus
  Orchard Oriole*
    Icterus spurius
  Ochre Oriole (A)
    I. fuertesi
  Black-headed Oriole*
    I. graduacauda
  Hooded Oriole*
    I. cucullatus
  Lichtenstein's Oriole*
  (Altamira Oriole)
    I. gularis
  Scott's Oriole*
    I. parisorum

Black-vented Oriole (A)†
  I. wagleri
Northern Oriole*
"Baltimore Oriole" "Bullock's Oriole"
  I. galbula
Rusty Blackbird
  Euphagus carolinus
Brewer's Blackbird*
  E. cyanocephalus
Boat-tailed Grackle*
  Quiscalus major
Great-tailed Grackle*
"Boat-tailed Grackle", in part
  Q. mexicanus
Common Grackle*
  Q. quiscula
Brown-headed Cowbird*
  Molothrus ater
Bronzed Cowbird*
  M. aeneus
THRAUPIDAE: Tanagers
Western Tanager*
  Piranga ludoviciana
Scarlet Tanager
  P. olivacea
Hepatic Tanager*
  P. flava
Summer Tanager*
  P. rubra
FRINGILLIDAE: Grosbeaks, Finches,
Sparrows, and Buntings
Crimson-collared Grosbeak (A)†
  Rhodothraupis celaeno
Cardinal*
(Northern Cardinal) (Red Cardinal)
  Cardinalis cardinalis
Pyrrhuloxia*
  C. sinuatus
Rose-breasted Grosbeak
  Pheucticus ludovicianus
Black-headed Grosbeak*
  P. melanocephalus
Blue Grosbeak*
  Guiraca caerulea
Blue Bunting (A)†
  Cyanocompsa parellina
Indigo Bunting*
  Passerina cyanea
Lazuli Bunting
  P. amoena
Varied Bunting*
  P. versicolor
Painted Bunting*
  P. ciris
Orange-breasted Bunting (H)†
  P. leclancherii
Dickcissel*
  Spiza americana
Evening Grosbeak
  Hesperiphona vespertina

Purple Finch
  Carpodacus purpureus
Cassin's Finch
  C. cassinii
House Finch*
  C. mexicanus
White-collared Seedeater
  Sporophila torqueola
Pine Grosbeak (A)
  Pinicola enucleator
Common Redpoll (H)
  Carduelis flammea
Pine Siskin*
  C. pinus
American Goldfinch
  C. tristis
Lesser Goldfinch*
(Dark-backed Goldfinch)
  C. psaltria
Lawrence's Goldfinch (A)
  C. lawrencei
Red Crossbill*
  Loxia curvirostra
White-winged Crossbill
  L. leucoptera
Olive Sparrow*
  Arremonops rufivirgatus
Green-tailed Towhee
  Pipilo chlorurus
Rufous-sided Towhee*
  P. erythrophthalmus
Brown Towhee*
  P. fuscus
Abert's Towhee (H)
  P. aberti
Lark Bunting*
  Calamospiza melanocorys
Savannah Sparrow
  Passerculus sandwichensis
Grasshopper Sparrow*
  Ammodramus savannarum
Baird's Sparrow
  A. bairdii
Le Conte's Sparrow
  Ammospiza leconteii
Henslow's Sparrow*
  A. henslowii
Sharp-tailed Sparrow*
  A. caudacuta
Seaside Sparrow*
  A. maritima
Vesper Sparrow
  Pooecetes gramineus
Lark Sparrow*
  Chondestes grammacus
Rufous-crowned Sparrow*
  Aimophila ruficeps

Bachman's Sparrow*
  A. aestivalis
Botteri's Sparrow*
  A. botterii
Cassin's Sparrow*
  A. cassinii
Black-throated Sparrow*
  Amphispiza bilineata
Sage Sparrow
  A. belli
Dark-eyed Junco
"Slate-colored Junco" "Oregon Junco"
  Junco hyemalis
Gray-headed Junco*
  J. caniceps
Yellow-eyed Junco (H)
"Mexican Junco"
  J. phaeonotus
Tree Sparrow
(American Tree Sparrow)
  Spizella arborea
Chipping Sparrow*
  S. passerina
Clay-colored Sparrow
  S. pallida
Brewer's Sparrow
  S. breweri
Field Sparrow*
  S. pusilla
Black-chinned Sparrow*
  S. atrogularis
Harris' Sparrow
  Zonotrichia querula
White-crowned Sparrow
  Z. leucophrys
Golden-crowned Sparrow
  Z. atricapilla
White-throated Sparrow
  Z. albicollis
Fox Sparrow
  Passerella iliaca
Lincoln's Sparrow
  Melospiza lincolnii
Swamp Sparrow
  M. georgiana
Song Sparrow
  M. melodia
McCown's Longspur
  Calcarius mccownii
Lapland Longspur
  C. lapponicus
Smith's Longspur
  C. pictus
Chestnut-collared Longspur
  C. ornatus
Snow Bunting (A)
  Plectrophenax nivalis

A Guide to
Regional Lists of Texas Birds

Llano Estacado

Field Check-list: Birds of Midland County, Texas, 7th edition, January 1978. Compiled by Frances Williams. Midland Naturalists, Inc., 3307 Neely, Midland, Texas 79703. 25¢ plus addressed, stamped envelope.

Field Check-list: Birds of Potter and Randall Counties, Texas, 3rd edition, April 1977, Texas Panhandle Audubon Society, Amarillo, Texas. % K. D. Seyffert, 2206 S. Lipscomb, Amarillo, Texas 79109. 25¢ plus addressed, stamped envelope.

Birds of the Texas South Plains, 4th edition, November 1978. Llano Estacado Audubon Society, P. O. Box 3603, Lubbock, Texas 79450. 25¢ each; 5 for $1.00 plus addressed, stamped envelope.

A Check-list of the Birds of Palo Duro Canyon State Park, August 1975. Compiled by Kenneth Seyffert, Peggy Acord, and Charles Smith. Texas Parks and Wildlife Department, Resource Management Section, 4200 Smith School Road, Austin, Texas 78744.

Birds of Buffalo Lake National Wildlife Refuge, July 1974. Buffalo Lake National Wildlife Refuge, P. O. Box 228, Umbarger, Texas 79091.

A Birder's Checklist: Lake Meredith Recreation Area, September 1976. Compiled in cooperation with the Texas Panhandle Audubon Society. Lake Meredith National Recreation Area, P. O. Box 2438, Fritch, Texas 79036.

Birds of Muleshoe National Wildlife Refuge, August 1979. Refuge Manager, Muleshoe National Wildlife Refuge, P. O. Box 549, Muleshoe, Texas 79347.

Trans-Pecos

Field Checklist: Birds of El Paso County, Texas and Adjacent Areas, 6th edition, June 1980. Compiled by Joe DiPasquale, Jeff Donaldson, John A. Sproul, Jr., Barry R. Zimmer, Kevin J. Zimmer. Published by El Paso/Trans-Pecos Audubon Society, 1305 Oak Drive, El Paso, Texas 79925. 30¢ (includes postage).

Birds of the Davis Mountains State Park: A Seasonal Checklist, July 1978. Compiled by Frances Williams and Pansy

Espy. Texas Parks and Wildlife Department, 4200 Smith School Road, Austin, Texas 78744.

Birds of Leaton State Historic Site, Presidio County, Texas: A Field Checklist, August 1979. Compiled by Steve West. Texas Parks and Wildlife Department, Resource Management Section, 4200 Smith School Road, Austin, Texas 78744.

Birds of Hueco Tanks State Historical Park: A Field Checklist, December 1977. Compiled by Kevin Zimmer. Texas Parks and Wildlife Department, 4200 Smith School Road, Austin, Texas 78744.

Bird Checklist: Big Bend National Park, Texas. Original list (July 1968) by Roland H. Wauer. Revised August 1973 by David A. Easterla. Revised September 1978 by Peter Scott. Big Bend Natural History Association, Inc., Big Bend National Park, Texas 79834. 10¢.

Check-list of Birds: Guadalupe Mountains National Park, Culberson County, Texas, 1974. Compiled by George A. Newman, Department of Biology, Hardin-Simmons University, Abilene, Texas, 79601. 25¢

Rolling Plains

Preliminary Checklist of the Birds of Coleman County, Texas, June 1978. Compiled by Charles W. Sexton, 4614 Hank Avenue, Austin, Texas 78745. Addressed, stamped envelope.

Field Checklist: Birds of the Concho Valley Region, Texas, 1979. Compiled by Terry C. Maxwell, Department of Biology, Angelo State University, San Angelo, Texas 76901. Addressed, stamped envelope.

The Birds of North Central Texas, 2nd edition, June 1976. Compiled by Kathleen S. Zinn and Nancy Moore, % North Texas Bird and Wildlife Club, 4434 Callfield Road, Wichita Falls, Texas 76308. 20¢ plus addressed, stamped envelope.

Checklist of Birds: Abilene State Recreation Area, September 1977. Compiled by George A. Newman. Resource Management Section, Texas Parks and Wildlife Department, 4200 Smith School Road, Austin, Texas 78744.

Edwards Plateau

Checklist of Birds of Kerr County, Texas (supplement dated November 10, 1977). Compiled by Col. L. R. Wolfe. Main Bookstore, 229 Earl Garrett Street, Kerrville, Texas 78028. $1.50 plus 20¢ postage.

Birds of Kerr County and Surrounding Area, March 1978. Compiled by Ernest and Kay Mueller, 207 Spanish Oak Lane, Kerrville, Texas 78028. Addressed, stamped envelope.

Check List and Seasonal Distribution: Birds of the Austin, Texas Region, 5th edition, May 1978. Compiled by Travis Audubon Society Bird Records Committee. Travis Audubon Society, % Mary Martin, 4915 Timberline, Austin, Texas 78746. 25¢ each; 5 for $1.00. Addressed, stamped envelope.

A Checklist of Birds of the Kerr Wildlife Management Area, Kerr County, Texas, May 1978. Compiled by Gregory L. Butts. Texas Parks and Wildlife Department, 4200 Smith School Road, Austin, Texas 78744.

Birds of LBJ State Historical Park: A Preliminary Seasonal Checklist, April 1976. Compiled by Stanley L. Archer. Resource Management Section, Texas Parks and Wildlife Department, 4200 Smith School Road, Austin, Texas 78744.

Birds of Lost Maples State Natural Area: Preliminary Field Checklist, October 1979. Contributors: Robert and Judy Mason, Warren Pulich, Ed Parrot, Kelly Bryan, Ed Kutac, John Sunder, Bruce Snyder, Travis Audubon Society, Fred and Nancy Gehlbach, and John Galley. Texas Parks and Wildlife Department, 4200 Smith School Road, Austin, Texas 78744.

Birds of Pedernales Falls State Park: A Seasonal Checklist, September 1976. Resource Management Section, Texas Parks and Wildlife Department, 4200 Smith School Road, Austin, Texas 78744.

Birds of Seminole Canyon State Historical Park: Preliminary Field Checklist, February 1980. Resource Management Section, Texas Parks and Wildlife Department, 4200 Smith School Road, Austin, Texas 78744.

Birding in Texas A comprehensive list of bird check lists available in Texas, March 1980. Compiled by David Riskind. For a free copy, write Resource Management Section, Texas Parks and Wildlife Department, 4200 Smith School Road, Austin, Texas 78744 (will be updated periodically).

Central Texas

A Check List of the Birds of Brazos and Adjacent Counties, Texas (Robertson, Grimes, Madison, Washington, and Burleson), 1977. Compiled by the Brazos Ornithological Society, P. O. Box 9181, College Station, Texas 77840. 25¢ plus addressed, stamped envelope.

Field Check List of Birds: Dallas County, Texas, December 1977. Compiled by Warren M. Pulich. % Bob Lanier, Dallas County Audubon Society, 2047 Christie Lane, Carrollton, Texas 75007, or % C. A. Smith, 2606 Burlington, Dallas, Texas 75211. 10¢ plus addressed, stamped envelope.

A Check List of the Birds of McLennan County, Texas, 1976. Waco Ornithological Society, % Strecker Museum, Baylor University, Waco, Texas 76798. 30¢ plus addressed, stamped envelope.

Field Check-List of the Birds of Tarrant County, Texas, 2nd edition, November 1967. Compiled by Bruce A. Mack, Fort Worth Audubon Society, % Fort Worth Museum of Science & History, 1501 Montgomery, Fort Worth, Texas 76107. 25¢ plus addressed, stamped envelope.

Birds of Buescher & Bastrop State Parks, June 1980. Compiled by Dr. Robert L. Neill. Texas Parks and Wildlife Department, Resource Management Section, 4200 Smith School Road, Austin, Texas 78744.

Birds of Lake Somerville State Recreation Area: A Field Checklist, April 1979. Compiled by Keith Arnold and Ken Ridlehuber. Texas Parks and Wildlife Department, Resource Management Section, 4200 Smith School Road, Austin, Texas 78744.

Birds of McKinney Falls State Park: A Field Checklist, 2nd edition, July 1977. Compiled by E. A. Kutac and D. H. Riskind. Texas Parks and Wildlife Department, Resource Management Section, 4200 Smith School Road, Austin, Texas 78744.

Mother Neff State Park: A Preliminary Bird Checklist, April 1979. Texas Parks and Wildlife Department, Resource Management Section, 4200 Smith School Road, Austin, Texas 78744.

Birds of Palmetto State Park, February 1977. Compiled by Rose Ann Rowlett, Ray Chancellor, and Fred Webster. Texas Parks and Wildlife Department, Resource Management Section, 4200 Smith School Road, Austin, Texas 78744.

Birds of the Hagerman National Wildlife Refuge, December 1975. Hagerman National Wildlife Refuge, % Refuge Manager, Route 3, Box B 123, Sherman, Texas 75090.

Checklist of Birds of Heard Wildlife Sanctuary. Heard Museum, Route 2, McKinney, Texas 75069. Addressed, stamped envelope.

Birds of the Fort Worth Nature Center and Refuge. Compiled by Tom Wood. Fort Worth Audubon Society, % Fort Worth Museum of Science & History, 1501 Montgomery, Fort Worth, Texas 76107.

Preliminary Checklist to the Birds of Eisenhower State Park, August 1975. Compiled by Resource Management Section, Texas Parks and Wildlife Department, 4200 Smith School Road, Austin, Texas 78744.

Birds of Meridian State Recreation Area: A Field Checklist, May 1980. Compiled by Dr. Warren M. Pulich. Texas Parks and Wildlife Department, Resource Management Section, 4200 Smith School Road, Austin, Texas 78744.

Birds of Lake Whitney State Recreation Area, May 1976. Compiled by Larry Barnett, Mr. and Mrs. S. T. Bozeman, John and Katie Casstevens, Tom Hakney, Bill Kirkpatrick, Warren Pulich, Jim and Grace Reeves, Jessie Mae Smith, and August and Mildred Twiest. Texas Parks and Wildlife Department, Resource Management Section, 4200 Smith School Road, Austin, Texas 78744.

Pineywoods

Checklist of the Birds: Nacogdoches County and Lake Sam Rayburn, January 1979. Compiled by Charles D. Fisher and David Wolf. University Bookstore, SFASU, Box 3057, Nacogdoches, Texas 75962. 10¢ plus addressed, stamped #10 envelope.

Field Checklist: Birds of Smith County, Texas, revised July 1976. Compiled by the Tyler Audubon Society. % Gerald Smith, 3100 S. Donnybrook, Tyler, Texas 75701. 25¢ plus addressed, stamped envelope.

A Checklist of the Birds of Walker County, Texas, September 1978. Compiled by Ralph R. Moldenhauer and Kelly B. Bryan. University Bookstore, Sam Houston State University, Huntsville, Texas 77341. 15¢ plus addressed, stamped envelope.

A Tentative Checklist of the Birds of the Gus A. Engeling Wildlife Management Area and Anderson County, Texas, November 1974. Compiled by George H. Veteto, Charles E. Davis, and Ray V. Hart. Texas Parks and Wildlife Department, Resource Management Section, 4200 Smith School Road, Austin, Texas 78744.

Birds of Huntsville State Park, May 1977. Compiled by Kelly Bryan. Texas Parks and Wildlife Department, Resource Management Section, 4200 Smith School Road, Austin, Texas 78744.

Gulf Coast

Checklist of the Birds: Central Coast of Texas, 1976. Compiled by Gene W. Blacklock (Welder Wildlife Foundation), Corpus Christi Museum, 1919 W. Water Street, Corpus Christi, Texas 78401. 25¢ plus addressed, stamped envelope.

Checklist of the Birds of Nueces County, Texas, 2nd edition, 1967. Compiled by Corpus Christi Outdoor Club, P. O. Box 3352, Corpus Christi, Texas 78404. 25¢ plus addressed, stamped envelope.

A Bird Checklist for the Lower Sabine-Neches Area (Southwest Louisiana-Southeast Texas), October 1978. Compiled by John M. Read. Sabine Audubon Society, % Treasurer, P. O. Box 758, Orange, Texas 77630. 10¢ plus addressed, stamped envelope.

Sea Gun Resort Hotel: Checklist of the More Abundant Area Birds. Compiled by Mrs. Connie Hagar. Sea Gun Resort Hotel, Route 1, Box 85, Rockport, Texas 78382. Addressed, stamped envelope.

A Birder's Checklist of the Upper Texas Coast, 6th edition, January 1980. Compiled by T. Ben Feltner and A. Noel Pettingell. Ornithology Group, Houston Outdoor Nature Club, % Mrs. J. M. Gillette, 5027 Longmont, Houston, Texas 77056. 10¢ plus addressed, stamped envelope.

Birds of Galveston Island State Park, September 1976. Compiled by Mrs. J. A. (Linda) Snyder. Texas Parks and Wildlife Department, Resource Management Section, 4200 Smith School Road, Austin, Texas 78744.

Birds of Goose Island State Recreation Area: A Field Checklist, January 1980. Compiled by Audubon Outdoor Club of Corpus Christi. Texas Parks and Wildlife Department, Resource Management Section, 4200 Smith School Road, Austin, Texas 78744.

Birds of Sea Rim State Park, October 1976. Compiled by Raymond Fleetwood, Dr. William Graber, Michael Hoke, Ornithology Group of the Outdoor Nature Club of Houston. Texas Parks and Wildlife Department, Resource Management Section, 4200 Smith School Road, Austin, Texas 78744.

Aransas Birds, March 1975. Aransas National Wildlife Refuge, P. O. Box 68, Austwell, Texas 77950. Addressed, stamped envelope.

Birds of the Anahuac National Wildlife Refuge, April 1976. Anahuac National Wildlife Refuge, P. O. Box 278, Anahuac, Texas 77514. Addressed, stamped envelope.

Birds of the Brazoria National Wildlife Refuge, October 1972. Brazoria National Wildlife Refuge, P. O. Box 1088, Angleton, Texas 77515. Addressed, stamped envelope.

Birds of Attwater Prairie Chicken National Wildlife Refuge, Texas, November 1980. Attwater Prairie Chicken National Wildlife Refuge, P. O. Box 518, Eagle Lake, Texas 77434. Addressed, stamped envelope.

Checklist of the Birds: Padre Island National Seashore, Texas, revised 1976. Compiled by Richard E. McCamant and Robert C. Whistler. Padre Island National Seashore, 9405 S. Padre Island Dr., Corpus Christi, Texas 78418.

Birds of San Bernard National Wildlife Refuge, August 1973. San Bernard National Wildlife Refuge, P. O. Drawer 1088, Angleton, Texas 77515. Addressed, stamped envelope.

Field Trip Record for the Birds of Texas' Golden Crescent, Compiled by Howard Pierce for the area surrounding Victoria from Rockport to Freeport, west to Luling, south to Three Rivers, then east to Rockport. Available from Dr. Peter Reisz, 6120 Country Club Drive, Victoria, Texas 77901 for 10¢ plus a stamped, addressed envelope.

South Texas

Checklist of the Birds of Jim Wells County, Texas, 1974. Compiled by Richard O. Albert, 1800 Newell Street, Alice, Texas 78332. 25¢ plus addressed, stamped envelope.

Birds of Bentsen-Rio Grande Valley State Park: A Field Checklist, January 1981. Compiled by John C. Arvin. Texas Parks and Wildlife Department, 4200 Smith School Road, Austin, Texas 78744.

Birds: A Field Checklist: Falcon State Recreation Area, March 1977. Compiled by John C. Arvin, Texas Parks and Wildlife Department, 4200 Smith School Road, Austin, Texas 78744.

Birds of Goliad State Historical Park: A Field Checklist, September 1979. Compiled by Gene W. Blacklock. Texas Parks and Wildlife Department, Resource Management Section, 4200 Smith School Road, Austin, Texas 78744.

Birds of Lake Corpus Christi State Recreation Area, May 1978. Compiled by Gene W. Blacklock. Texas Parks and Wildlife Department, Resource Management Section, 4200 Smith School Road, Austin, Texas 78744.

Birds of Laguna Atascosa National Wildlife Refuge, Texas, July 1973. Laguna Atascosa National Wildlife Refuge, P. O. Box 2683, Harlingen, Texas 78550.

Birds of Santa Ana National Wildlife Refuge, January 1978. Refuge Manager, Route 1, Box 202A, Alamo, Texas 78516.

Checklist of the Birds: Welder Wildlife Refuge, 1978. Compiled by G. W. Blacklock, Welder Wildlife Foundation, Drawer 1400, Sinton, Texas 78387. Addressed, stamped envelope.

Check List of Bexar County Birds, 1980. Prepared by San Antonio Audubon Society, San Antonio Garden Center, 3310 North New Braunfels, San Antonio, Texas, 78209. 15¢ plus addressed, stamped envelope.

Bird Organizations

National Bird Organizations

National Audubon Society
950 Third Avenue
New York, New York 10022
(Publishes *American Birds*, a bimonthly journal covering birds and birding in America.)

American Birding Association
P.O. Box 4335
Austin, TX 78765
(Publishes *Birding*, a bimonthly that promotes the hobby and sport of birding.)

American Ornithologists' Union
National Museum of Natural History
Smithsonian Institution
Washington, DC 20560

Cooper Ornithological Society
Department of Zoology
University of California
Los Angeles, CA 90052

Wilson Ornithological Society
Museum of Zoology
University of Michigan
Ann Arbor, MI 48104

Cornell Laboratory of Ornithology
159 Sapsucker Woods Road
Ithaca, NY 14850

State Bird Organization

Texas Ornithological Society, 1736 Albans, Houston, Texas 77005. Newsletter: *T.O.S. Newsletter*, monthly except summer. Field trips at semi-annual meetings. Publish *T.O.S. Bulletin* on Texas bird research semi-annually. Semi-annual meetings in various locations around the state. 750 members.

Local Texas Bird Organizations

The following organizations answered a questionnaire mailed to all groups for which an address was known.

They are arranged alphabetically by principal city of the area represented. If the address is a different city, the principal city is shown in parentheses.

Abilene Naturalist Society, % Mr. Jack Joy, Director, Abilene Zoological Gardens, P. O. Box 60, Abilene, Texas 79064. Participates in Christmas Bird Count. 10–15 members.

Alice Audubon Society, Richard O. Albert, President, 1800 Newell, Alice, Texas 78332. Field trips twice a month. Meetings first Tuesday of each month at Alice Public Library, Conference Room 1930. 20 members.
Big Bend Birders, % John R. Schmidt, Box 1438, Alpine, Texas 79830. Field trips: six or seven a year, especially in spring and fall. Participates in Alpine Christmas Bird Count and two Nesting Bird Surveys each June: "Longfellow" and "Altuda." 30 members. For bird information phone: John R. Schmidt (915) 837–2983, or Hal Flanders (915) 837–5656.

Texas Panhandle Audubon Society, 1400 Streit Drive, Amarillo, Texas 79106. Newsletter: *The Prairie Horned Lark*, monthly except summer. Field trips every other weekend. Participates in "Big Days," Christmas Bird Counts, and Festival of Trees. 110 members. For bird information phone: Kenneth Seyffert (806) 373–9580, or Peggy Acord (806) 352–6372.

Travis Audubon Society, % Natural Science Center, 401 Deep Eddy, Austin, Texas 78703. Newsletter: *Signal Smoke*, monthly. Operates 600-acre sanctuary; sponsors Audubon Wildlife Film Series, educational programs, conservation projects and field trips twice each month. Has monthly meetings. 1200 members. For bird information phone: E. A. Kutac (512) 926–3126.

Highland Lakes Birding Society, Burnet, Texas. Field trips once or twice per month, and spring and fall camping trips. Monthly meetings on first Thursdays, 10:00 A.M., Burnet Library (with nature programs). 30 members. For bird information phone: Keith Ackley (512) 793–2386, or Ursula Kramer (512) 756–2872.

Rio Brazos Audubon Society (formerly Brazos Ornithological Society), P. O. Box 9181, College Station, Texas 77840. Newsletter: *El Chaparral*, monthly except summer.

Field trips first Sunday of each month, October-May. Monthly meetings, September-May. 40 members. For bird information phone Keith Arnold (713) 845–6751, office, or (713) 846–3226, home; or Doug Slack (713) 845–6751, office, or (713) 693–2438, home.

Audubon Outdoor Club of Corpus Christi, P. O. Box 3352, Corpus Christi, Texas 78401. Field trips twice per month except in summer. Regular meetings. Sponsors four Audubon films per year. Supports a few organizations by contributions. 110+ members. For bird information phone: Sheriton Burr (512) 853–3287, Corpus Christi; or Charles Clark (512) 729–3396, Rockport.

Dallas County Audubon Society, 3544 Haynie, Dallas, Texas 75205. Newsletter: *Wood, Wings and Water*, monthly. Field trips weekly. Participate in conservation activities. 1400 members. For bird information phone: Charles Potter (214) 321–2176.

El Paso/Trans-Pecos Audubon Society, P. O. Box 9655, El Paso, Texas 79986. Newsletter: *The Roadrunner*, monthly except July and August. Field trips twice each month. Monthly general meetings except summer. Maintains Feather Lake Wildlife Sanctuary. Conducts El Paso and Hueco Tanks Christmas Bird Counts. 250 members. For bird information phone: Al and Madeline Gavit (915) 852–3119, El Paso; or Kevin Zimmer (505) 646–1735, Las Cruces, NM.

Fort Worth Audubon Society, Route 10, Box 53, Ft. Worth, Texas 76135. Newsletter: *Ft. Worth Audubon Newsletter*, monthly. Field trips twice monthly, September-May. Participates in Christmas and Spring Bird Counts. 650 members. For bird information phone: Tom Wood (817) 237–1111 or 246–9284; or Bob Coggeshall (817) 236–7407.

Bird Research Group, 5409 Braeburn, Bellaire (Houston), Texas 77401. Strictly a research organization, funded by Ornithology Group and the Houston Audubon Society. Involved presently in shorebird banding project on Bolivar Peninsula. 50 members. For information phone: Jim Morgan (713) 461–3080, or Ted Eubanks (713) 666–7639.

Ornithology Group of the Outdoor Nature Club, 4141 South Braeswood, Houston, Texas 77025. Newsletter: *Spoonbill*, monthly. Field trips monthly. Monthly meetings. Every other month's program is a seminar. Shorebird banding project. 250 members in Ornithology Group and 600 members in Outdoor Nature Club. For bird information phone: Margaret Anderson (713) 668–6405; Ron Braun (713) 496–3108; or David Dauphin (713) 383–3955.

Houston Audubon Society, 440 Wilchester, Houston, Texas 77079. Newsletter: *Houston Audubon Society Bulletin*, monthly. Field trips monthly. Monthly membership/program meetings; occasional classes and workshops.

Tours of Edith L. Moore Nature Sanctuary. 2900 members.

Llano Estacado Audubon Society, P. O. Box 6066, Lubbock, Texas 79413. Newsletter; *The Scissor-tail*, 10 times a year. Field trips twice each month. Members participate in several weekend birding/camping trips, annual pot luck dinners, 4th of July picnic and campout. 225 members. For bird information phone: Cliff Stogner (806) 795–2196, or Darleen Stevens (806) 797–8774.

Frontera Audubon Society, P. O. Box 4186, McAllen, Texas 78501. Newsletter: *The Alta Mira*, monthly. Field trips. Maintain natural trails in Methodist Camp. Sponsor bird trips to Central America. Sells houses to encourage Purple Martins in lower Rio Grande Valley. 350 members.

Midland Naturalists, Inc., Rt. 3, Box 667, Midland, Texas 79701. Field trips at least twice each month, January-May, and September-December; once a month in June, July, and August. One yearly meeting, usually in August or September. Other meetings as programs are available. Newsletter: *The Phalarope*, 10 times a year. 153 subscribers to *The Phalarope*. 15 active birders.

Nacogdoches County Aubudon Society, 306 Northgate, Nacogdoches, Texas. Newsletter: *Pinewoods Scissor-tales*, 8 issues a year. Regular Sunday morning field trips and other special events. Meetings on first Thursday evenings during school year. Participate in Christmas Bird Count and Spring Bird Count. 30 members. For bird information phone: Dr. C. D. Fisher (713) 569–7276, home, or 569–3601, office; or Susie Lower (713) 564–1744.

Sabine Audubon Society, Box 758, Orange, Texas 77630. Newsletter: *Wingbeat*, monthly, August-May. Field trips every two months, August-May. Sponsors Audubon Wildlife Film Series. 291 members.

San Antonio Audubon Society, 3310 North New Braufels, San Antonio Texas 78209. Newsletter: *San Antonio Audubon News*, monthly. Field trips, twice each month except summer. Monthly meetings, sponsors Audubon Wildlife Films, rare bird alert, educational programs for children, Bluebird Trail established and monitored by members, beginner bird walks. 250 members.

Texoma Outdoor Club, 2205 Ridgewood, Sherman, Texas 75090. Newsletter: *Warbler*, periodically. Field trips once or twice a month. Sponsors camping and canoeing trips, etc. 40 members.

Tyler Audubon Society, Tyler, Texas. Newsletter: *The Pine Warbler*, monthly, September-May. Field trips twice a month in fall and spring. Maintains Langley Island Sanctuary. Monthly meetings, September-May. Participates in Spring Bird Count and Christmas Bird Count.

90–95 members. For bird information phone: Gerald Smith (214) 592–8904, or Bill McClellan (214) 592–9816.

Golden Crescent Nature Club, Route 1, Box 84E, Victoria, Texas 77901. Newsletter: *De Rerum Natura*, monthly except during summer months. Field trips monthly. Participates in Christmas Bird Count and Breeding Bird Surveys. 35 members. For bird information phone: Frank or Jean Frankenburger (512) 575–5789; or Byron M. Griffin (512) 573–3477.

Central Texas Audubon Society, 4823 Hillcrest Drive, Waco, Texas 76710. Newsletter: *The Roadrunner*, monthly except summer. Field trips monthly, except summer; every two weeks in spring. Monthly meetings except summer. Participates in two Christmas Bird Counts and four Breeding Bird Surveys. Maintains a Bluebird Trail. Sponsors several educational projects in public and private schools and for senior citizens. 225 members. For bird information phone: Lillian Brown (817) 753–1670, Yvonne Daniel (817) 772–0077, or June Osborne (817) 772–0728.

North Texas Bird and Wildlife Club, 516 W. Aldine, Iowa Park (Wichita Falls), Texas 76367. Newsletter: *The Cardinal*, monthly. Monthly meetings. Participates in Christmas Bird Count. Members work with city and SCS to improve habitat at Lucy Park. 15 members. For bird information phone: Esther Crawford (817) 692–2023, or Margaret Broday (817) 723–9384.

Scientific Bird Collections in Texas

The following is a list of museums, institutions, and other locations of study skins, skeletons preserved in fluid, mounted birds, and egg set collections in Texas. These collections are maintained primarily for research by biologists; however, they are also very useful to persons interested in identification and variations within species. The collections are listed in descending order by number of study skins.

Texas A&M University, Department of Wildlife Science, College Station 77843. 10,750 skins, 50 skeletons, 220 in fluid, one mounted, 150 egg sets. Collection available to interested persons by prearrangement. Contact Dr. K. A. Arnold. Texas and Mexico represented in collection with approximately 450 Texas species.

Dallas Museum of Natural History, Fair Park Station, Box 26193, Dallas 75226. 7000 skins, 1000 mounted, 400 egg sets. Collection available to interested persons by prearrangement. Contact Steve R. Runnels, Curator of Ornithology. Texas is best represented in the collection with approximately 525 Texas species.

Texas Technological University, Department of Biology, Lubbock 79409. 3500 skins, 300 skeletons, 150 in fluid, 25 mounted, 30 egg sets. Collection available to interested persons by prearrangement. Contact Dr. Michael K. Rylander. Northwest Texas best represented with approximately 290 Texas species.

Stephen F. Austin State University, Dept. of Biology Box 3003, Nacogdoches, Texas 75961. 3000 skins, 15 mounted birds. Collection available to interested persons by prearrangement. Contact Charles D. Fisher. East Texas best represented with approximately 375 Texas species.

Welder Wildlife Refuge, Drawer 1400, Sinton 78387. 2500 skins, 4000 egg sets. Collection available to interested persons by prearrangement. Contact Gene W. Blacklock, Curator. South Texas well represented with approximately 500 Texas species.

University of Dallas, Department of Biology, Irving 75060. 2000 skins. Collection available Monday-Friday to scientists or persons doing special studies (only when curator present). Contact Warren Pulich. North-central Texas and parts of Texas Middle Coast best represented with 400+ Texas species.

Texas Memorial Museum, The University of Texas, Austin 78705. 1750 skins, 50 mounted, 500 egg sets. Collection available for research purposes (otherwise by exception). Contact Dr. R. F. Martin. Southwest U. S. and Northern Mexico best represented with approximately 296 Texas species.

Baylor University, Strecker Museum, Waco 76798. 1500 skins, 40 skeletons, 250 mounted, 1500 egg sets and nests. Collection available to interested persons by prearrangement. Contact Dr. Bryce C. Brown, Director. Texas best represented with approximately 200 Texas species.

Fort Worth Museum of Science and History, 1501 Montgomery Street, Ft. Worth 76107. 1370 skins (100 African), three skeletons, 200 mounted, 150 egg sets. Collection available to interested persons by prearrangement. Contact William J. Voss, Curator. Texas and Southwest best represented with approximately 80% Texas species.

Sam Houston State University, Huntsville 77341. 1300 skins, 10 skeletons, 65 mounted. Also have approximately 200 species of recorded bird sounds in Sound Library. Collection available to interested persons by prearrangement. Contact Ralph R. Moldenhauer. East Texas best represented with approximately 300 Texas species.

Corpus Christi Museum, 1919 N. Water Street, Corpus Christi 78401. 1217 skins, 10 entire skeletons, 40 skulls only, five in fluid, 107 mounted, 3301 egg sets. Collection available to interested persons by prearrangement. Contact Mr. Carrol L. Williams. Central Coast of Texas best represented with approximately 220 Texas species.

Sul Ross University, Alpine 79830. 1050 skins, 30 skeletons, 20 mounted, one egg set. Collection available to interested persons by prearrangement. Contact Dr. James F. Scudday. Trans-Pecos Texas and Chihuahuan Desert best represented with approximately 280 Texas species.

Midwestern University, Department of Biology, Wichita Falls 76308. 780 skins, 150 skeletons. Collection available to interested persons by prearrangement. Contact Dr. Walter W. Dalquest. Texas, Mozambique best represented.

University of Texas at Arlington, Arlington 76010. 750 skins, 150 in fluid. Collection available to interested persons by prearrangement. Contact John L. Darling. Texas, Guatemala best represented with approximately 130 Texas species.

Lamar State College of Technology, Department of Biology, Beaumont 77704. 670 skins. Collection available to interested persons by prearrangement. Contact Jed J. Ramsey. East Texas best represented.

Big Bend National Park, 79834. 309 skins, two egg sets. Collection available to interested persons. Contact Raymond Olivas. Big Bend National Park best represented with 220 Texas species.

Austin College, Biology Department, Sherman 75090. 250 skins. Collection available to interested persons by prearrangement. Contact Karl Haller. Local area represented with approximately 100 Texas species.

Spring Branch School System, Houston 77024, 250 skins, 60 skeletons, 150 mounted, 10 egg sets. Collection available to interested persons. Contact Randy Beavers. Texas best represented with 175 Texas species.

University of Texas at El Paso, Museum of Arid Land Biology, El Paso 79999. 200 skins, 600 skeletons, 10 egg sets. Collection available to interested persons by prearrangement. West Texas, Southern New Mexico best represented with approximately 400 Texas species.

Muleshoe National Wildlife Refuge, Muleshoe 79347. 57 skins. Collection available to interested persons by prearrangement. Contact Refuge Manager, Allen C. Jones. Muleshoe National Wildlife Refuge best represented with approximately 35 Texas species.

Tarleton State College, Stephenville 76402. 50 skins. Collection available to interested persons by prearrangement. Contact E. O. Morrison. North Central Texas best represented with 25 Texas species.

Abilene Christian College, Abilene 79601. 50 skins, six skeletons, 15 in fluid, six mounted. Collection available to interested persons by prearrangement. Contact Roy E. Shaye. Local area and Taylor County best represented with 30 Texas species.

McMurray College, Abilene 79605. 46 skins. Collection available to interested persons by prearrangement. Contact Dr. C. W. Beasley. Taylor County best represented with approximately 25 Texas species.

El Paso Centennial Museum, University of Texas at El Paso, El Paso 79999. Approximately 200 mounted, 600 egg sets. Collection available to interested persons by prearrangement. Contact Thomas C. O'Laughlin, Curator. El Paso, Gulf Coast best represented with 80 Texas species.

Fort Concho Museum, San Angelo 76901. 100 mounted, approximately 50 assorted eggs. Collection available to interested persons by prearrangement. Contact Kathleen Roland. Texas coast and West Texas best represented with approximately 20 Texas species.

The Texas Cooperative Wildlife Collections

The Texas Cooperative Wildlife Collections are housed in the Department of Wildlife and Fisheries Sciences, Texas A&M University, College Station. Dr. Keith A. Arnold is Curator of Birds. The bird collection contains more than 11,000 specimens, mostly study skins. A large portion of the bird specimens added each year result from salvage efforts. Most of the other birds added are collected in relation to research efforts.

This collection not only includes a wide representation of Texas birds, but also significant holdings from Colorado, Mexico, and to a lesser extent, other parts of the world. Most orders and a large number of families of birds are represented.

The collections are open to the public. However, to facilitate visits, the curator should be contacted in advance for arrangements. Since special permits are necessary to hold bird specimens, even salvaged birds, persons interested in donating such specimens to the collection should arrange this with those persons holding the necessary permits or through local game wardens. Dr. Arnold will furnish names of such persons upon request.

The Texas Photo-Record file is maintained as part of the Texas Cooperative Wildlife Collections. The file contains photographs of rare and unusual bird records (usu-

ally distributional records) which are important to Texas ornithology. Such records may include first documentation for a several county area, a bird that has been documented less than 10 times in the state, first breeding record for an area, etc. Persons wishing to submit a photograph should consult Oberholser's *The Bird Life of Texas* to establish the worthiness of the record and should submit as many details as possible with the photographs and appropriate data, such as locality, date, who discovered, who identified, who photographed, weather conditions, and any other pertinent details. If desired, the sender can also send the type of camera, film, f-stop and speed, and lens. In the instance of a very rare or unusual record, it would be best to submit a completed Texas Ornithological Society Verifying Document of an Unusual Record, a certificate available from Dr. Arnold.

Photographs may be submitted in color or black-and-white, as slides, prints or movies; prints should not exceed 8 × 10 inches. Copies of the current contents of the file may be obtained from Dr. Arnold for $2.50 to cover printing and mailing. Make checks payable to Keith A. Arnold, Department of Wildlife and Fisheries Sciences, Texas A & M University, College Station TX 77843 (713) 845-6751.

The Texas Bird Sound Library

A Texas Bird Sound Library has been established in the Department of Life Sciences at Sam Houston State University. The purpose of the library is to provide a depository for recorded bird sounds available for researchers, educators, and the general public. Presently, there are five major institutional collections of bird sounds recordings in the United States, but none are located in Texas or the south central states. It is not the intent of the library to compete with any of the other larger established libraries but instead to serve as a regional library and primarily a Texas library. The major objectives of the library are:

1. To establish a collection of Texas bird songs, calls, and other sounds that, with adequate corresponding data, will be made available to research scientists, educators, and other persons interested in bird acoustics.

2. To serve as a repository for recorded bird sounds resulting from completed individual research projects. The recordings are catalogued and properly stored so that they will be available for future use.

3. To establish a Texas Bird Sound Record File for documentation of unusual species, state records, or declining species.

4. To provide audiospectrographs or sonagrams of bird sounds for those in need of such information but who do not have access to an audiospectrograph. A sonogram provides a three-dimensional picture of frequency, time, and amplitude of the bird sound which then can be analyzed qualitatively and quantitatively.

The collection has grown from 110 species in 1979 to more than 200 in 1981, and additions are received every day. While the collection contains mostly Texas birds, other states are also represented as well as the Yucatan. Research scientists, educators, and other persons interested in bird acoustics are encouraged to use as well as contribute to the library.

For further information contact Ralph R. Moldenhauer, Ph.D., Department of Life Sciences, Sam Houston State University, Huntsville, Texas 77341 (713) 295–6211, ext. 1539.

Selected References

Bull, John and Farrand, John, Jr., *The Audubon Society Field Guide to North American Birds, Eastern Region*, New York: Alfred A. Knopf, Inc., 1977.

Davis, L. Irby, *A Field Guide to the Birds of Mexico and Central America*, Austin: University of Texas Press, 1972.

Kutac, Edward A. and Caran, S. Christopher, *A Bird Finding and Naturalist's Guide for the Austin, Texas, Area*, Austin: Travis Audubon Society and Austin Natural Science Association, 1976.

Lane, James A., *A Birder's Guide to the Rio Grande Valley of Texas*, Sacramento: L & P Photography, 1978.

Lane, James A. and Tveten, John, *A Birder's Guide to the Texas Coast*, Sacramento: L & P Photography, 1980.

Oberholser, Harry C. and Kincaid, Edgar B., Jr., *The Bird Life of Texas*, Austin: University of Texas Press, 1974.

Peterson, Roger Tory, *A Field Guide to the Birds of Texas and Adjacent States*, Boston: Houghton Mifflin Co, 1963.

Peterson, Roger Tory, *A Field Guide to Western Birds*, 2nd revised edition, Boston: Houghton Mifflin Co, 1961.

Peterson, Roger Tory, *A Field Guide to the Birds, Fourth Edition*, Boston: Houghton Mifflin Co, 1980.

Peterson, Roger Tory and Chalif, Edward L., *A Field Guide to Mexican Birds*, Boston: Houghton Mifflin Co, 1973.

Peterson, Roger Tory, et al., *A Field Guide to Bird Songs* (Phonograph records keyed by page number to *A Field Guide to the Birds (eastern), second edition*. Also available on cassettes) Boston: Houghton Mifflin Co.

Peterson, Roger Tory, et al., *A Field Guide to Western Bird Songs* (Phonograph records keyed by page to *A Field Guide to Western Birds, 2nd revised edition*. Also available on cassettes) Boston: Houghton Mifflin Co.

Pettingill, Olin Sewell, Jr., *A Guide to Bird Finding West of the Mississippi, 2nd edition*, New York: Oxford University Press, 1981.

Pulich, Warren M., *Birds of Tarrant County*, 2nd edition, 1979.

Riskind, David, *Birding in Texas*, Austin: Texas Park and Wildlife Department (A compilation of all bird checklists available in Texas. Will be updated periodically), 1980.

Robbins, C., et al, *Birds of North America: A Guide to Field Identification*, New York: Golden Press, 1966

Udvardy, Miklas D. F. *The Audubon Society Field Guide to North American Birds: Western Region*, New York: Alfred A. Knopf, Inc, 1977.

Wauer, Roland H., *Birds of Big Bend National Park and Vicinity*, Austin: University of Texas Press, 1973.

Wolfe, Col. L. R., Pulich, Warren M., and Tucker, James A., compilers; Arnold, Dr. Keith A. and Kutac, Edward A., editors, *Check-list of the Birds of Texas*, Texas Ornithological Society, 1975.

Unique Wildlife Ecosystems of Texas, U.S. Fish and Wildlife Service, 1979.

Index

Birds (Locations are on page 109.)

This index is of common English names only. Page numbers in bold indicate the page on which orders, families, and/or scientific names may be found in A Check-List of Texas Birds.

A

Albatross, Yellow-nosed, **84**
Anhinga (American), 54, 57-58, 68, 74, **85**
Ani
  Groove-billed, 71, 79-80, 83, **87**
  Smooth-billed, **87**
Avocet, American, 1, 3, 6, 8, 41, 47, 65, 67, **87**

B

Becard
  Jamaican, **88**
  Rose-throated, 80, **88**
Bittern
  American, 26, 62, 65, **85**
  Least, 7, 26, 62-63, 65, 71, 74, **85**
Blackbird
  Brewer's, 69, 78, **91**
  Red-winged, x, xi, 46, 61, 67, **90**
  Rusty, 67-68, **90**
  Yellow-headed, 8, 13, 24, 26, 46, **90**
Bluebird
  Eastern, 5, 14, 24, 33, 47-48, 68, **89**
  Mountain, 5, 7, 14, 19, 24, **89**
  Western, 10, 14, 16, 19, 24, **89**
Bobolink, 46, **90**
Bobwhite (Common), x, 3, 6, 26, 77, **86**
Booby
  Blue-faced, 64-65, 72-73, **84**
  Blue-footed, **84**
  Brown, 72-73, **85**
  Masked. *See* Blue-faced Booby.
  Red-footed, **85**
Brant, 43, 64, **85**
Bufflehead, 5, 24, 27, 41, 62, **85**
Bunting
  Blue, **91**
  Indigo, 22, 37, 45-46, 49, 53, 56, 63-64, 68, 83, **91**

Lark, 6, 10, 13, 15, 19, 24, 27, **91**
Lazuli, 13, 19, **91**
Orange-breasted, 91
Painted, x, 5, 7, 10, 12, 23-24, 45-46, 48-49, 56, 77, **91**
Snow, **91**
Varied, 11-13, 35, 83, **91**
Bushtit (Black-eared, and Common), 4, 7, 10-11, 23, 27-28, 30, 32, 34, 77, **89**

C

Canvasback, 8, 24, 27, 38, 47, 62, 67, 72, 76, 78, **85**
Caracara (Crested), 49, 69, 71, 74, 76, 81, 83, **86**
Cardinal (Northern and Red), x, xi, 12, 41, 42, 78, **91**
Catbird
  Black, **89**
  Gray, 47, 63, **89**
Chachalaca (Plain), 79-80, 83, **86**
Chat, Yellow-breasted, 12-13, 30, 43, 45, 47-48, 53, 56, 59, 65, 77, 80, **90**
Chickadee
  Black-capped, **89**
  Carolina, x, 5, 22, 31, 41, 48, 78, **89**
  Gray-sided. *See* Mexican Chickadee.
  Mexican, **89**
  Mountain, 3, 10, 14-16, 19, **89**
Chuck-will's-widow, 29, 31, 46-48, 50, 53, 78, **88**
Chukar, **86**
Condor, California, **85**
Coot, American, xi, 5, 24, 30, 41, 46, 63, 69, **86**
Coquette, Black-crested, **88**
Cormorant
  Double-crested, 23, 26-27, 38, 41, 47-48, 57, 63, 76, **85**

Neotropic. *See* Olivaceous Cormorant.
  Olivaceous, 26, 48, 63, 71-72, 76, 81, **85**
  Red-footed, **85**
Cowbird
  Bronzed, 76, 83, **91**
  Brown-headed, x, xi, 32, 46, **91**
Crake, Paint-billed, **86**
Crane
  Sandhill, 3, 8, 27, 47, 61, 64, 68-69, 71-72, 81, **86**
  Whooping, 31, 69, 71, 78, **86**
Creeper, Brown, 16, 23, 38, 42, 45, 47, 49, 50, 66, 68, 78, **89**
Crossbill
  Red, 16-17, 49, **91**
  White-winged, **91**
Crow
  American. *See* Common Crow.
  Common, 38, 66, **89**
  Fish, 52, **89**
  Mexican, 83, **89**
Cuckoo
  Black-billed, 29, 45, 64, 68, **87**
  Mangrove, **87**
  Yellow-billed, x, 12, 24, 31, **87**
Curlew
  Eskimo, **86**
  Long-billed, 1, 5-6, 8, 65, 72, **86**

D

Dickcissel, 46-47, 67, 69, **91**
Dipper (American and North American), **89**
Dove
  Blue Ground, **87**
  Common Ground. *See* Ground Dove.
  Ground, 12, 68, 74, 76, **87**
  Inca, 12, 17, 46-47, 66-67, 74, 78, **87**
  Mourning, x, xi, 13, 32, **87**
  Ringed Turtle, **87**

Locations

Hermann Park, 66-67
Memorial Park, 66
Mercury Drive, 66-67
Spring Creek Park, 66-67
Houston, Sam, National Forest, 51, 56-57
Hueco Tanks State Historical Park, 9, 18-19
Huntsville, 51, 55-56
Sam Houston Park, 55
Huntsville State Park, 55-56

I

Inks Lake State Park, 28, 31

J

Jones, W. G., State Forest, 54-56

K

Kerrville, 28, 32-33
Dewberry Hollow, 32-33
RR 479, 32
Scenic Drive, 33
Kerrville State Recreation Area, 33
Kirby, John K., State Forest, 59

L

Laguna Atascosa National Wildlife Refuge, 81-83
Lajitas, 9, 11-12
Lake Abilene, 21
Lake Arrowhead State Recreation Area, 22-23
Lake Balmorhea, 9, 14-15
Lake Buchanan, 28, 31
Lake Conroe, 51, 56-57
Lake Livingstone, 51, 57
Lake Livingston State Recreation Area, 57
Lake Marvin, 1, 4
Lake Meredith, 1, 4-5
Lake of the Pines, 51-52
Lake Somerville, 36, 48
Lake Somerville State Recreation Area, 49
Lake Texoma, 36, 43-44
Larsen, Roy E., Sandyland Sanctuary, 59
Llano Estacado, 1ff
Lost Maples State Natural Area, 33-34
Lower Rio Grande Valley, 75, 79
Lubbock, 1-2
Boles Lake, 2-3
Buffalo Springs Lake, 1-3
City Cemetery, 2
Clapp Park, 2
Mackenzie State Recreation Area, 2
Maxey Park, 2

M

McCardell's Lake, 57-58
McFaddin National Wildlife Refuge, 61-62
McKinney Falls State Park, 29, 50
Marfa, 9, 13
Marshall, 51-52
Meridian State Recreation Area, 48
Midland, 1, 7-8
Hogan Park, 8
Interstate Pond, 8
Midland County, 8
Monahans Draw, 7-8
Monahans Sandhills State Park, 9, 19
Muleshoe National Wildlife Refuge, 1, 3
Mustang Island, 70, 72
Mustang Island State Park, 73

N

Nacogdoches, 51-53
Oil Springs, 53

P

Padre Island National Seashore, 70, 73
Palmetto State Park, 49
Palo Duro Canyon State Park, 1, 4-5
Pedernales Falls State Park, 28, 31-32
Pineywoods, 51ff
Port Aransas, 60, 70, 72
Port Arthur, 60-61
Presidio, 9, 12-13
Presidio County, 12-14

R

Rayburn, Sam, Reservoir, 51, 53-54
Angelina National Forest, 51, 53-54
Marion Ferry Park, 53-54
Ralph McAllister Park, 53-54
Townsend Recreation Site, 53-54
Redford, 12-13
Rita Blanca National Grasslands, 6-7
Rockport, 60, 70, 72
Rolling Plains, 21ff
Rollover Pass, 63, 64
Ruidosa, 12-13

S

San Angelo, 21, 25
Civic League Park, 26
Fairmont Cemetery, 26

Lake Nasworthy, 25-26
O. C. Fisher Lake, 25-26
Pugh Park, 27
Twin Buttes Reservoir, 21, 25
San Antonio, 75-76
Botanical Center, 78
Brackenridge Park, 78
Braunig Lake, 76
Calaveras Lake, 76
Emilie and Albert Friedrich Park, 77
Jack Judson Nature Trail, 78
Mitchell Lake, 76
Southside Lions Park, 78
W. W. McAllister Park, 78
San Bernard National Wildlife Refuge, 65
San Jose Island, 70, 72
San Luis Pass, 63, 65
Santa Ana National Wildlife Refuge, 75, 79-80
Santa Margarita Ranch, 81
Sea Rim National Wildlife Refuge, 61
Sea Rim State Park, 61-62
Seminole Canyon State Historical Park, 28, 35
Shafter, 12-13
Shoshoni Park, 22, 23
South Texas, 75ff
Spence, E. V., Reservoir, 25, 27
Stonewall Jackson Camp, 22-23

T

Texas City Dike, 63-64
Tishomingo National Wildlife Refuge, 44
Trans-Pecos, 9ff
Twin Buttes Reservoir, 21, 25

V

Village Creek State Park Site, 59

W

Waco, 36, 44
Cameron Park, 44-45
Camp Val Verde, 44, 46
Lake Waco, 44, 47-48
McLennan Community College, 44, 46
Steinbeck Bend Area, 44-46
Welder Wildlife Foundation, 73-74
White River Lake, 21, 27
Wichita Falls, 21-22
Jaycee Park, 22-23
Lake Wichita, 22-23
Lake Wichita Dam, 23
Lucy Park, 22